Essential Components of Cognitive–Behavior Therapy for Depression

Essential Components of Cognitive–Behavior Therapy for Depression

Jacqueline B. Persons

Joan Davidson

Michael A. Tompkins

American Psychological Association

Washington, DC

First Printing August 2000
Second Printing March 2001
Third Printing March 2002

Published by
American Psychological Association
750 First Street, NE
Washington, DC 20002

Copies may be ordered from
APA Order Department
P.O. Box 92984
Washington, DC 20090-2984

In the U.K., Europe, Africa, and the Middle East, copies may be ordered from
American Psychological Association
3 Henrietta Street
Covent Garden, London
WC2E 8LU England

Typeset in Meridien by EPS Group Inc., Easton, MD

Printer: Automated Graphic Systems, White Plains, MD
Dust jacket Designer: Minker Design, Bethesda, MD
Technical/Production Editor: Amy J. Clarke

The opinions and statements published are the responsibility of the authors, and such opinions and statements do not necessarily represent the policies of the American Psychological Association.

Library of Congress Cataloging-in-Publication Data

Persons, Jacqueline B.
    Essential components of cognitive–behavior therapy for depression / Jacqueline B. Persons, Joan Davidson, and Michael A. Tompkins.—1st ed.
        p.   cm.
    Includes bibliographical references and index.
    ISBN 1-55798-697-5 (hardcover: acid-free paper).
        1. Depression, Mental—Treatment.   2. Cognitive therapy.   I. Davidson, Joan, 1960–   .   II. Tompkins, Michael A.   III. Title.
    RC537.P436 2001
    616.85'270651—dc21
                                                                    00-038045
                                                                    CIP

British Library Cataloguing-in-Publication Data
A CIP record is available from the British Library.

Printed in the United States of America

Contents

7

Preface

This book and the accompanying video series had their origins in our teaching efforts, in our daily struggles to provide top quality care for our depressed patients, and in the synergy resulting from the fact that we do both these things (train and treat) almost daily. We provide training in cognitive–behavior therapy to students and clinicians in numerous settings in the San Francisco Bay area and elsewhere. Trainees often fall into one of two groups: (a) experienced clinicians who were originally taught to use psychodynamic models and methods and (b) novice clinicians who are learning about therapy for the first time. The process of training both these groups pushed us to specify explicitly the essential elements of cognitive–behavior therapy and to elucidate the precise behaviors that are required to conceptualize and intervene in a cognitive–behavioral manner.

Our daily efforts to provide our patients with high-quality care also shaped the material presented here. Our ideal is an empirically based mode of clinical work that draws on the results of the randomized controlled trials while meeting the needs of the individual patient. Surprisingly little has been written about the precise steps required to implement this ideal. We spell out in the first chapter a conceptual model underpinning an empirically based clinically flexible mode of working. In the remainder of the book, we show how to use it to develop an individualized case conceptualization and provide cognitive–behavior therapy for the depressed patient.

Acknowledgements

We are grateful to dozens of individuals who have contributed to our thinking, to our professional development, and to this project. Our patients, by entrusting us with their difficulties, offered innumerable insights and opportunities to practice and extend our skills. Similarly, we often feel that we learn more from our students than they do from us. Students (many of whom are now colleagues) who made particularly important contributions to our thinking include Andrew Bertagnolli, Michelle Hatzis, David M. Fresco, Douglas S. Mennin, and Kristen L. Valus. Teachers and mentors who laid out the path ahead of us and guided us along the way include Aaron T. Beck, David H. Barlow, David D. Burns, Edna B. Foa, Gerald C. Davison, the late Neil S. Jacobson, and Marsha M. Linehan.

Several collagues and students generously played the role of patient in the therapy sessions we taped for our videos: Thomas Farnsworth, Joshua Kirsch, Chad W. LeJeune, Simone K. Madan, Georgia Maslowski, Alexandra Matthews, Kristen Valus, and Julie Weiss. Our local professional community provides an important source of collegial support and stimulating discussion; colleagues include W. Stewart Agras, Bruce A. Arnow, Polly Bloomberg-Fretter, Anita Eagleton, Eileen Gambrill, Lynne Henderson, Stephen P. Hinshaw, Lorrin Koran, Hanna Levenson, Matthew McKay, Paul Malkin, Lynn Martin, Ricardo F. Muñoz, Stewart Nixon, Robin O'Heeron, M. Gail Price, Jason M. Satterfield, Sharon Smith, Margo Thienemann, John White, Melinda White, Linda Zaruba, Antonette M. Zeiss, Steve Zlutnick, and Elke Zuercher-White.

The Association for Advancement of Behavior Therapy (AABT) provides a professional home and platform for our efforts. AABT colleagues who have been particularly important to us include Constance V. Dancu,

Keith S. Dobson, Randy O. Frost, Richard G. Heimberg, Robert L. Leahy, Ralph M. Turner, Zindel V. Segal, and Gail S. Steketee. Colleagues in our national and international professional community who have made important contributions to our thinking include Stephen N. Haynes, Christine A. Padesky, Paul M. Salkovskis, and Ira D. Turkat.

We thank Julia Frank-McNeil, Director of APA Books, for her stewardship of this project from development to publication and Amy J. Clarke at APA Books for her work to bring the project from manuscript to finished form. We thank John Quick, indefatigable and unflappable, for his outstanding video work.

We are grateful for the remarkable synergistic collaborative relationships that allow the three of us to accomplish projects like this one, move forward together professionally, and have some fun as we go. Our therapist colleagues at the San Francisco Bay Area Center for Cognitive Therapy, Chad W. LeJeune, Simone K. Madan, and Alexandra Matthews, provide clinical care we are proud of and are essential to our center's growth and development.

Finally, we thank our families for allowing us to work long hours to complete this project.

Essential Components of Cognitive–Behavior Therapy for Depression

Introduction

This book provides hands-on training in the essential components of cognitive–behavior therapy[1] (CBT) for depression, emphasizing the theory and practice of Aaron T. Beck. It is intended for trainees and practitioners in the mental health professions, including the fields of clinical, counseling, and health psychology; social work; psychiatry and psychiatric nursing; marriage and family counseling; and pastoral counseling. The two primary aims of the book are to present an evidence-based approach to clinical work and to teach basic clinical skills.

Evidence-based clinical work uses the findings from empirical studies, including randomized controlled trials (RCTs). Reliance on the RCTs supports the use of Beck's (1976) CT for depression, of course, because it has been shown to be effective in more RCTs than any other psychosocial treatment for depression (as shown in chap. 1). We teach four basic interventions of the therapy: activity scheduling, using the Thought Record, schema change methods, and use of a structured therapy session. Our choice of these four components was based on our reading of Beck's (1976; Beck, Rush, Shaw, & Emery, 1979) theory, the RCT-validated protocol (Beck et al., 1979), and the results of empirical studies evaluating the theory and therapy, as described in chapter 1.

An evidence-based approach to the individual case is one in which the clinician adopts a hypothesis-testing, scientific mode of working (see Haynes & O'Brien, 2000; and Barlow, Hayes, & Nelson, 1984). An individualized case formulation serves as the clinician's hypothesis about the factors causing and maintaining the patient's problems and as the basis for an individualized treatment plan for the patient. As treatment proceeds, the therapist monitors outcome using objective measures. The results of outcome monitoring determine whether changes in the

---

[1]We use the terms *cognitive–behavior therapy* and *cognitive therapy* (CT) interchangeably.

formulation and treatment plan are needed. The approach to CBT for depression presented in this book integrates the use of the individualized case formulation and treatment plan into the protocol for Beck's (1976) CT.

The book begins with a description of Beck's (1976) theory of depression and its treatment and reviews the data underpinning the theory, the efficacy of the therapy, and the mechanisms of action of the therapy (chap. 1). Chapter 2 describes how to develop an individualized case formulation and use it to plan treatment. Chapters 3–6 describe four basic components of the therapy: structuring the therapy session, activity scheduling, using the Thought Record, and schema change methods. The final chapter presents a case example that illustrates how a therapist uses the formulation to plan and carry out treatment for Nancy, a depressed editorial assistant.

We emphasize training in basic skills. We describe in detail the basic assessment and intervention strategies of the therapy, and we provide step-by-step guidelines for replicating many of them. Whenever possible, we describe simple, straightforward strategies that are easy to teach and learn. Activity scheduling (chap. 4) and the Positive Data Log intervention for promoting schema change (chap. 6) are particularly easy to learn and use. The steps required to carry out a structured therapy session (chap. 3) are also simple and straightforward—but there are a lot of them. Two components are complex and more difficult to learn: individualized case formulation and treatment planning (chap. 2) and using the Thought Record (chap. 5).

To aid in skill acquisition, we provide numerous clinical examples; we also offer practice exercises to be used in class or in consultation groups of practitioners. To make it easy to implement the skills in routine clinical practice, we provide forms that clinicians can use to carry out the intervention or assessment strategy and examples of the completed forms. We describe strategies for overcoming common obstacles to implementing each strategy. In the final chapter, we provide a case description providing more examples of each intervention and demonstrations of how the assessment and intervention strategies are woven together over the course of treatment.

Because we focus on basic skills in this book, we assume that the patient is able to establish a collaborative working relationship with the therapist and is reasonably receptive to the interventions and able to use them. We do not provide extensive discussions of nonadherence, problems in the therapeutic relationship, treatment failure, or other types of difficulties. We do teach the clinician to develop a case formulation; certainly one of the major roles of formulation is to assist the clinician in handling setbacks and glitches in treatment. We also include in each chapter a brief discussion of obstacles to the assessment and intervention strategy described. However, extensive discussion of the handling of complex cases is beyond the scope of this basic text.

Our videotape series, *Cognitive–Behavior Therapy of Depression,* accompanies this book. The series and the book can be studied alone or can be used together. The chief contribution of the videos is to bring alive the assessment and intervention strategies described in the book through demonstrations of patient–therapist interactions. For those wishing to use the book and video series together, we recommend that the clinician read the chapter paired with each video before watching the video. After watching the video, we recommend that the clinician work through with a colleague or fellow student the practice exercises in the book chapter that corresponds to the video. The precise sequence of training experiences required to produce competency in CBT for depression are not yet known and must be empirically determined. We hope the training materials provided here will facilitate that work.

We emphasize the theory and practice of Aaron T. Beck's approach to CT for several reasons. Beck's (1976; Beck et al., 1979) CT has been studied and shown effective in more RCTs than any other psychosocial treatment for depression (Agency for Health Care Policy and Research, 1993). Beck's CT has been shown in RCTs to provide effective treatment for numerous clinical problems and disorders, including many that are frequently comorbid with depression, including anxiety disorders, substance abuse, couples problems, pain disorders, and irritable bowel syndrome (see the February 1998 special issue of the *Journal of Consulting and Clinical Psychology,* entitled Empirically Supported Psychological Therapies).

Empirical studies of the theory's major tenants, which continue to be published at a rapid rate in the *Journal of Abnormal Psychology, Cognitive Therapy and Research,* and elsewhere, provide considerable support for cognitive theory. Beck's (1976) theory and the therapies based on it are developing and thriving, with new developments that include the treatment of bipolar illness (Basco & Rush, 1996), schizophrenia (Kingdon & Turkington, 1994), Axis II disorders (Beck, Freeman, & Associates, 1990), and atypical depression (Jarrett et al., 1999). Topics of particular current interest include individualized case formulation (see J. S. Beck, 1995; and Persons, 1989), schema-focused therapies (see Padesky, 1994; and Young, 1999), and training (see the Summer 1998 special issue on supervision of the *Journal of Cognitive Psychotherapy*). Beck's theory and therapy are clearly here to stay.

Empirical and Theoretical Underpinnings

1

> The truth of a knowledge claim is not determined by the strength of belief held by the individual putting forth the claim. (K. Stanovich)

We begin this book with a review of data from randomized controlled trials (RCTs) of cognitive therapy (CT) for depression. Why do we begin this way? Because we view RCTs as the gold standard for evaluating the evidence of a treatment's benefits, and we encourage clinicians to evaluate evidence from RCTs before learning any type of psychotherapy. We also review evidence from other types of outcome studies of cognitive–behavior therapy (CBT) for depression.

The clinician's challenge is to adapt the standardized therapies shown effective in RCTs to meet the needs of the individual patient in an evidence-based way. In the second section of this chapter, we describe a systematic way of using an individualized case formulation as the foundation of a hypothesis-driven mode of clinical work.

Developing an individualized case formulation and treatment plan requires that the therapist have a strong understanding of the theory underpinning a protocol. Therefore, we conclude the chapter with a detailed description of Beck's (1976; Beck, Rush, Shaw, & Emery, 1979) cognitive theory and therapy of depression.

Evidence Base for Cognitive–Behavior Therapy for Depression

Efficacy studies examine the outcome of CT when it is used to treat highly selected research samples in carefully controlled research settings, and effectiveness studies examine the outcome of the therapy when used to treat naturalistic samples in clinical settings (Howard, Moras, Brill, Martinovich, & Lutz, 1996; Seligman, 1996). Studies of clinical significance examine the degree to which individual patients obtain reliable and meaningful benefits from the therapy. We review all three of these types of outcome studies of CT for depression.

EFFICACY

The RCT is widely viewed as the experimental design providing the strongest demonstration that a therapy is efficacious (Chambless & Hollon, 1998; Frazier & Mosteller, 1995). In an RCT, patients with a given clinical problem or diagnosis (e.g., major depressive disorder [MDD]) are randomly assigned to treatment conditions (e.g., CBT, pharmacotherapy), and all aspects of the treatment and environment except for differences between the two treatment conditions are controlled to the greatest degree possible. Using this experimental design, we can conclude that any posttreatment differences in depression between patients in the two treatment conditions are likely due to the differences between the treatment conditions.

Numerous RCTs of CT for depression show that it is more effective than no treatment and as effective as antidepressant medication (Agency for Health Care Policy and Research [AHCPR], 1993; DeRubeis & Crits-Christoph, 1998; Persons, Thase, & Crits-Christoph, 1996; Schulberg, Katon, Simon, & Rush, 1998).[1] The demonstration that patients treated with CT do as well as those treated with antidepressant medication is an important finding because antidepressant medication is a well-established therapy that has been shown effective in RCTs with thousands of patients (Nemeroff & Schatzberg, 1998). Traditionally, most researchers have examined White adults; a few have studied children and adolescents (see reviews by Speier, Sherak, Hirsch, & Cantwell, 1985; and Stark, Rouse, & Kurowski, 1994), and in a recent investigation researchers studied a sample of Puerto Rican adolescents (Rossello & Bernal, 1999).

A handful of other psychosocial treatments have been shown in RCTs to provide effective treatment for depression; these are the interpersonal therapy developed by Klerman, Weissman, Rounsaville, and Chevron (1984); other varieties of CBTs; and two or three specific types

---

[1]In this chapter, CT and CBT are used interchangeably. Thus, this review includes studies both of the A. T. Beck et al. (1979) protocol and of other varieties of CBT, such as Nezu's (1986) problem-solving therapy. The A. T. Beck et al. protocol is the most frequently studied single protocol in this group.

of brief psychodynamic therapies.[2] Researchers who compared these psychosocial therapies in the treatment of depression have generally failed to find differences among them (AHCPR, 1993; DeRubeis & Crits-Christoph, 1998). Given this failure to find differences, it may be tempting to conclude that all therapies are equally effective for treating depression. However, we do not draw that conclusion.

We conclude that only a few psychosocial therapies (CBTs, interpersonal therapy, two or three brief psychodynamic therapies) have been shown in RCTs to provide effective treatment for depression.[3] No good evidence of efficacy (i.e., evidence from RCTs) is available for other psychosocial treatments for depression. Unfortunately, psychosocial therapies for depression that have not been studied in RCTs include many therapies routinely provided by practicing clinicians, including supportive psychotherapy (AHCPR, 1993) and long-term psychodynamic psychotherapy (APA, 1993).

In addition to the demonstrations that CT provides effective treatment of depression, several studies show that CT is superior to brief (12 weeks) treatment with antidepressant medications in preventing relapse in patients who have recovered from depression (Blackburn, Eunson, & Bishop, 1986; Evans et al., 1992; Simons, Murphy, Levine, & Wetzel, 1986). CT provides relapse protection equal to long-term pharmacotherapy (Blackburn & Moore, 1997; Evans et al., 1992) and superior to clinical management (Fava, Rafanelli, Grandi, Conti, & Belluardo, 1998).

The question of whether CT is efficacious for treating severe, as opposed to mild to moderate, depression is a controversial one (Craighead et al., 1998). The NIMH [National Institute of Mental Health] Treatment of Depression Collaborative Research Program (TDCRP; Elkin et al., 1989) concluded from post hoc analyses that CT was as efficacious as pharmacotherapy for the treatment of mild to moderate depression but less efficacious than pharmacotherapy for the treatment of severe depression. On the basis of this finding, the *Practice Guideline for Major Depressive Disorder in Adults* (APA, 1993) evaluates CT as effective only for the treatment of less severe depression. In contrast, data from Hollon, DeRubeis, Evans, et al. (1992); results of a recent meta-analysis by DeRubeis, Gelfand, Tang, and Simons (1999); and a recent review by Schulberg et al. (1998) indicate that CT is as efficacious as pharmacotherapy for severely depressed patients.

---

[2]Some evidence also supports the efficacy of couple and family therapy for depression (AHCPR, 1993; American Psychiatric Association [APA], 1993); however, we focus on individual treatment in this review.

[3]On the basis of findings from RCTs that met their stringent standards, Craighead, Craighead, and Ilardi (1998) concluded that only behavior therapy, CBT, and interpersonal psychotherapy have been shown to provide effective treatment for depression.

The value of combined psychotherapy plus pharmacotherapy is also a controversial topic. The most recent large study of this question was conducted by Thase et al. (1997). These investigators, reanalyzing data from six RCTs, found that combined treatment is superior to psychotherapy alone for severely depressed and chronically ill patients.

In addition to its effectiveness when provided in a standard patient–therapist interaction, CT provided through a self-help book (Burns's *Feeling Good,* 1999) has been shown in RCTs to be effective (vs. no treatment) in alleviating mild to moderate depression in community samples. These gains were maintained for 6–12 months (Jamison & Scogin, 1995; Scogin, Hamblin, & Beutler, 1987; Scogin, Jamison, & Gochneaur, 1989).

The cost of CT compares favorably with the cost of pharmacotherapy. A recent comparison of CBT and fluoxetine (Prozac) for the treatment of depression indicates that fluoxetine is more expensive than individual CT (Antonuccio, Thomas, & Danton, 1997). Hollon (1999) presented preliminary data from a study he conducted showing that although over the first 12 weeks of treatment CT is more expensive than fluoxetine, over the long-term CT is cheaper because it can be discontinued sooner.

Thus, CT's well-deserved reputation in the treatment of depression rests on several facts:

- CT is one of the few psychosocial treatments for depression that has been shown effective in RCTs.
- CT has been shown to provide effective treatment for depression in more RCTs than any other psychosocial treatment.
- CT has been shown to be as effective as a well-validated treatment (e.g., antidepressant medication).
- CT has been shown to be superior to antidepressant medication in preventing relapse in depressed patients.
- CT is cost effective.

EFFECTIVENESS

The effectiveness of CBT refers to the question of whether CBT alleviates depressive symptoms when it is used to treat heterogeneous samples of patients in routine clinical practice settings (Howard et al., 1996; Seligman, 1996). Patients in RCTs (at least those conducted to date; Jacobson & Christensen, 1996) typically meet extensive selection criteria that are not met by patients treated in a routine clinical practice. For example, patients participating in the TDCRP met the following criteria: a diagnosis of definite MDD; Beck Depression Inventory (BDI) score of 20 or greater; Hamilton Rating Scale for Depression score of 14 or greater; no psychotic subtype of MDD; no active suicidality or other need for immediate treatment; no definite bipolar disorder; no current generalized anxiety disorder, panic disorder, phobic disorder, or obsessive–compulsive disorder that is predominant over MDD; no alcoholism or drug use disorder within the last year; no hallucinations, delusions, or stupor; no antisocial personality disorder; no more than two schizotypal features; no past or current schizophrenia; no organic brain syndrome; no mental retardation; no concurrent treatment; no medical contraindication for the use of imipramine; and no recent (within 3 months) failure to respond to an adequate trial of imipramine. As a result of these extensive selection criteria, large numbers of potential study participants were ineligible for the study. Of the 252 patients screened, 145 (58%) were excluded because they did not meet the selection criteria.

In contrast, depressed patients treated in routine clinical practice often do not meet the criterion for MDD or other selection criteria typically used in the RCTs. Therefore, the results of RCTs (at least, those conducted to date) do not provide clear evidence that therapy is effective in routine clinical practice.

In a handful of published studies, researchers have evaluated the effectiveness of CT for depression in clinical settings. Two studies of private practice patients, one sample treated by David Burns and Jacqueline Persons (Persons, Burns, & Perloff, 1988) and another treated by Persons (Persons, Bostrom, & Bertagnolli, 1999), show that depressed patients who had completed treatment ended their treatment with BDI scores similar to the scores of patients treated in several important RCTs. This was true despite the fact that the private practice patients were drawn from a more heterogeneous sample than those treated in the RCTs and most of them would not have met the criteria for the RCTs. Patients in the Persons et al. (1988, 1999) private practice samples were both more severely ill (had more comorbid conditions, including panic disorder and significant medical problems) and less severely ill (less severely depressed) than patients treated in the RCTs. Haaga, DeRubeis, Stewart, and Beck (1991) reported that an unselected sample of patients suffering from depression treated by trainees at the Center for Cognitive Therapy at the University of Pennsylvania showed outcomes similar to those of patients in the RCTs.

In contrast, Organista, Muñoz, and Gonzalez (1994) found that low-income, ethnic minority, medical patients treated at San Francisco (CA) General Hospital had significantly poorer outcomes than patients treated in the RCTs. Researchers conducting subsequent work with this population are evaluating whether adding pharmacotherapy and case management to CT can improve outcomes for these patients (Miranda & Dwyer, 1994).

Thus, there is some evidence that CT for depression can be successfully transported to private practice and university clinic settings, but evidence of effectiveness of CT with low-income, minority, medically ill patients is weaker. More effectiveness data are needed.

CLINICALLY SIGNIFICANT BENEFITS

As Howard et al. (1996) pointed out, the efficacy and effectiveness trials answer the following nomothetic question: Is the standardized protocol effective for the average patient? In contrast, clinicians ask Is the treatment helpful to particular individual patients?

Another question of interest to clinicians not typically addressed in RCTs (although that is changing; see Ogles, Lambert, & Sawyer, 1995, and below) is the question of whether a treatment produces clinically significant (i.e., large and meaningful) benefits. To address these two issues (what happens to individual patients and does the treatment make a clinically significant difference in patients' lives), Jacobson and Truax (1991), and others (e.g., Fishman, 1999; Howard et al., 1996), developed some new data analysis strategies.

Jacobson and Truax (1991) defined a change in a measure (e.g., BDI) in a particular patient over the course of treatment as clinically significant if it met two criteria: (a) the change was sufficiently large that it was unlikely due to chance, and (b) the change moved the patient outside the range of scores of the dysfunctional population or into the range of scores of a functional population. When Ogles et al. (1995) used Jacobson and Truax's methodology to examine clinically significant change in the patients treated in the TDCRP, they found that 50% of depressed patients treated with CT showed a clinically significant change on the BDI, where "clinically significant change" was defined as a change that (a) was unlikely due to chance and (b) resulted in a posttest score on an outcome measure that was low enough to place the patient's score in the range of scores of the general population. In addition, 28% of the patients showed reliable change and a posttest score on an outcome measure that was sufficient to place their scores in the distribution of scores of an asymptomatic population. Persons et al. (1999) reported that 57% of their private practice patients showed reliable change on the BDI that was sufficient to place their scores in the range of scores of the general population, but only 17% of the scores could be placed in the scores of an asymptomatic population.

SUMMARY

RCTs, effectiveness studies, and studies of clinical significance show that CT provides effective treatment for depression that produces clinically significant benefits for substantial proportions of patients. At the same time, the controlled studies indicate that additional developments are needed to strengthen the therapy. Furthermore, none of these studies address the question that clinicians ask every day: Will the patient who is in my office right now benefit from CT for depression? To address this question, we recommend that clinicians use an empirical, hypothesis-testing approach for the treatment of each patient, which is described in the next section of this chapter.

Evidence-Based Clinical Practice

The task of the clinician is to translate the nomothetic (general) to the idiographic (individual), that is, to tailor RCT-validated standardized protocols to the treatment of an individual patient and to do this in an evidence-based way. To accomplish this task, we recommend an evidence-based case formulation-driven approach to treatment. Our method relies heavily on the elegant conceptual model (see Figure 1.1) developed by behavior analysts (e.g., Barlow, Hayes, & Nelson, 1984; Haynes & O'Brien, 1990, 2000; Nelson & Hayes, 1986).

In an *evidence-based formulation-driven* approach to treatment, the therapist views the treatment of each individual case as an experiment. Treatment begins with an assessment, which leads to a hypothesis about the nature of the mechanisms causing or maintaining the problem behaviors. The hypothesis is the individualized case formulation. The therapist uses the individualized formulation to develop an individualized treatment plan. As treatment proceeds, the therapist collects data (more

FIGURE 1.1

Conceptual model describing an empirical approach to the treatment of a single case.

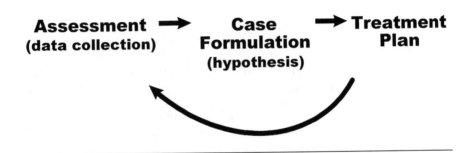

assessment) to evaluate the effects of this treatment plan. Evidence that the treatment is unsuccessful cues the clinician to reformulate the case, develop a new treatment plan on the basis of the results of the reformulation, and continue monitoring outcome. Thus, clinical work is carried out in a systematic, hypothesis-testing way. Although we described the behavior analytic view of the process of assessing, formulating, treating, and monitoring outcome, similar views of the treatment process have been described by therapists of many therapeutic orientations (Eells, 1997).

In addition to the hypothesis-driven approach to the individual case, an evidence-based approach to treatment has other components (which are not discussed in detail because of space limitations), including providing informed consent for treatment and using results from the empirical literature to guide clinical decision making (Persons, 1999; Persons & Silberschatz, 1998; Sackett, Richardson, Rosenberg, & Haynes, 1997).

The formulation-driven approach to treatment is a principle-driven approach to treatment rather than a treatment consisting of a list of interventions to deliver in a predetermined order (Eifert, Evans, & McKendrick, 1990). That is, the therapist is guided by a principle (the case formulation) rather than simply by a list of interventions. There are several advantages of a principle-driven approach to treatment (we discuss this issue in more detail in chap. 2). A primary advantage is that when the therapist encounters setbacks during the treatment process, he or she can follow a systematic strategy to make a change in treatment (consider whether a reformulation of the case might suggest some new interventions) rather than simply making hit-or-miss changes in the treatment plan.

A weakness of the formulation-driven approach to treatment is that the clinician, while monitoring treatment outcome systematically, may nevertheless rely on idiosyncratic, non-evidence-based formulations and interventions. To secure individualized formulation-driven treatment to a solid evidence base and to minimize clinical judgment errors (see Wilson, 1996), we make the following two recommendations to clinicians when developing individualized case formulations and treatment plans:

- Base your initial idiographic formulation on a nomothetic formulation with a strong evidence base
- Base your initial idiographic treatment plan on a nomothetic protocol that has been shown effective in RCTs.

These two modifications strengthen the evidence base of the individualized, formulation-driven approach to treatment. However, it is important to acknowledge that individualized formulation-driven treatment has itself rarely been evaluated in RCTs (Persons, 1991; see a review by Haynes, Leisen, & Blaine, 1997). RCTs evaluating the effect of formulation-driven treatment on therapy outcome, dropout, compliance, and relapse are urgently needed.

The formulation and intervention methods we describe in this book are based on Beck's (1976) cognitive theory and therapy. Therefore, a thorough understanding of Beck's theory of depression and its treatment is recommended; we review them in the next part of this chapter. Beck's theory and therapy meet the two criteria proposed above. As shown in the first part of this chapter, protocols based on the theory are well supported by RCTs. As shown in the next section, the theory itself has a solid evidence base.

Beck's Cognitive Theory and Therapy of Depression

Aaron Beck (1976; Beck et al., 1979) proposed that depressive symptoms result when a vulnerable individual's maladaptive schema are activated by external life events, as depicted in Figure 1.2. Schema are deep cognitive structures that enable an individual to interpret his or her experiences in a meaningful way. For example, a restaurant owner who believes that "I'm a worthless person unless others value and care for me" is vulnerable to depression if his wife tells him she does not love him and wants a divorce. Symptoms of depression are conceptualized in Beck's model as consisting of behaviors (e.g., passive moping), thoughts (e.g., "I'm unlovable"), and mood (e.g., depressed, discouraged). Beck's CT entails interventions designed to change behaviors, thoughts, and schema, which are all carried out in the context of a highly structured therapy session.

SCHEMA AND ACTIVATING LIFE EVENTS

Schema are depicted near the bottom of Figure 1.2 because they are viewed as "underlying" or "latent"—even unconscious—constructs (Beck, 1976). Beck proposed that negative views of self, others, the world, and the future are important in causing symptoms of depression. Measures of dysfunctional attitudes developed to assess the schema of depressed individuals have supported Beck's predictions (Imber et al., 1990). We have noted in our clinical experience that depressed patients also often hold schema of the sort described as typical of patients with anxiety disorders (Beck, Emery, & Greenberg, 1985), substance abuse

FIGURE 1.2

Beck's cognitive theory of depression.

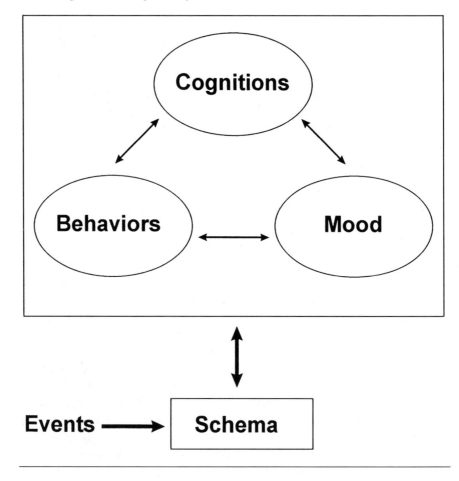

problems (Beck, Wright, Newman, & Liese, 1993), and Axis II disorders (Beck, Freeman, & Associates, 1990). All of these disorders, of course, frequently coexist with depression.

Beck's (1976) theory specifies that the external life event must "match" the schema to activate it. That is, a person whose belief is that he is worthless unless he is loved by others would not be expected to become depressed following a professional setback but might become depressed following his wife's announcement that she no longer cares for him and wants a divorce. Testing the matching aspect of the theory in the most direct manner requires prospective longitudinal studies in which individuals' schema are assessed and their life events monitored over time. Ambitious and careful studies by Constance Hammen and colleagues (G. P. Brown, Hammen, Craske, & Wickens, 1995; Hammen, Marks, Mayol, & deMayo, 1985; Hammen, Ellicott, & Gitlin, 1989; Hammen, Ellicott, Gitlin, & Jamison, 1989), Zindel Segal and colleagues (e.g., Segal, Shaw, Vella, & Katz, 1992), and others (e.g., Hewitt, Flett, & Ediger, 1996) provide good evidence supporting this matching hypothesis, although results are not unequivocally supportive.

Beck (1983) described two typical types of depressed patients: the dependent or sociotropic and the autonomous. The *dependent* type holds such schema as "I must be loved by others or I'm worthless," is vulnerable to depressive symptoms following an interpersonal loss or rejection, and experiences a typical pattern of depressive symptoms that includes sadness, feelings of unattractiveness, and crying. The *autonomous* type believes that "I must be independent or accomplish significant achievements or else I am worthless," is vulnerable to depressive symptoms following a significant loss of independence or a significant failure, and experiences feelings of failure, self-blame, self-hate, guilt, loss of interest in others, and hopelessness. The theory does allow for individuals to hold both dependent and autonomous types of beliefs simultaneously.

Good evidence supports the existence of the sociotropic and autonomous subtypes of depression (see the studies of the matching hypothesis above and Imber et al., 1990). Therefore, therapists can use these conceptualizations as initial schema hypotheses. However, Beck's (1976) predictions about the patterns of depressive symptoms experienced by the two types of depressives have received only mixed support (Persons, Burns, Perloff, & Miranda, 1993; Robins, Block, & Peselow, 1989). Thus, observations about the topology of the patient's depressive symptoms do not appear to yield reliable information about underlying schema.

According to Beck's (1983) cognitive theory, schema can be present but latent. Unless the vulnerable individual experiences events that match and activate his or her schema, the vulnerable individual may not experience any symptoms. Several empirical studies support this aspect of the theory (Hedlund & Rude, 1995; see reviews by Persons & Miranda, 1992; and Gotlib & Krasnoperova, 1998). Important clinical implications flow from the proposition that schema can be present but latent. One implication is that depressed patients when they recover from depression (especially if they are not treated with CT) may retain latent schema that make them vulnerable to depression should the schema become activated at a later time. For this reason, cognitive therapists treat both overt symptoms of depression using behavioral and cognitive interventions (see chap. 4 and 5) and underlying schema (see chap. 6).

The depressed individual's schema, according to Beck's (1976) theory, are beliefs that the individual learned as a child in response to negative life events and circumstances. For example, a woman who grew up in a family in which she was abandoned by her father and neglected by her mother may develop schema such as "I am worthless" and "Others don't care about me." In a review, Ingram, Miranda, and Segal (1998) concluded that a significant body of data supports Beck's prediction that many depressed individuals experienced negative events in childhood.

Beck (1976) predicted that distorted, negative schema learned in childhood are not readily changed, despite disconfirming evidence in later life. This notion is consistent with evidence from cognitive and social psychology showing that individuals are more likely to notice and remember schema-consistent information than to notice and remember schema-inconsistent information (Williams, Watts, MacLeod, & Mathews, 1988). Thus, Susan, who believes "others are unreliable and don't come through for me," tends to ignore and minimize evidence (e.g., friends calling to check on her at home after she has a car accident) that disconfirms her schema. Instead, she focuses on evidence (e.g., the auto repairman made a mistake) that supports her schema. This aspect of the theory supports the use of active, intentional interventions to change schema in individuals who are vulnerable to depression and suggests that overcoming the biases of schema-driven information processing is difficult therapeutic work (see chap. 6).

DEPRESSIVE SYMPTOMS

As shown in Figure 1.2, Beck (1976) proposed that depressive symptoms consist of cognitions ("automatic thoughts"), behaviors, and moods. *Behaviors* consist of both motor behaviors (e.g., sitting passively, calling to cancel a therapy session, crying) and physiological responses (e.g., palpitations, sweating). The term *mood* in this part of the model corresponds to the layperson's usual understanding of that term. Mood states commonly experienced by depressed patients include depression, sadness, irritability, anxiety, guilt, anger, jealousy, and hopelessness. A mood state may be momentary or prolonged.

Beck (1976) labeled the *cognitions* of depressed patients as automatic thoughts because they seem to arise automatically, without effort or intention. The double arrows linking automatic thoughts, behaviors, and mood in Figure 1.2 reflect the cognitive theory's statement that all of these aspects of depression are linked in reciprocal causal relationships. That is, change in any one of the elements is expected to produce changes in the others. Persons and Miranda (1992) reviewed data supporting the theory's proposal that mood and cognitions change in tandem. More studies of this part of the theory are needed.

ACTIVATING EVENTS AND SITUATIONS

External situations activate latent schemas and give rise to symptoms. Thus, Beck's (1976) theory, like behavioral theories, gives a prominent role to the external environment. In addition to specifying the external large-scale life events (e.g., death of a parent) that activate schema to produce an episode of depressive symptoms, Beck's theory also attends to *small-scale situations* (e.g., your boss did not say hello) that activate negative mood, problematic automatic thoughts, and maladaptive behaviors. The *large-scale life events* are occurrences that precipitate an episode of illness and appear on the left-hand side of Figure 1.2. The *activating situations* are small-scale events that precipitate a negative mood state. Both the large-scale life events and the small-scale activating situations can appear in the Situation column of a Thought Record (see chap. 5). The cognitive–behavioral case formulation format described in chapter 2 asks the therapist to specify both the large-scale life events and the small-scale situations that activate negative mood, maladaptive behavior, and distorted thinking. Good evidence supports the role of both large-scale life events, particularly negative and uncontrollable events (G. W. Brown & Harris, 1989; Monroe & McQuaid, 1994), and small-scale events (see Kanner, Coyne, Schaefer, & Lazarus, 1981) in causing depressive episodes and symptoms.

A CLINICAL EXAMPLE

The saga of Garrett, a country–western musician, illustrates the relationships among large-scale life events, small-scale situations, schema, and the mood, behavioral, and cognitive features of depression described by cognitive theory and shows how the relationships among these elements described by the theory have direct intervention implications. Garrett began experiencing depressive symptoms after a meeting with the top executives of a record company in which they reneged on a record contract they had promised him (large-scale negative life event). This setback activated his schema ("I'm a loser," "Others don't respect me," and "The future is hopeless; things never work out for me."). He felt especially low (negative mood) after receiving a phone call canceling his gig in a local saloon (small-scale situation). After getting that call, Garrett began spending a lot of time lying around his mobile home watching TV (maladaptive behavior). He briefly considered working on a new song but was impeded by his thoughts: "What's the point? My career is in the toilet. I'm going nowhere but down. Anyway, I can't write until the muse returns, and she seems to have gone south for good" (negative automatic thoughts). He felt depressed, discouraged, and listless (depressed mood).

The cognitive theory's view of depression as consisting of reciprocally linked mood, cognitive, and behavioral elements activated by external situations has two primary intervention implications. It suggests that if Garrett were able to change his thinking ("Maybe I could spend a few minutes on a song today before I turn on the TV"), he would be more likely to take some productive action and feel better. The theory also suggests that if Garrett were to become more active (go to the No Tell Motel Café for breakfast instead of staying in bed all day), his mood might lighten and his thinking might become more optimistic. Thus, the theory leads directly to the behavioral (chap. 4, Activity Scheduling) and cognitive (chap. 5, Using the Thought Record) interventions of the therapy. The therapy focuses on changing cognitions and behavior rather than mood for the pragmatic reason that it is easier to design interventions that target behaviors and cognitions than to design interventions that target mood directly.

According to cognitive theory and as the example of Garrett illustrates, external life events play a role in causing symptoms (cognitions, moods, and behaviors). In addition, as the example of Garrett shows, an individual's cognitive, behavioral, and mood responses to negative life events can have feedback effects, changing the situation itself. For example, the recent cancellations activated Garrett's beliefs that he is a "no-talent loser," causing him to lie around passively, to avoid his buddies, and to postpone returning phone calls from the manager of the saloon in the next town who would like to hire Garrett. The result of this behavior, of course, is to exacerbate the situation; now Garrett is not doing any local gigs, is not seeing his buddies (who like him and tell him how good he is), and is not out and about where he would have a chance to "rustle up" some business. Thus, his passive behavior generates more evidence that supports his belief that he is a loser. In this cycle, negative external events activate schema, which lead to behaviors, moods, and cognitions that generate more evidence to support the schema, which in turn generate more problematic behaviors, mood, and cognitions, and so on, in a downward spiral.

Thus, the cognitive and behavioral interventions of the therapy, if successful, lead to changes in the external situations and events that depressed individuals experience in a positive feedback loop that counters the negative feedback loop described above. For example, if Garrett can take some action, he may get some positive feedback from his environment (an offer for a local gig, a buddy who invites him to join in a song-writing session) that will disconfirm his negative automatic thoughts and serve as an impetus for further activity, leading to more positive feedback from the environment, and so on, in an upward spiral. Similarly, cognitive restructuring can play a role in the upward spiral.

RELATIONSHIPS AMONG SCHEMA AND DEPRESSIVE SYMPTOMS

According to Beck's (1976) theory, activation of underlying schema leads to overt symptoms; this causal relationship is depicted in Figure 1.2 by the arrow leading from schema to symptoms. Note that the figure also includes an arrow from symptoms to schema, suggesting that changes in symptoms can lead to changes in schema. This arrow reflects the theory's proposal that changes in mood–cognition–behavioral elements of depression contribute to schema change.

For example, imagine that Garrett's friend (or his cognitive therapist) convinces him to go out one evening to the No Tell Motel Café, where he runs into some friends who tell him that the mayor has expressed an interest in hiring him for the Fourth of July town jubilee. Garrett calls the mayor the next day and finalizes the arrangements. As a result of taking this action (going out to the café), Garrett gets positive feedback from the environment that weakens his self-schema that he is a loser and his views of others as not respecting him. When he takes more action (calls the mayor), he gets even more positive feedback. That is, changes in the behaviors, automatic thoughts, and moods that make up depressive symptoms at the overt, or surface, level contribute to schema change at the latent, or underlying, level.

This reasoning suggests that interventions intended to produce changes in automatic thoughts and overt behavioral symptoms of depression can contribute to schema change. This hypothesis is consistent with the results of the dismantling study of CT conducted by Jacobson et al. (1996), in which the researchers found no superior outcome or relapse protection for patients who received schema change interventions in comparison with patients who received behavioral and cognitive interventions alone. However, more direct tests of this interesting hypothesis are needed.

The cognitive theory's statement that overt behavioral change leads to underlying cognitive change is similar to Foa and Kozak's (1986) account of the effectiveness of behavioral exposure treatment for clinical fears. Seligman and Johnston (1973) proposed a similar cognitive account of avoidance learning. According to Foa and Kozak, behavioral exposure therapy is effective because the emotional activation and behavior change required by exposure treatment activate the cognitive fear structure and present the patient with information that disconfirms key elements of the fear structure. That is, the phobic who believes that "I will die if I experience panic" learns by experiencing panic that he does not die. This line of reasoning suggests that the behavioral interventions of CT for depression and exposure treatment for anxiety work through the same mechanism, namely, cognitive change.

Foa and Kozak (1986) proposed that change in a cognitive fear structure cannot occur if the fearful individual learns new information in an emotionally neutral context. Instead, they argued that therapeutic cognitive change can only occur if the individual's fear structure is activated during treatment, so that the individual actually experiences fear during the treatment process. Foa and Kozak used the term *emotional processing* to describe what happens during effective treatment. Similarly, the cognitive therapist treating the depressed patient strives for emotional processing of new information, that is, an effectively charged (not emotionally sterile or intellectual) therapy session or homework experience during which the patient acquires information that disconfirms key cognitions that drive his or her depressive symptoms.

OVERVIEW OF THE THERAPY

The protocol for CT (Beck et al., 1979) consists of interventions directed at behaviors and at automatic thoughts to alleviate symptoms and modify schema to prevent relapse. All interventions are carried out in the context of a structured therapy session. The protocol suggests that treatment components be introduced in the following order: behavioral interventions, interventions directed at producing changes in automatic thoughts, and schema change interventions.

Beck et al. (1979) recommended that the therapist begin treatment with behavioral interventions, particularly when patients are severely depressed and functioning at a very low level. The rationale for this is that so long as the patient is not functioning, the lack of functioning serves as compelling evidence to support the depressed patient's negative cognitions (e.g., "I'm a hopeless case" or "I can't do anything"); therefore, behavioral change must come before cognitive interventions. Schema change interventions are introduced near the end of therapy because they are intended to reduce the patient's vulnerability to future depression; the first interventions of the therapy focus on alleviating depressive symptoms. In an individualized, formulation-driven approach to CT, as described in this book and specifically in more detail in the next chapter, the order of introduction for the components of CT may be modified depending on the needs of the individual patient.

EMPIRICAL STUDIES OF THE MECHANISMS OF ACTION OF COGNITIVE THERAPY

Some data support the value of each of the treatment components of Beck's (1976) CT (behavioral interventions, restructuring of automatic thoughts, schema change methods, and use of the structured therapy session). We review them in each chapter devoted to these components.

At the same time, it is important to acknowledge that not all of the available data unequivocally support the proposed mechanisms of action of the therapy. In a dismantling study, Jacobson et al. (1996) produced some findings that are not consistent with cognitive theory. Jacobson et al. compared outcomes of depressed patients treated with (a) behavior activation, (b) behavioral activation plus cognitive restructuring, or (c) behavioral activation plus cognitive restructuring plus schema change interventions. Outcomes for the three groups did not differ at posttreatment or 6 months later. These findings suggest that contrary to cognitive theory, cognitive restructuring and schema change interventions do not confer benefits to patients over and above the benefits of behavioral activation. Furthermore, some data support the role of nonspecific mechanisms, including the therapeutic alliance (Burns & Nolen-Hoeksema, 1992) and the therapist's allegiance to the therapy (Robinson, Berman, & Neimeyer, 1990). Finally, significant methodological difficulties (see Hollon, DeRubeis, & Evans, 1987) make it hard to unravel the precise mechanisms of action of the therapy. Thus, although cognitive theory provides a compelling account of the mechanisms of action of the therapy, it is undoubtedly not the whole story.

Summary and Conclusion

We reviewed outcome studies of CT for depression, presented a conceptual model for adapting RCT-validated protocols to an individual case, and reviewed Beck's cognitive theory and the evidence underpinning it. In the next chapter, we describe in detail the process of using Beck's cognitive theory and therapy protocol to develop an individualized case formulation and treatment plan for a depressed patient.

Individualized Case Formulation and Treatment Planning | 2

You've got to be careful if you don't know where you're going because you might not get there. (Yogi Berra)

A case formulation is an idiographic (individualized) theory that explains a particular patient's symptoms and problems, serves as the basis for an individualized treatment plan, and guides the therapy process. In this chapter, we teach the process of formulating and treatment planning based on Beck's (1976) cognitive theory of depression. We present

- a rationale for the use of an individualized case formulation
- levels of cognitive–behavioral case formulation
- components of the cognitive–behavioral case formulation and treatment plan
- guidelines for developing an initial formulation
- the process of developing a cognitive–behavioral formulation
- solving problems arising in formulation and treatment planning
- practice exercises
- further readings
- an example of a completed case formulation and treatment plan
- list of assessment tools for measuring therapeutic progress in depressed patients
- Cognitive–Behavioral Formulation and Treatment Plan form
- Progress Plot form.

Rationale for the Use of an Individualized Case Formulation

We recommend that clinicians develop an individualized case formulation to guide treatment rather than relying solely on a standardized protocol or working in an unplanned way for three reasons. The formulation provides a systematic method for individualizing the treatment, allows the therapist to take an empirical approach to the treatment of each case, and provides assistance during the treatment process.

SYSTEMATIC METHOD FOR INDIVIDUALIZING TREATMENT

Although the standardized treatment protocols studied in the randomized controlled trials (RCTs) are themselves based on a formulation, it is a nomothetic (general), not idiographic (individualized), formulation. In carrying out the protocol, the therapist must individualize it for the patient at hand. A case formulation provides a systematic method for doing this. When based on Beck's (1976) cognitive theory, the individualized case formulation specifies *which* life events activated *which* schema to produce *which* symptoms and problems and describes some of the cognitive–behavioral–mood components of the patient's depressive symptoms.

The format we provide for the individualized case formulation includes an exhaustive list of all of the patient's problems in all domains and describes some of the relationships among these problems. This information is particularly useful to therapists treating patients with multiple problems. Depressed patients frequently have multiple psychiatric, medical, and psychosocial problems, especially those treated in clinical practice rather than RCTs. An exhaustive problem list is helpful when setting and prioritizing treatment goals and when developing a working hypothesis (see p. 32) for these types of cases.

We use Beck's (1976) cognitive theory of psychopathology as a template for an individualized case formulation that explains all of the depressed patient's presenting problems and symptoms, as shown in Figure 2.1 (Persons, 1989). This use of Beck's theory is supported by the fact that his theory, originally developed as an account of depressive symptoms (Beck, 1976), has also been shown to provide useful accounts of numerous other psychiatric and behavioral symptoms and problems, including anxiety (Beck et al., 1985), substance abuse (Beck et al., 1993), couples problems (D'Attilio & Padesky, 1990), personality disorders (e.g.,

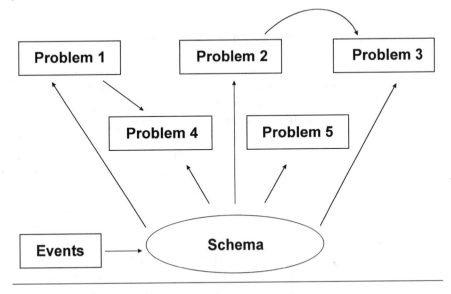

FIGURE 2.1

Applying Beck's cognitive theory of psychopathology to the multiple-problem case.

Beck et al., 1990), anger (Beck, 1999), and irritable bowel syndrome (Blanchard, Schwarz, & Neff, 1988).

AN EMPIRICAL APPROACH TO THE INDIVIDUAL CASE

A formulation-driven approach to treatment allows the therapist to take an empirical approach to the treatment of each case. In an empirical, hypothesis-testing approach to treatment using a case conceptualization, the therapist views the treatment of each case as an experiment, with $N = 1$. The therapist's hypothesis is the case formulation; the treatment plan is based on the formulation (see Hayes, Nelson, & Jarrett, 1987; Persons & Tompkins, 1997; and Turkat, 1985). The therapist collects data to assess the patient's response to interventions as the therapy proceeds. When the treatment response is poor, the therapist reviews the formulation, considers whether an alternative formulation might generate some new treatment interventions, and collects data to evaluate the patient's response to the new interventions. When proposing a new formulation, a therapist might rely on the nomothetic model on which the original formulation was based or he or she might draw on other empirically supported models of depression, including Lewinsohn's (Lewinsohn, Hoberman, & Hautzinger, 1985) behavioral theory, Nezu and Nezu's (1993) problem-solving theory, and Rehm's (1977) self-control theory. Without such a formulation, the therapist would make clinical decisions in a hit-or-miss manner and would have no systematic way of proceeding when treatment does not go smoothly (see Kendall, Kipnis, & Otto-Salaj, 1992).

ASSISTANCE DURING THE TREATMENT PROCESS

The case formulation assists the therapist during the treatment process in numerous ways. A formulation shared by the patient and therapist can strengthen the therapeutic alliance and enhance the patient's motivation to comply with treatment. The formulation guides treatment planning, as we emphasize later in this chapter (see also Haynes & O'Brien, 2000; and Turkat & Maisto, 1985). The formulation, particularly the Problem List, guides the choice of treatment goals, which in turn guides the choice of agenda items in the therapy session.

The specification of problems in terms of mood, behavioral, and cognitive components, as described later, often leads directly to behavioral (see chap. 4) and cognitive (chap. 5) intervention suggestions. For example, one student's procrastination problem may be a consequence of his belief that "there's no point tackling this project unless I have at least 3 hours to devote to it," whereas another may procrastinate because of his belief that "I can't learn this material."

The working hypothesis section of the formulation describes relationships among presenting problems and can yield suggestions about the order in which problems are best treated (see Haynes, 1992). For example, a working hypothesis that proposes that a woman's marital conflicts are caused in part by excessive drinking leads to a treatment plan that includes interventions to address the alcohol abuse. A working hypothesis that proposes that one cause of a lawyer's depression is self-critical thoughts about procrastination leads to a treatment plan that includes interventions to address both procrastination and self-criticism.

The formulation guides the therapist when he or she chooses a line of attack on a clinical problem, as in the case of Flora, a depressed housewife. Flora came to her therapy session complaining that she felt too depressed to drive to Sacramento to visit her cousin Rose, as she had promised to do. The therapist, guided by his formulation that Flora's view of herself was "my needs don't count; my role in life is to care for others" chose to work with her on this aspect of her problem and to encourage her to call Rose to say she would not be coming to visit. In contrast, the therapist operating without a formulation or with a different formulation ("I'm weak and fragile and can't do anything") might have chosen to help Flora "push" through her depression to make the visit.

The case formulation guides the clinician as he or she makes clinical decisions throughout the treatment process. For example, when a patient proposes to end his treatment, the formulation helps the therapist evaluate whether the proposed termination is premature (driven by a schema such as "my needs and health are unimportant"), appropriate (treatment goals have been met), or overdue (treatment goals have been met except that the patient believes that "if a problem arises, I won't be able to solve it on my own").

The formulation helps the therapist anticipate, understand, and effectively manage problems that arise in the therapy, including homework noncompliance and problems in the therapeutic relationship (Tompkins, 1997; Turkat & Brantley, 1981). For this reason, the case formulation includes a section in which the therapist uses the formulation to predict and anticipate potential obstacles to therapeutic success in the hope that if the therapist can anticipate them, some of these obstacles might be forestalled or prevented.

An example of the clinical value of an individualized case formulation is provided in the case of Ginger. When her therapist asked her in an early session to propose items for the agenda, Ginger, whose self-schema was "I am unimportant; no one is interested in me," stammered hesitantly that there was nothing in particular she wanted to discuss. After some probing, however, she revealed that just prior to the session, she had sat in the waiting room and made a list of things she wanted help with but then tore it up, believing the therapist would not be interested in her concerns. The therapist who guides interventions by a formulation can remain alert for, understand, and make therapeutic use of this type of event.

Levels of Cognitive–Behavioral Case Formulation

Cognitive–behavioral case formulation can occur at three levels: the case, the syndrome or problem, and the situation. The formulation at the level of the *case* is an attempt to understand the entire case as a whole, particularly the relationships among the patient's presenting problems and the schema that appear to underlie many or all of the problems. In this chapter, we primarily focus on the formulation at the level of the case, which uses the format described in the next section of this chapter (see Appendix 2A).

A formulation at the level of the *syndrome or problem* provides a conceptualization of a particular syndrome or problem, such as depressive symptoms, social anxiety, fatigue, or binge eating. Beck's (1976) cognitive theory of depression is a formulation at this level. In fact, when we use Beck's theory to conceptualize at the case level, we are extrapolating from his theory of the depressive syndrome, as noted above.

The third level of formulation occurs at the level of the *situation*; a situation-level formulation based on Beck's (1976) model contains information about a particular situation and information about the cognitive, behavioral, and mood components of the patient's reaction to that situation. For example, an insurance salesman came to his therapy session wanting to understand why he had suffered from insomnia the previous night and what could be done to prevent this from happening again. To answer these questions, the therapist using Beck's model would collect information about the details of the situation and about the cognitive, behavioral, and mood components of the salesman's reaction to the situation in an attempt to obtain a hypothesis about what happened. We sometimes call a formulation at this level of situation a "miniformulation."

At all levels, the formulation yields intervention suggestions. The therapist's hypotheses about the elements of the formulation at the level of the syndrome or the case are often based on observations of behaviors, moods, and cognitions that recur frequently in formulations at the situation level (J. S. Beck, 1995). Themes that emerge in multiple situations may reflect general schema, and recurring behaviors and moods may reflect syndromes or problems that belong on the Problem List of a case-level formulation.

Components of the Cognitive– Behavioral Case Formulation and Treatment Plan

A complete Cognitive–Behavioral Case Formulation and Treatment Plan has several components, as shown in Appendix 2A and described in detail here. In the following discussion, we describe each component of the formulation in detail; we provide the details therapists need as they write a formulation and treatment plan for a patient.

IDENTIFYING INFORMATION

This is where the therapist lists the patient's name, age, marital status, ethnicity, gender, occupational status, and living situation. Referral source is sometimes indicated here as well.

PROBLEM LIST

A comprehensive problem list describes any problems the patient is having in any of the following domains: psychological–psychiatric symptoms, interpersonal, occupational, medical, financial, housing, legal, and leisure. A comprehensive problem list allows the therapist to develop a formulation that provides the therapist (and patient) with a "big picture" view of the entire case.

Linehan (1993) provided a useful set of guidelines for ranking clinical problems; it can be used to prioritize the problem list items and treatment goals. Linehan's list in priority order includes the following:

- **Suicidality**. Suicidality is a high priority problem because if the patient is dead, none of his or her other problems will get solved.
- **Therapy-interfering behaviors**. Examples of these include homework noncompliance, medication noncompliance, repeatedly arriving late to the therapy session, not working collaboratively in the therapy session, and not getting along with the therapist. These behaviors are given a high priority, with the rationale that if they are not solved, the patient will not receive help solving any of the other problems on the problem list.
- **Behaviors that are dangerous or that interfere with quality of life**. These problems if not solved will likely prevent the patient from solving any other problem. Examples of these behaviors include major substance abuse, shoplifting or other criminal behavior, high-risk sexual behaviors, staying with a physically abusive partner, repeatedly getting fired, being unemployed, being homeless or at risk of being homeless, and not showing up for work.
- **Other problems**. These are problems the therapist observes or the patient describes that are not included in any of the other categories.

Because we are using Beck's (1976) theory as a template for the formulation, we describe as many of the problems on the problem list as possible using the three-component system Beck used of cognition, behavior, and mood to describe depressive symptoms. Viewing problems in these terms leads directly to intervention suggestions.

DIAGNOSIS

Psychiatric diagnosis is not, strictly speaking, a component of a case formulation. We include it on our form because diagnosis is helpful in formulating a case and planning treatment. Empirical findings suggest that depressed patients hold certain typical schema about themselves, others, the world, and the future (Ingram et al., 1998); therefore, a diagnosis of depression can suggest some schema hypotheses. The diagnosis can help the therapist with the problem list by alerting the therapist to look for typical disorders and problems that are comorbid with a depressive disorder. A psychiatric diagnosis also serves as a link to RCTs, in which researchers generally select patients on the basis of psychiatric diagnosis. Thus diagnosis, through its link to the RCTs, suggests empirically supported nomothetic formulations and treatment interventions.

WORKING HYPOTHESIS

This section has four subheadings: schema, precipitants and activating situations, origins, and summary; we describe each briefly here. These subheadings, of course, flow from Beck's (1976) theory. If the therapist were using a different cognitive–behavioral theory, the subheadings of this section would differ. A functional formulation, for example, would include sections for antecedents and consequences and would describe functional relationships (Haynes & O'Brien, 2000).

Schema

Schema or core beliefs are deep cognitive structures that enable an individual to interpret his or her experiences in a meaningful way (Beck et al., 1979). On the basis of Beck et al.'s work, we recommend that therapists propose hypotheses about the patient's views of self, others, the world, and the future. Sources of schema hypotheses for depressed patients include descriptions of clinical depression and writings about common comorbid conditions seen in depressed patients, including anxiety disorders (Beck et al., 1985), substance abuse problems (Beck et al., 1993), and Axis II disorders (Beck et al., 1990; Young, 1999).

Precipitants and Activating Situations

Precipitating events and activating situations are two types of external events. The term *precipitant* refers to large-scale events that appear to have caused an episode of illness. For example, a depressive episode might be precipitated by leaving home to go to college or by the breaking up of an important relationship. Sometimes the depressed person is not able to report precipitants of his symptoms, which may be chronic and longstanding, but can report what caused him to seek treatment, perhaps because the symptoms got worse or their presence became more intolerable than in the past. For example, a chronically depressed executive sought treatment when he found himself in a new, more challenging job in which his usual passive style of working was no longer tolerated by his superiors.

The term *activating situations* refers to small-scale events that trigger negative mood or maladaptive behaviors. Often these are smaller scale events that trigger the same schema activated by the precipitating event: For example, a student whose depression was precipitated by the breakup of his relationship with his girlfriend finds his mood is particularly low when he is sitting home alone on Saturday night, a time he and his girlfriend usually spent together. In this example, the precipitating event (rejection by girlfriend) and an activating situation (alone on Saturday night) both trigger his self-schema ("I'm worthless.").

The matching hypothesis (see chap. 1, p. 16) suggests that careful attention to the types of events and situations that are problematic for an individual can yield schema hypotheses, as in the example of the jilted student just given. Information about the activating circumstances and the schema hypotheses leads to intervention suggestions: Activity scheduling (see chap. 4) can help the student make some plans for Saturday night that he will enjoy more than staying home and moping, and a Thought Record (see chap. 5) can be used to identify the maladaptive schema and cognitive distortions and to begin to change them.

Origins

In the origins section, the therapist provides information from the patient's early learning history that explains how the patient might have learned his or her problematic schema. The therapist does this with a simple statement or with a brief description of one or two particularly poignant or powerful incidents that capture the patient's early experience. For example, "Janet's parents abused alcohol, neglected her, and had frequent angry outbursts over minor infractions when they were drinking. As a result, Janet learned that 'my needs are unimportant' and 'others cannot control their emotional reactions.'" Origins can also include modeling experiences or failures to learn important behaviors, as in the case of a patient who has significant social skills deficits due in part to growing up in a family in which both parents had marked social skills deficits.

Summary of the Working Hypothesis

This is the heart of the formulation. Here the therapist "tells a story" that describes how the patient learned the schema that are now being activated by external events to cause the symptoms and problems on the patient's problem list. The summary of the working hypothesis can be stated verbally or with a diagram with arrows linking the components of the formulation (see Haynes, 1992; and Persons & Davidson, 2000). In the summary of the working hypothesis, the therapist may explain some problems as resulting from schema activation and some from other problems. For example, depressive symptoms may result from activation of the schema that "I'm a failure" by a job setback; the depressive symptoms and resulting passivity may contribute to marital problems.

STRENGTHS AND ASSETS

This section of the formulation appears between the working hypothesis, which describes the psychopathology, and the treatment plan. This placement is intended to encourage the therapist to draw on the patient's strengths and assets when designing interventions to treat the psychopathology. Strengths and assets can include good social skills, the ability to work collaboratively, a sense of humor, a good job, financial resources, a good support network, a regular exercise regimen, intelligence, personal attractiveness, and a stable lifestyle.

TREATMENT PLAN

We place the treatment plan after the formulation because it flows from and is based on the formulation. This section has several subheadings, some of which are a standard part of any clinical writeup (modality, frequency, and adjunctive therapies) but are not specific to a cognitive–behavioral case formulation. We focus here on the components of the treatment plan that are specific to the cognitive–behavioral approach.

Goals (Measures)

Treatment goals must be mutually agreed on. The patient and therapist do not always agree on the problem list (we discuss this problem later, in the section titled Patient and Therapist Disagree About the Problem List or Treatment Goals). However, we believe patient and therapist must agree on the goals, for the reason stated by Yogi Berra at the beginning of this chapter; namely, a patient and therapist are unlikely to be very successful in accomplishing their goals if they do not agree on what they are.

It is important to describe goals concretely for several reasons. Clear, concrete goal statements facilitate the work of the therapy. For example, a vague goal statement that reads "Frida will feel better about herself" does not provide much guidance about what is or is not a relevant agenda item for the therapy session. However, specific goal statements, such as, "Frida will feel more confident at work and will contribute more often in staff meetings," "Frida will have fewer depressive symptoms," and "Frida will feel less upset and recover more quickly following arguments with her husband," provide clear guidance to the agenda-setting process (see chap. 3).

Stating goals concretely also facilitates outcome assessment. After stating each goal, we recommend that the therapist note what measures are used to track progress toward the goal. The topic of assessing progress in treatment is a substantial one that is beyond the scope of this book (to learn more about this topic, see Barlow et al., 1984; Bloom, Fischer, & Orme, 1995; and Ogles, Lambert, & Sawyer, 1995).

We recommend that clinicians ask their depressed patients to complete a self-report scale to assess depressive symptoms prior to each therapy session. Widely used measures include the BDI and the Burns Anxiety Inventory (details about these and other measures are provided in Exhibit 2.1). Other self-report measures can be used to track progress on other treatment goals; Fischer and Corcoran (1994a, 1994b) provided a useful compendium of measures. All these measures, of course, are nomothetic measures; to address the specific needs of the patient at hand, the therapist may wish to work with the patient to develop an idiographic measure tailored to the patient's particular difficulties. Self-monitoring methods (see Foster, Laverty-Finch, Gizzo, & Osantowski, 1999) are invaluable in this regard.

We recommend the use of a graph to track the patient's progress on depressive symptoms and other problems addressed in treatment; we provide a Progress Plot for this purpose (see Appendix 2B). A plot, where the session date is noted on the X axis, and the patient's score on the measure (e.g., a measure of depressive symptoms) is noted on the Y axis, is extremely useful in many ways (Kazdin, 1993). For example, if there is a marked perturbation (improvement or deterioration) in the patient's score, the clinician can ask about this; if a cause is ascertained (e.g., a vacation, a fight with the spouse, a change in the treatment plan), this can be noted on the plot and its implications for treatment can be discussed.

Interventions

The conceptual model used here states that the interventions of the therapy flow from the formulation. Thus, the interventions proposed in the treatment plan should be related to the deficits described in the working hypothesis, address some of the problems on the problem list, and facilitate the accomplishment of the goals. For example, assertiveness training is a logical intervention for a depressed woman whose symptoms are viewed as due in part to inhibited assertion because of her beliefs that her needs are unimportant and others will not be responsive to her. The depressed patient who is passive and inactive, spending hours every day in bed watching television, is likely to benefit

EXHIBIT 2.1

List of Assessment Tools for Measuring Therapeutic Progress in Depressed Patients

- *Beck Depression Inventory (BDI)*. Forms I and II are available from the Psychological Corporation, 555 Academic Court, San Antonio, TX 78204-9990. The BDI is a 21-item self-report scale assessing the severity of depressive symptoms. An advantage is that it is widely used in the randomized controlled trials (RCTs); therefore, clinicians who use it can compare their findings with those in the RCTs. BDI Form I is in Beck et al.'s (1979) book *Cognitive Therapy of Depression.* The BDI was revised in 1996 and relabeled "BDI-II." The Psychological Corporation catalogue describes the relationship between the BDI and BDI-II as follows: "Items on the new scale replace items that dealt with symptoms of weight loss, changes in body image, and somatic preoccupation. Another item on the BDI that tapped work difficulty was revised to examine loss of energy. Also, sleep loss and appetite loss items were revised to assess both increases and decreases in sleep and appetite." ·
- *Burns Anxiety Inventory, Burns Depression Checklist.* These and other cognitive therapy forms are available from David Burns, MD, as part of the Therapist's Toolkit (see Dr. Burns's webpage on the World Wide Web: http://www.feelinggood.com).
- *Symptom Checklist-90 Revised (SCL-90R).* This 90-item instrument was developed by Leonard Derogatis in 1975 to assess overall psychological distress. It measures symptoms on nine dimensions: somatization, obsessive-compulsive, interpersonal sensitivity, depression, anxiety, hostility, phobic anxiety, paranoid ideation, and psychoticism. The SCL-90R may be purchased from National Computer Systems, Inc., P. O. Box 1416, Minneapolis, MN 55440; 800/627-7271.
- *CAGE Questionnaire.* This questionnaire is a 4-item screening tool developed by Mayfield, McLeod, and Hall (1974) to assess for alcohol problems.
- *Yale–Brown Obsessive Compulsive Scale (Y-BOCS).* For permission to use Y-BOCS, contact Dr. Wayne Goodman, University of Florida College of Medicine, Gainesville, FL 32610. The original version was published by Goodman et al. (1989) in their article "The Yale–Brown Obsessive Compulsive Scale I: Development, Use, and Reliability."

Note. For other useful measures, see Fischer and Corcoran's (1994) *Measures for Clinical Practice: A Sourcebook. Vol. 1: Couples, Families and Children* and *Vol. 2: Adults.*

from activity scheduling. Data supporting the notion that interventions tailored to the patient's deficits are particularly helpful when treating depressed patients were provided by McKnight, Nelson, Hayes, and Jarrett (1984) in their single-case study entitled "Importance of Treating Individually Assessed Response Classes in the Amelioration of Depression." McKnight et al.'s depressed patients who had social skills deficits benefited most from social skills training and those with cognitive deficits benefited most from cognitive restructuring. To strengthen the empirical foundation of the therapy, we recommend that therapists use, when possible, interventions described in protocols that have been shown in RCTs to provide effective treatment for depression.

Obstacles

In this section of the formulation, the clinician uses information from any part of the formulation (e.g., problem list, schema) to make predictions about difficulties that might arise in the therapy. If the therapist can anticipate obstacles, he or she may be more successful in preventing or overcoming them than if they are unanticipated. For example, we have learned from experience that depressed patients who believe that "my needs don't count; my role in life is to care for others" tend to wish to terminate treatment prematurely. Although these patients sometimes seek treatment when they are extremely uncomfortable, as soon as they get some relief and their distress is manageable, their view of themselves as unimportant and not worth caring for causes them to want to end their treatment. If the therapist can anticipate and predict this tendency, he or she can initiate a discussion of this issue with the patient early in the treatment in an attempt to prevent a premature termination. For an example of a completed Cognitive–Behavioral Case Formulation and Treatment Plan form, see Exhibit 2.2.

Guidelines for Developing an Initial Formulation

Formulation and treatment planning are an ongoing, iterative process, with the formulation leading to a treatment plan, data evaluating the outcome of the treatment plan leading to revisions of the formulation and to new intervention ideas, and so on. This process occurs throughout treatment. Although the formulation is constantly subject to revision, we do recommend that after three or four sessions, the therapist write down an initial formulation and treatment plan using the format in Appendix 2A. We also recommend that the therapist review the formulation and treatment plan periodically, especially if the process or outcome of treatment is problematic.

The initial part of the formulation and treatment planning process is particularly important to the success of the treatment; therefore, we focus on it here. We recommend that the therapist use the following general guidelines (see Exhibit 2.3) during the initial formulation process.

1. *Make a comprehensive problem list.* We believe it is important to collect a comprehensive problem list, even though the treatment plan is likely to focus on only some of the patient's problems (Linehan, 1993; Nezu & Nezu, 1993; Turkat & Maisto, 1985). Without a comprehensive problem list, the therapist may fail to

EXHIBIT 2.2

Cognitive–Behavioral Case Formulation and Treatment Plan for "Jenna"

Name: Jenna

Identifying Information: 34 MWF, not working, living with husband and 5-year-old daughter.

Problem List:

1. Depressive symptoms. BDI = 22. Sadness, lack of enjoyment, feeling like a failure, self-criticism, lack of energy, suicidal thoughts but no plan or intent, difficulty making decisions, loss of interest in others, insomnia, loss of appetite. "Things are not good. Nothing much matters. Sometimes I don't care if I live or die."

2. Not working. Believes work would help "pull her out" of depression, as it did in the past, but "I don't know what I want to do, and I don't have any energy to do it. I just can't get moving." Enjoyed working as an editor for 5 years, "but I don't know what my long-term career goals are."

3. Marital problems. Following a stillbirth, she wanted to consider adoption, but her husband did not and refused to discuss it. He wanted her to "let go [of her distress about the stillbirth] and move on"; she is resentful that he does not acknowledge her pain, loss, suffering. She describes the miscarriage as a "black hole" in their marriage. She fears asserting herself with him, saying that when she speaks up about her resentment, "he just throws it back at me." They do not fight, but they are distant, estranged.

4. Fear of freeway, bridge driving. "There are a lot of bad drivers, and I'm very vulnerable in a car on the freeway." "I could turn the steering wheel and slam into a wall." Fear of panic attacks while driving, onset following several panic attacks while driving several years ago. She avoids busy streets, freeways, and bridges and rarely drives outside a 2-mile radius surrounding her home.

5. Socially isolated. Jenna has two women friends, mothers of children that are her daughter's friends, but she is not close to either, does not initiate any activities with them.

Diagnosis:

Axis I: Major depressive disorder, panic disorder with agoraphobia

Axis II: Dependent personality disorder

Axis III: None. History of miscarriage, stillbirth.

Axis IV: Unemployed, marital problems, socially isolated.

Axis V: 50

Working Hypothesis:

Schema:

Self: "I'm not ready for and can't handle adult responsibilities." "I can't make good choices/decisions." "I'm weak and vulnerable and need lots of nurturing, support."

Other: "My husband doesn't care, doesn't want to be supportive of my needs." "My husband is to blame for my unhappiness; he must change if I am to be happy."

World: "Life shouldn't be so hard; it should be easier."

World/future: "Bad things can happen to me, my child, such as disease, death, accident."

Precipitants: Move to California about 5 years ago; as part of this transition, Jenna gave up her job that had been a confidence builder. Other precipitants include several miscarriages and a stillborn child.

(continued)

E X H I B I T 2 . 2 continued

Activating situations: Challenging driving situations (freeways, bridges), a need to speak up to her husband about her emotional distress, wanting to seek work.

Origins: Parents modeled difficulty handling loss of a child who died of leukemia; it was never discussed in the family, and the patient learned about her dead brother from her grandmother when she was 9 years old. The patient's mother was fearful and overprotective: "Don't try some thing if you're not sure you can do it—something bad might happen."

Summary of the working hypothesis: Jenna's move to California and the loss of her job that had given her some direction, satisfaction, and feedback that she can make decisions and handle adult responsibilities activated her beliefs that she cannot handle adult/demanding decisions/responsibilities. In response to these beliefs and the anxiety they produced when activated, she withdrew from responsibilities, including looking for a job and driving in challenging freeway and bridge situations, which left her isolated, resulting in a loss of potential sources of gratification, leading to her depression. Jenna's beliefs that she cannot make good choices and cannot choose a career path, coupled with driving problems, inertia from depression, and resentment toward her husband, block her from seeking work. The stillbirth and miscarriages and resulting unhappiness supported or activated Jenna's beliefs that she needs lots of support/nurturing, that her husband is unsupportive, and that he is responsible for her unhappiness, contributing to her depression, inertia, and marital problems.

Strengths and Assets: Stable life circumstances (husband who supports the family), a good network of friends, well educated, bright, psychologically minded.

Treatment Plan:

Goals (measures):
1. Reduce depressive symptoms (BDI).
2. Increase comfort while driving freeways and bridges (measured through patient's ratings of items on a fear hierarchy). Increase the distance (now about 2 miles) she is willing to drive from home.
3. Return to work.
4. Reduce marital tension and estrangement, as measured by spending more enjoyable time together as a couple.

Modality: Individual cognitive–behavior therapy   *Frequency:* Weekly

Interventions
1. Activity scheduling to increase sources of pleasure and mastery, alone and perhaps with husband.
2. Build a hierarchy and use gradual exposure to alleviate driving fears.
3. Teach anxiety-management skills, including diaphragmatic breathing.
4. Interceptive exposure (exposure to internal somatic sensations; see Barlow, Craske, Cerny, & Klosko, 1989).
5. Cognitive restructuring to work on fears that she cannot handle driving or other challenges, beliefs that her happiness depends on her husband, fears that bad things could happen, beliefs she cannot choose and act on a professional goal.
6. Schema change methods to tackle her belief that she is weak/vulnerable.
7. Assertiveness training, especially with her husband.

Adjunct therapies: Consider antidepressant medications, couples therapy.

Obstacles:
1. Jenna's view that others are responsible for her happiness may make it difficult for her to work aggressively in treatment to overcome her problems.

Note. MWF = married, white female; BDI = Beck Depression Inventory; 50 = score on Global Assessment Functioning Scale.

EXHIBIT 2.3

Guidelines for Developing an Initial Formulation

- Make a comprehensive problem list.
- Describe problems in concrete, behavioral terms.
- Base the formulation on a well-validated theory.
- Begin formulating early.
- Share the formulation with the patient.

obtain important pieces of the puzzle needed to understand the case (hence to develop a good working hypothesis) and propose an effective treatment plan. If the therapist is not aware of the larger context of the patient's disorder (what Taylor, 1971, called the "predicament"), the treatment may be derailed when a problem the therapist had not anticipated (e.g., the patient cannot pay the rent) suddenly becomes a crisis.

2. *Describe problems in concrete, behavioral terms.* Beck (1976) proposed that depressive (and other symptoms) consist of cognitive, behavioral, and mood components. Therefore, we recommend that therapists attempt to describe patients' problems in these terms. Describing problems in terms of mood–cognition–behavior components can readily lead to interventions (cognitive restructuring and activity scheduling) to modify those components of the problem. Concrete, behavioral descriptions also make it easier to translate problems into measurable goals and into therapy session agenda items.

3. *Base the formulation on a well-validated theory.* We recommend that therapists base their formulation on a nomothetic theory that is well-supported empirically, underpins a therapy that has been shown effective in RCTs, or both. This strategy strengthens the empirical foundation of the therapist's clinical work. If treatment based on the well-validated nomothetic theories fails, treatment plans that are based on unvalidated theories can be attempted after informing the patient about the experimental nature of the treatment.

4. *Begin formulating early.* We (and others; see Sackett et al., 1997; Turkat & Maisto, 1985) recommend that clinicians begin developing a formulation right away, as soon as any information is collected, rather than collecting a lot of information before beginning to hypothesize about the case. Studies of medical problem solving (Elstein, Shulman, & Sprafka, 1978) indicate that highly competent physicians develop initial diagnostic hypotheses very early in the assessment process.

5. *Share the formulation with the patient.* A shared formulation builds collaboration and the patient's allegiance to the treatment plan. In addition, the patient's reaction to and input about the formulation can provide valuable feedback. One of us (J. B. P) once proposed to her patient, a personnel manager who was having panic attacks in response to stressful work conflicts, the hypothesis that the manager appeared to believe, "I can't cope with these conflicts." When the therapist proposed this formulation, the manager responded resentfully: "No, that's not it. My belief is 'I shouldn't have to cope with this nonsense!'" This feedback was invaluable—in fact, the manager's formulation was superior to the therapist's. The manager's formulation explained not only her panic symptoms but also her resentful, frustrated mood and her reluctance to work hard in treatment to overcome her panic symptoms. It is not possible or useful to share with the patient every formulation hypothesis the therapist entertains. However, we encourage therapists to use their patient's self-knowledge and problem-solving abilities when developing and testing formulations.

The Process of Developing a Cognitive–Behavioral Case Formulation

A complete cognitive–behavioral case formulation contains a lot of information, as Appendix 2A's format shows. A fully elaborated discussion of the assessment strategies the clinician can use to obtain this information is beyond the scope of this book (see J. S. Beck, 1995; Bellack & Hersen, 1998; Bloom et al., 1995; Haynes & O'Brien, 2000). We focus here on a few highlights of the process of gathering information for formulation and treatment planning.

Collecting some of the information needed for the formulation is straightforward. For example, as illustrated in the videotape *Cognitive–Behavior Therapy for Depression: Individualized Case Formulation and Treatment Planning* (Persons, Tompkins, & Davidson, 2000), the therapist can ask the patient directly about problems in all the various domains to be assessed. In addition, the therapist can ask the patient and perhaps others to complete rating scales or collect monitoring data, interview family members or others (e.g., teachers), conduct behavioral assessments (e.g., measuring in feet how close to a snake the snake-phobic patient will go), and collect physiological data.

Therapists find the process of developing schema hypotheses to be a particularly challenging one. We recommend three general strategies: attend to repeated automatic thoughts (particularly to those that occur across a variety of situations), use the "downward arrow" method, and use self-report scales. We describe each in turn.

As an example of the strategy of attending to repeated automatic thoughts, an attorney who came to his therapy session quite anxious and agitated about several work stresses began speaking rapidly and agitatedly about his situation. As the therapist listened carefully, she heard the patient repeatedly say "I'm out of control; I can't handle this." When the therapist pointed this out to the attorney, he immediately evaluated his self-statement as incorrect, asserting "I *can* handle all this stuff. I always do." He admitted, however, that the thought "I can't handle it" was a frequent one and, based on the brief sample observed in the therapist's office, probably recurred dozens of times a day. Because of the prominence of the "I'm out of control; I can't handle this" thought in the attorney's stream of thinking, the therapist hypothesized that it reflected an aspect of his self-schema.

Cognitive theory and current models of information processing suggest that automatic thoughts occurring in multiple and diverse situations are more likely to arise from underlying schema than are automatic thoughts activated only in certain particular situations. One of us (J. B. P.) treated a depressed chemist (Dr. P.) who had multiple problems: His marriage was in trouble, he was not performing up to par at work, and he was procrastinating on many minor and major personal matters (e.g., filing his income tax return). When the therapist asked him to propose an agenda item for his therapy session, Dr. P. was silent. When asked about this, he reported "I don't know where to start. Nothing I try will help anyway." Dr. P. also had great difficulty completing therapy homework assignments, finding himself easily overwhelmed and immobilized if an unanticipated obstacle arose; when this happened, he simply shut down and stopped trying. These problems in therapy and many of Dr. P's problems outside of therapy appeared to be related to his prevailing automatic thought, namely, "I can't tackle that task. I'll fail." This recurring pattern of thinking in multiple situations suggested that Dr. P.'s schema about himself was "I'm a failure. I can't do anything right" and that his schema about the world was "the world is overwhelming, unsolvable, unmanageable."

To pinpoint themes in patients' thinking, we recommend that the therapist retain in the patient's clinical record copies of their completed Thought Records done as homework or during the therapy session (see chap. 5) and review them periodically to search for themes. If patients are keeping a notebook for their therapy materials, they can review them as well. Frequently repeated automatic thoughts yield good schema hypotheses.

Another useful method for arriving at schema hypotheses from automatic thoughts is the "downward arrow," or "vertical arrow," method described by David Burns (1999). To use the downward arrow method, choose an automatic thought that occurs in a particular situation, ideally one that recurs frequently and in multiple situations. Begin by saying to your patient, "Assume that thought is true. Tell me why is this upsetting to you? What does it mean about you?" Repeat as often as necessary until you seem to reach "the bottom"—a core belief about the self, others, the world, or the future.

For example, a depressed graduate student who used the downward arrow method produced the following series of automatic thoughts: "If I try that project, I won't be able to do it," "If I'm not able to do it, this means I'm incompetent," "If I'm incompetent, this means I'm a loser," and "If I'm a loser, no one will want to be with me."

Self-report scales can also serve as sources of schema hypotheses. The two best known measures of this sort are the Dysfunctional Attitude Scale, a version of which is published in *Feeling Good* (Burns, 1999), and the Young Schema Questionnaire developed by Jeffrey Young (1999).

Solving Problems Arising in Formulation and Treatment Planning

TIME

Individualized formulation and treatment planning is time consuming. Writing up a complete formulation and treatment plan can require $1\frac{1}{2}$ hours or more, and this time is not usually directly billable. Spending this amount of time on a formulation and treatment plan is particularly demanding when treatment is brief. One solution to the time problem is to carry out at least some of the formulation work in the session; this is consistent with the goal of making the formulation process as collaborative as possible. For example, the patient and therapist can work together during an early therapy session to make a comprehensive problem list. Some patients can be asked to make a list of goals as an early homework assignment; in other cases, a patient and therapist can develop these together in the therapy session.

DIFFICULTY OBTAINING A PROBLEM LIST

Most depressed patients are quite responsive to the therapist's request to make a comprehensive problem list. However, some patients have difficulty tolerating this task and assiduously avoid it. In our experience, some of the patients who avoid this task do so because they hold beliefs such as "If I acknowledge any weakness, this means I'm a total loser and I'm vulnerable to domination (or humiliation, attack, or criticism) by others, including my therapist." That is, the process of describing problems activates the patient's schema, produces negative emotions, and prompts escape, avoidance, defensive, or even aggressive behaviors. When working with these patients, it is often necessary to proceed slowly and provide a lot of empathy and support in addition to the usual problem-solving strategies (Linehan, 1993). The therapist may wish to accommodate this patient by approaching the collection of a problem list a bit at a time rather than in a single session. If the patient and therapist are able to form a solid, trusting working relationship, it may be possible to get the patient's fear of discussing problems and vulnerabilities "out on the table" and work on it as a problem in its own right.

PATIENT AND THERAPIST DISAGREE ABOUT THE PROBLEM LIST OR TREATMENT GOALS

A patient and therapist do not always hold the same view of the patient's problem list or goals of treatment. Common areas of disagreement include substance abuse and marital problems. Sometimes the patient and therapist can handle a disagreement by simply monitoring it or by agreeing to disagree, but occasionally the disagreement aborts the treatment altogether.

Disagreement about goals is highly undesirable because treatment goals are often difficult to accomplish even when patient and therapist agree on them. Disagreement about items on the problem list is common and sometimes can be problematic. A useful principle for deciding whether a problem list disagreement is manageable or not is the following: If the disagreement is not likely (in the therapist's judgment or as determined empirically) to prevent the patient from reaching his or her goals or to lead to a catastrophe (e.g., financial insolvency), then divergence is acceptable.

For example, a graphic artist who sought treatment for depression described his marriage as happy but also described frequent arguments with his wife, which suggested that his marriage was probably not going smoothly. When the therapist pointed out this discrepancy, the patient became defensive and insisted he had a happy marriage. In this case, the therapist placed the item "possible marital problem" on the patient's problem list and moved forward to work with the patient on his depression, keeping the marital issue in mind as a problem that might need to be taken up if the patient did not make good progress with a treatment plan that ignored the marital issue. As often happens, the marital problem boiled up again, more seriously, several weeks later; at that point, the patient agreed to seek couples therapy to address it.

Similarly, a young computer programmer sought treatment for anxiety and was eager to learn relaxation and time-management skills. This young executive also had a significant social skills deficit, but when the therapist raised this issue for discussion, the executive denied that social interactions were a problem for him. The therapist agreed to move ahead with a treatment plan to address the young man's anxiety; after making good progress on these problems, the executive was able to acknowledge his social skills problem and agreed to tackle it.

Although disagreement about the items on the problem list can be benign, as in the examples just presented, disagreement about treatment goals is more problematic. However, sometimes a successful treatment can be carried out even when the patient and therapist disagree about the goals, particularly if the disagreement is about a lower priority goal. Sometimes, as in the examples just presented, the therapist has a covert goal that the patient acknowledge and agree to tackle a certain problem that the therapist perceives but the patient does not.

Substance abuse is a common area of disagreement. It is not uncommon for the therapist to view a patient's substance use as a problem and to want the patient to set a treatment goal to reduce or stop it, but the patient insists that it is not a problem and refuses to address it. Sometimes a disagreement of this sort can be addressed through an empirical test, as in the case of Terry, a depressed attorney. Terry drank nearly a bottle of wine a day, usually while socializing after work with his colleagues. He sought treatment for depressive symptoms, which were making him miserable and interfering with his work. He also had a tumultuous and conflictual relationship with a girlfriend. The therapist hypothesized that Terry's alcohol use was contributing to his various difficulties and recommended that Terry set a treatment goal of reducing his drinking. Terry refused, insisting that he wanted to work on his depression and that the drinking was not a problem and, in fact, helped him cope.

The therapist adopted an empirical approach, proposing to Terry "I'll work with you on the depression for 3 months. I'll ask you to complete a Beck Depression Inventory (BDI) weekly to monitor your progress. If after 3 months we are making good progress, I will continue working with you. If at that point we have not made good progress, I will not be willing to continue treating you unless you agree to renegotiate your treatment plan to address your alcohol use." Terry was agreeable to this plan and tried it. Unfortunately, after 3 months of treatment, Terry's depression, as evaluated with the BDI, was essentially unchanged, and his life was increasingly dominated by chaotic interactions with his girl-friend. He had stopped drinking for 1 week during the 3-month treat-ment period, and he admitted that during that week his mood improved and his relationship settled down considerably. However, he resumed drinking. When treatment was reviewed at the end of 3 months, he had to admit that he had not made any gains in alleviating his depression. However, Terry was still not willing to work on his drinking, so he re-luctantly terminated his treatment.

PATIENT AND THERAPIST DISAGREE ON THE FORMULATION AND TREATMENT PLAN

We recommend that the therapist share all or parts of the proposed formulation, especially the working hypothesis, with the patient (see Guideline 5). This can provide the therapist with information leading to a useful reworking of the formulation. But sometimes the patient and therapist disagree on key elements of the formulation or treatment plan.

When the patient and therapist disagree on the working hypothesis, it is ideal if this disagreement can be put out on the table and examined collaboratively. A depressed young architect with a major marital prob-lem was drinking nearly a bottle of wine 1 or 2 evenings a week. The therapist's formulation was that this drinking contributed to her marital problems because the architect became irritable and feisty when she drank and provoked nasty verbal conflicts with her husband. When the therapist proposed this hypothesis, the patient did not agree with it—but she did agree to collect data to test it. After 3 weeks of data collec-tion, the architect saw that fights with her husband were, after all, linked to her drinking, and she agreed to set a treatment goal of reduc-ing her drinking.

Occasionally the disagreement between the patient and therapist on the formulation or treatment plan is so fundamental that the treatment cannot go forward. A depressed freelance copy editor sought treatment for depression. He lived alone and worked at home. He was quite iso-lated, with only one friend he saw rarely. He experienced debilitating pain following a botched surgical procedure, and he was drinking large quantities of alcohol to manage his pain. He had filed a lawsuit against the physician whom he believed was responsible for his condition. He owned a gun and was contemplating using it to kill himself if things got too bad. After evaluating the case, the therapist proposed a treatment plan that required the patient to surrender the gun, to meet for twice-weekly therapy sessions, to agree that reducing his alcohol intake was a top priority, and to do homework outside the therapy session. In addition, the therapist warned the patient that if he did not make rapid improvement, a day treatment or pain treatment program would be necessary. The patient refused to agree to this treatment plan, insisting that he could not do homework outside the therapy session. His therapist then secured treatment for the patient with another provider.

As these examples illustrate, the process of formulating and treatment planning is complex and obstacles do arise. The case formulation itself can be a fruitful source of hypotheses about the obstacles to the process of formulation and treatment planning, as illustrated in the example of the patient who was unable to make a problem list because acknowledging problems activated his fears of being dominated and humiliated.

Summary and Conclusion

In this chapter, we described in detail the reasons for, format of, and process of developing an individualized Cognitive–Behavioral Case Formulation and Treatment Plan. The formulation guides the use of the activity scheduling, cognitive restructuring, and schema change interventions described in the next three chapters of this book.

Practice Exercises

These exercises are intended for the use of clinicians who wish to practice the formulation and treatment planning strategies taught in this chapter.

1. Choose the case of a patient who is not making good progress in treatment and take the time to write up a complete case formulation and treatment plan using the format presented in Appendix 2A. After completing that task, follow these steps:
   (a) List in the obstacles section of your treatment plan any new ideas you have about why this patient is not making progress.
   (b) List in the interventions section of your treatment plan any new intervention ideas that arise from this formulation.
   (c) Discuss with the patient the issue of treatment progress and your ideas about why he or she is not making progress and what new interventions might be attempted.
   (d) If you attempt new interventions, monitor outcome to evaluate the value of the new formulation and treatment plan.

2. Choose a complex, multiproblem case. Then walk through the following steps:

    (a) Write down, alone or working collaboratively with your patient, a complete list of the patient's problems in all of the following domains: psychological–psychiatric symptoms, interpersonal, occupational, medical, financial, housing, legal, and leisure.

    (b) Using the problem list, work with your patient to arrive at a clear list of treatment goals.

    (c) Develop with your patient a collaborative agreement about the priority order of the goals.

3. Choose one of your cases and suggest to your patient that you work together to make a short list of treatment goals. Do this in one of the therapy sessions or ask the patient to do this task as a homework assignment and bring the list of goals to the next session for review. For as many of the goals as possible, devise a method to measure progress toward the goal.

4. Obtain a self-report scale of depressive symptoms (see Exhibit 2.2. Assessment Tools for Measuring Therapeutic Progress in Depressed Patients). Ask one of your depressed patients to complete the scale prior to each session. Or ask your patient to provide daily ratings on a mood scale, ranging from 0 (*feeling fine*) to 100 (*totally depressed*). Graph the scores on the Progress Plot (Appendix 2B). Review the plot each week with your patient. To remind yourself to give the measure to the patient the next time you meet, place the depression scale and the Progress Plot in the front of the patient's chart.

5. If you believe your patients will dislike the process of completing a self-report scale to measure depressive symptoms and bringing it to the therapy session, collect some data to test your hypothesis. Provide the rationale for collecting weekly assessments of progress, obtain a measure of depressive symptoms (see Exhibit 2.2), and propose to your patient that he or she complete the measure weekly. Track scores on a Progress Plot (Appendix 2B). Afterward, ask your patient the following: "Was this helpful? How did it feel?" Ask yourself the same questions.

6. Read the following two vignettes and answer the accompanying questions. (Answers are provided at the end of this question.)

    (a) Sam, a retired businessman, described two recent problematic situations. On Sunday evening, after a weekend in which he had cancelled some dates with friends because he felt too depressed to go out, he felt really down and had the following thoughts: "I can't do anything; I can't get anything done; I make plans, but then I can't follow through. I'll never get better." The following day he received a call from a client who wanted him to provide some business advice. He put off meeting with his client because of the following thoughts: "I have nothing to contribute, and it will be a huge effort to drive to his office to see him."

(b) Jeannie, a married, working mother, reported two problematic situations. On Friday afternoon, she had planned to visit with her best friend after work, something she and her friend rarely found the time to do. In the late afternoon, her daughter called, needing a ride home after school. When her mother asked her to take the bus, the child became angry, complaining "You never help me out when I need you!" Her husband also called, asking her to cook dinner so that he could have more time to work at home during the evening. In response to these two calls, Jeannie canceled her plans to visit her friend, picked her daughter up at school, and cooked dinner for her family. She felt depressed that evening and had the following thoughts: "My daughter is angry and pulling away from me. I'm not a very good mother. I try hard, but it's never enough. It's never going to change."

At work the next day, her boss asked her to take on a new project that would require lots of overtime for the next 2 months. Jeannie did not want to accept the project, but she agreed to do it anyway. Later, she felt upset, thinking "I should have said 'no'; I'm already dropping too many balls at home. But if I don't take on this project, my boss will be disappointed in me, and I might get a negative evaluation and lose my job."

Question: As the therapist, on the basis of this information, propose a hypothesis about Sam's and Jeannie's self-schema. Propose a preliminary Working Hypothesis about the relationship among activating situations, schema, automatic thoughts, mood, and behaviors for these patients.

Answers

(a) Sam's view of himself appears to be the following: "I can't do anything; I'm helpless, ineffectual, ineffective, impotent." When situations require him to take action, his negative self-schema are activated, he feels anxious and depressed, and he has thoughts about how hard it will be to take action and how ineffectual his actions will be. Behaviorally, he withdraws and avoids; these behaviors provide further support for his belief that he is incapable and ineffective.

(b) Jeannie's view of herself appears to be the following: "My needs are not important; I'm not worthy." Her view of others appears to be that "others are demanding, needy, unable to manage on their own." She also appears to believe that "If I do not meet others' needs, they will reject me." When others make requests of her, her schema are activated and she has thoughts that drive her to accommodate others before herself. As a result of pushing herself to meet others' needs, she feels emotionally unsupported, overwhelmed, and depressed. Taking action to meet others' needs and ignoring her own produces more evidence supporting her view of herself as unworthy.

Further Readings and Videotapes

Barlow, D. H., Hayes, S. C., & Nelson, R. O. (1984). *The scientist–practitioner: Research and accountability in clinical and educational settings*. New York: Pergamon.

Beck, J. S. (1995). *Cognitive therapy: Basics and beyond*. New York: Guilford Press. Chap. 1, Cognitive conceptualization.

Freeman, A. (1992). Developing treatment conceptualizations in cognitive therapy. In A. Freeman & F. Dattilio (Eds.), *Casebook of cognitive–behavior therapy* (pp. 13–23). New York: Kluwer Academic/Plenum Press.

Haynes, S. N., & O'Brien, W. H. (1990). Functional analysis in behavior therapy. *Clinical Psychology Review, 10,* 649–668.

Haynes, S. N., & O'Brien, W. H. (2000). *Principles and practice of behavioral assessment*. New York: Plenum Press.

Persons, J. B. (1989). *Cognitive therapy in practice: A case formulation approach*. New York: Norton.

Persons, J. B., & Davidson, J. (2000). Cognitive–behavioral case formulation. In K. Dobson (Ed.), *Handbook of cognitive–behavioral therapies* (pp. 86–110). New York: Guilford Press.

Persons, J. B., & Tompkins, M. A. (1997). Cognitive–behavioral case formulation. In T. D. Eells (Ed.), *Handbook of psychotherapy case formulation* (pp. 319–339). New York: Guilford Press.

Persons, J. B., Tompkins, M. A., & Davidson, J. (2000). *Cognitive–behavior therapy for depression: Individualized case formulation and treatment planning* [Videotape]. Washington, DC: American Psychological Association.

Sackett, D. L., Haynes, R. B., Guyatt, G. H., & Tugwell, P. (1991). *Clinical epidemiology: A basic science for clinical medicine*. Boston: Little, Brown.

Tompkins, M. A. (1997). Case formulation in cognitive–behavioral therapy. In R. Leahy (Ed.), *Practicing cognitive therapy: A guide to interventions* (pp. 37–59). Northvale, NJ: Aronson.

Turkat, I. D. (Ed.). (1985). *Behavioral case formulation*. New York: Plenum Press.

Turkat, I. D., & Maisto, S. A. (1985). Personality disorders: Application of the experimental method to the formulation and modification of personality disorders. In D. H. Barlow (Ed.), *Clinical handbook of psychological disorders: A step-by-step treatment manual* (pp. 502–570). New York: Guilford Press.

APPENDIX 2A: COGNITIVE–BEHAVIORAL CASE FORMULATION AND TREATMENT PLAN

Name: _____

Identifying information: _____

Problem List

1. _____
2. _____
3. _____
4. _____
5. _____
6. _____
7. _____
8. _____

Diagnosis

Axis I: _____

Axis II: _____

Axis III: _____

Axis IV: _____

Axis V: _____

Working Hypothesis

Schema

Self: _____   Others: _____

World: _____   Future: _____

Precipitants: _____

Activating situations: _____

Origins: _____

_____

Summary of the Working Hypothesis: _____

Strengths and Assets: _____

Treatment Plan:

Goals (measures)

1. _____

2. _____

3. _____

4. _____

Modality: _____ *Frequency:* _____

Interventions: _____

_____

Adjunct therapies: _____

Obstacles: _____

APPENDIX 2B: PROGRESS PLOT

Progress Plot for

Score on measure

25	50	75
20	40	60
15	30	45
10	20	30
5	10	15
4	8	12
3	6	9
2	4	6
1	2	3
0	0	0

Session date

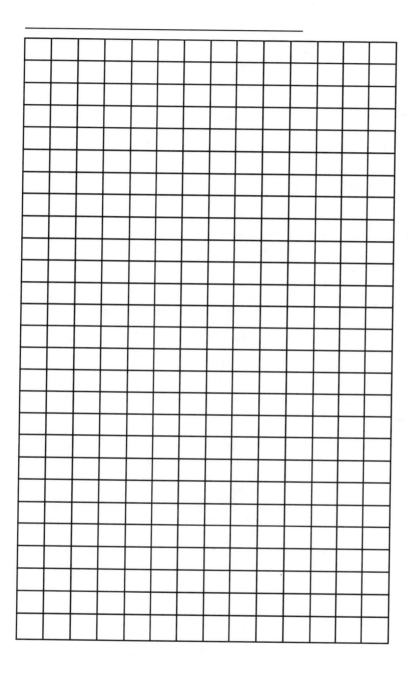

Structure of the Therapy Session

3

Action to be effective must be directed to clearly conceived ends.
(Jawaharlal Nehru)

Perhaps nothing distinguishes cognitive–behavior therapy (CBT) from other psychotherapies more than its use of a carefully, explicitly structured therapy session. Most sessions (the usual exceptions being the initial session and the final session) of CBT follow the structure described in this chapter; even the initial and final sessions include most of the structural elements described here.

In this chapter, we present

- theoretical and empirical underpinnings for using a structured session
- components of a structured CBT session
- guidelines for implementing two components: agenda setting and assigning homework
- strategies for overcoming common obstacles to the use of a structured therapy session
- practice exercises
- further readings and videotapes
- Therapy Session Log.

Underpinnings of the Use of a Structured Therapy Session

THEORETICAL

The use of a carefully and explicitly structured therapy session reflects the structured nature of the therapy itself. CBT is a goal-oriented, active approach to treatment. The patient and therapist together set explicit goals for treatment, and they work together collaboratively to attempt to accomplish these goals. The therapist's role is to teach the patient skills helpful in reaching these goals—skills that often involve making changes in cognitions and behaviors. The patient is expected to practice the skills and do other tasks outside the therapy session.

To prepare the patient for and obtain the patient's agreement to the structured and goal-directed nature of the therapy, the therapist can describe the features of the therapy in an early session. When describing the skills to be learned in the therapy, the therapist might tell the depressed patient the following:

> I recommend that we begin the therapy with activity scheduling to get you moving and to decrease your social isolation. Once your mood has improved a bit, I'll teach you strategies to manage the thoughts that may be maintaining your depression. Later in treatment, we can tackle the core beliefs that may make you vulnerable to future episodes of depression. How does this sound?

The use of a structured therapy session facilitates the therapist's efforts to teach skills to help the patient accomplish the goals of treatment. The therapist who uses a structured therapy session also models for the patient the types of skills and behaviors that the therapist is trying to teach: goal-oriented, active, problem-solving behaviors focused on concrete, specific difficulties.

EMPIRICAL

When the adequacy of cognitive therapy (CT) is evaluated in research settings, investigators often use the Cognitive Therapy Scale (CTS; Young & Beck, 1980). The CTS is also used by the Academy of Cognitive Therapy to certify cognitive therapists.[1] The CTS includes several of the components of the structured therapy session described in this chapter, including agenda setting, asking for feedback from the patient, and reviewing and assigning homework. The presence of these items on the CTS reflects how central they are to the definition of competent CT.

Brian Shaw et al. (1999) recently provided evidence that supports the notion that structured therapy sessions are helpful to depressed patients. Examining data from the NIMH (National Institute of Mental Health) Treatment of Depression Collaborative Research Program, Shaw et al. showed that the outcome of patients treated with CBT was positively related to the therapist's competency ratings on the structural

---

[1]The CTS may be obtained from the Academy of Cognitive Therapy's website (http://www.academyofct.org). The Academy of Cognitive Therapy is a nonprofit body that certifies competent cognitive therapists.

items of the CTS. In fact, patient outcome was more strongly related to the therapist's ability to structure the session than it was to the therapist's skill, as measured by items assessing both general therapeutic skills (e.g., interpersonal effectiveness) and cognitive–behavioral intervention skills (e.g., focusing on cognitions). Similarly, Robert DeRubeis and colleagues (DeRubeis & Feeley, 1990; Feeley, DeRubeis, & Gelfand, 1999) showed in two studies that those elements of CT they termed "concrete" predicted symptom reduction early in the treatment of depressed patients. Concrete elements of CT include (a) setting and following the agenda and (b) assigning and reviewing homework.

Homework is the most frequently studied structural component of CT. Several studies show that depressed patients treated with CT have better outcome if they complete homework assignments outside the therapy session (Burns & Nolen-Hoeksema, 1991; Fennell & Teasdale, 1987; Harmon, Nelson, & Hayes, 1980; Neimeyer & Feixas, 1990; Persons et al., 1988; Startup & Edmonds, 1994; see a review by Detweiler & Whisman, 1999). In recent studies, David Burns (Burns & Nolen-Hoeksema, 1992; Burns & Spangler, 2000), using structural modeling techniques, found that homework compliance is not simply a concomitant of recovery but plays a direct causal role in reducing the depressive symptoms of patients treated with CT.

Components of a Session

An effective CBT session includes the following components (Davidson, Persons, & Tompkins, 2000a):

- Orient the patient to the structure of the session
- Check in
- Set the agenda
- Review homework
- Work the agenda
- Give periodic summaries
- Assign homework
- Summarize the session and ask for feedback.

We describe each component here, giving special emphasis to setting the agenda and assigning homework—two of the most important components.

ORIENT THE PATIENT TO THE STRUCTURE OF THE SESSION

It is difficult for patients to follow a structure or format if they do not know what it is. In the orientation part of the therapy session, the therapist explicitly tells the patient what will happen in the first part of the therapy session. To do this, the therapist can say the following:

> Let's start with a brief check in: I want to hear about how you're feeling and how your week went and to take a look at your measures [if the patient has brought any self-report measures or logs]. Then let's set an agenda; one thing we want to be sure to put on the agenda is to review your homework from last time.

A statement such as this sets the tone of the session and tells the patient that the session, like the rest of the therapy, will be structured, orderly, and problem focused.

CHECK IN

Each therapy session begins with a brief check in during which the therapist inquires about the following:

- any significant events today and since the last session
- current mood
- objective measures completed (e.g., depression or anxiety scales)
- significant discrepancies (between the scores on measures and the verbal check in)
- significant changes (improvement or worsening).

We encourage therapists to limit the time spent on these items to about 5–10 minutes. If one or more of the topics listed here requires a more extended discussion, we recommend that it be placed on the therapy session agenda. It is important that the therapist clearly distinguish the check in (which is a prelude to working on the agenda) from the rest of the therapy session to ensure that the primary focus of each session is a mutually agreed-on agenda item. Handling this part of the session effectively is challenging; we discuss problems that often arise in this part of the session later in this chapter. The check in serves many purposes, including a ready way to build and maintain a solid therapeutic alliance. A bit of chit chat and the opportunity for the therapist to express warmth and concern for the patient helps to build the rapport essential for carrying out the cognitive–behavioral interventions that follow.

The check in may lead to relevant agenda items. For example, a patient might tell his therapist that a new problem has arisen or that he is upset about a recent event. Or in reviewing the patient's objective measures (e.g., suicide item on a depression scale), the therapist may note a change in the patient's status. These data can alert the therapist to important matters that merit attention but that the patient may not propose as agenda items for whatever reason. Finally, the check in offers the therapist an opportunity to observe the patient's mental status and nonverbal cues (e.g., if the patient looks distressed or happy) that may be worth commenting on and may lead to an agenda item for the session.

SET THE AGENDA

A therapy session agenda is a short list of topics that the patient and therapist agree will be the focus of the therapy session. The agenda may include a new situation or problem, further work on an old situation or problem, or a piece of housekeeping related to the therapy itself (e.g., a report from the patient about a meeting with an adjunct therapist). A typical agenda for a good therapy session might be the following: review homework from last time, work on recent upset with mother-in-law, and plan for the upcoming weekend. Although it is not included on the agenda, the session also should include working to develop a new homework assignment.

Agenda setting is one of the most important components of the session and can make the difference between a structured session and an unstructured one. Initially, the therapist may play a very active role and model effective agenda setting. As the therapy proceeds, the responsibility for setting the agenda usually shifts, as patients learn to do this for themselves.

Agenda setting can often be accomplished with a simple, direct question from the therapist: "What would you like to put on the agenda for your therapy session today?" In some situations (e.g., when working with a patient who has difficulty maintaining a clear focus on therapy goals, managing time, or making decisions or who tends to avoid discussing important topics), the therapist may wish to suggest agenda items: "I suggest we follow up on the work we did last time with your time-management problems. Can we put that on our agenda for today?" Or the therapist can limit the patient's choices by asking "Would you prefer to work on A or B?" (instead of "What should we work on today?").

Guidelines for Successful Agenda Setting

Successful agenda setting depends on the effective implementation of a set of simple guidelines we provide here (for easy reference, see Exhibit 3.1).

Work Collaboratively

Successful agenda setting begins with a straightforward invitation by the therapist, such as "Let's make an agenda for our session today." We

Guidelines for Successful Agenda Setting

- Work collaboratively.
- Prioritize agenda items.
- Always review homework (this is an excellent first agenda item).
- Be realistic about what can be accomplished.
- Keep treatment goals in mind when setting agenda items.

recommend that both the patient and therapist play an active role in contributing to the agenda. Sometimes after each contributes potential items, it may be necessary to conduct a brief negotiation to arrive at a mutually agreeable agenda. We cannot stress enough the importance of collaboration when setting the agenda. If the therapist sets the agenda without inviting input from the patient, the patient may not feel motivated to put much energy into the session. If the patient sets the agenda without input from the therapist, the patient's automatic maladaptive patterns may prevent him or her from using the therapy time effectively.

Prioritize Agenda Items

Once agenda items are agreed on, it is helpful to prioritize the items so that the most important items receive sufficient time and emphasis. Prioritizing is ideally done collaboratively, of course. Prioritizing agenda items for the therapy session is usually fairly straightforward. However, when working with complex, difficult patients who present a different set of urgent problems each week, the therapist may become confused or uncertain about what issues to tackle in what order. For these patients, Linehan (1993) provided a useful heuristic for ranking clinical problems, with suicidal behavior and therapy-interfering behaviors, such as homework noncompliance, as the top two positions (see chap. 2, page 31).

Always Review Homework; This Is an Excellent First Agenda Item

We recommend that the therapist suggest that the first item on the agenda be a review of the previous week's homework assignment. It is helpful to discuss homework early in the therapy session because it provides a useful bridge from the previous session and it may otherwise be forgotten. Following this step also emphasizes the importance of homework to the patient. In addition, a review of homework can open up important issues that need attention. In fact, sometimes the patient and therapist will agree to change the therapy session agenda to focus on handling the problems that came up in the homework.

For example, Jason, a depressed college student who lived at home with his mother, agreed to activity scheduling homework (see chap. 4) to help him increase his school attendance and spend more time with friends on weekends. During the homework review, Jason's therapist examined Jason's Activity Schedule, which showed that he had gone to school during the week but had failed to go out at all over the weekend. Jason admitted that he had made plans to go out with his friends on Saturday but had canceled the plans at the last minute when his mother complained that she was not feeling well. In fact, this happened frequently. After careful questioning, the therapist learned that "not feeling well" meant that Jason's mother feared she might have a panic attack while Jason was away. This discovery led to a very useful agenda item focused on how Jason could respond to his mother's requests in the future.

Be Realistic About What Can Be Accomplished

It is important that the therapist play an active role in setting a realistic agenda. Many patients cannot manage their time effectively; this may be part of why they are seeking treatment. Time management can be difficult for patients who are perfectionistic, have difficulty with decision making, are unassertive, or tend to avoid unpleasant feelings or matters. Realistically, a workable therapy session agenda can only include homework review and one or two substantial items.

Keep Treatment Goals in Mind When Setting Agenda Items

This guideline may seem too obvious to mention, but it is not unusual for patients to wish to spend the session on agenda items that do not help them reach their treatment goals. Reasons include the patient's difficulty keeping treatment goals in mind, tendencies to avoid, the wish to focus on immediate emotional upsets that may not be related to therapy goals, or experience with previous unstructured therapies. The therapist has a responsibility to play an active role in contributing items for the agenda that will help the patient make progress toward his or her treatment goals.

REVIEW HOMEWORK

The fastest way to discourage patients from completing homework assignments is for the therapist to fail to review the homework in the next session. Suppose your therapist or clinical supervisor made homework assignments but did not review them with you. How motivated would you be to complete them? How important would they seem to you? For this reason, we consider homework review a must for every therapy session. Homework review can be brief or can take up most or all of a session. The therapist and patient may spend the time discussing what was learned in the homework or what problems arose in the homework plan and how they might be solved. We discuss strategies for handling homework noncompliance later in this chapter (see Completing a Homework Assignment).

We recommend that the review of the previous week's homework follow the agenda-setting component of the session and that homework review appear as the first item on the therapy session agenda. The advantage of this strategy is that patient and therapist work together to set an agenda before any significant piece of work (i.e., homework review) is undertaken.

An alternative ordering of the homework review deserves consideration, however; therapists may find that they prefer it for some of their patients. An alternative order is to review the homework before setting the agenda for the session. This strategy can be particularly helpful for patients who tend to bring up a new problem or crisis every session. For these patients, reviewing the homework before setting the agenda can help keep the therapy on track and prevent it from being derailed by the "crisis of the week."

WORK THE AGENDA

The heart of the session involves working on the agreed-on agenda items. The therapist is likely to use one of the main intervention strategies (e.g., activity scheduling, using the Thought Record, schema change methods) of CBT. We describe each of these interventions in detail in later chapters of this book.

As the therapist works on the agenda items, he or she is responsible for managing the time in the session. Summaries (discussed in more detail in the next section) can help here, and decisions about how to use therapy time can be negotiated collaboratively. The following statement is an example of what a therapist could say:

> We've been working on the conflict with your boss, and we've identified a couple of strategies you can try. We have about 15 minutes left before we need to start wrapping things up. We could work more on this issue with your boss, or we could take up the medication question. Which would you prefer?

Sometimes when patients take up an agenda item, they become lost in recounting the details of the problem and their feelings about it. Some patients have a view of themselves as powerless and the world as all powerful; these schema may underpin an individual's tendency to use the therapy session to complain about the unfairness of it all rather than to adopt a problem-solving stance. Other patients may have been socialized in previous nondirective therapies to engage in a process of unstructured free association or to explore the early origins of their difficulties.

In general, the cognitive–behavior therapist strives to help the patient adopt a problem-solving approach to agenda items. At the same time, it is important to recognize that when people are upset, they often need time to "vent" and receive some empathic support from the therapist before they are ready to move on to solving a problem. To help patients make the transition to a problem-solving stance, sometimes venting and griping can be labeled explicitly for what it is and placed on the therapy session agenda: "I need to spend a few minutes moaning and groaning about this problem before I can work on it." To help patients make the transition to problem solving, Burns (1999) suggested that the therapist address this issue explicitly: "I hear you saying you're pretty upset about the argument with your boss yesterday. Is that something you would like some help with?" The validation strategies developed by Linehan (1993) for working with individuals who have borderline personality disorder are also helpful in managing this situation.

Often after choosing an agenda item, a significant amount of therapy time can be spent making the item more explicit or setting up the item so that it can become a solvable problem. We recommend that therapists use Socratic questioning to turn a vague agenda item, such as "problems at work," into a solvable problem or goal to be tackled in the therapy session, such as "I'd like to waste less time on email at work" or "I'd like to work on how I could get along better with my coworkers."

Attention to the case formulation can be helpful when choosing what tack to take to help a patient with a problem. For example, a busy office manager who is overwhelmed with too many things to do may need help saying *no* to requests from others, delegating to subordinates, responding to negative automatic thoughts that invalidate her own judgments about priorities, and scheduling her time. The case formulation can yield hypotheses about the schema that are driving these difficulties and may lead to some intervention ideas.

Burns (1999) recommended that the therapist work collaboratively with the patient to decide how to tackle agenda items, saying, for example,

> We could work on the problem with your boss by using a
> Thought Record to help you develop some ways to calm yourself
> down when you're feeling angry with her. We could do some
> role-plays to help you be assertive with your boss. Or perhaps
> you have another idea about how to work on this. How should
> we work on this today?

GIVE PERIODIC SUMMARIES

Summaries can be useful at several points during the therapy session. A summary after the agenda is set clarifies what the session will cover. A summary during the session provides a review of what has been learned, clarifies what will be covered next, and improves collaboration and time management. A summary at the end of the session is the most important; we discuss this later in more detail.

We recommend that the therapist provide a summary at least once during the main part of the session for several reasons. Because therapy material is often highly charged, patients may have difficulty concentrating or processing information in the session and brief summaries during the session help patients focus on and remember what has been learned. For this same reason, some patients benefit from taking notes in the therapy session or audiotaping the session and listening to the tape later. We recommend giving each patient a bound or spiral notebook or folder in which to keep therapy notes and materials. Patients can use the therapy notebook to record the summaries provided by the therapist at the end of each session, to review before a therapy session, to jot notes about what they would like to work on in the next session, to check their homework assignment if they are not clear about it, and to read during times of need instead of or before calling the therapist.

Summaries can strengthen collaboration between therapist and patient by clearly acknowledging what has been accomplished in the session and offering the patient options for how he or she would like to spend the remainder of the session time. For example, the therapist might say "We used the Thought Record to list the thoughts that were making you feel hopeless, and we've gotten some answers that you say seem helpful. Would you like to spend more time on this, or would you rather go on to talk about how to handle the weekend?" Summaries provide valuable assistance with time management because at the time of a summary, the patient and therapist can look at the clock as they decide how to spend the balance of the session.

ASSIGN HOMEWORK

One of the chief objectives of CBT is to teach new skills. Therapy homework permits the patient to practice newly learned skills in his or her natural environments and to work daily on resolving problems. For example, a housewife whose depression is due in part to her difficulty being appropriately assertive with others can try out new assertive behaviors in the therapy session. However, the new skills will have little impact on her life if she cannot use the skills outside the session with her coworkers, husband, and mother-in-law. We define homework as any task that (a) is collaboratively devised by the therapist and patient, (b) is intended to facilitate new learning or to enable the patient to practice a new skill and apply it to differing situations over time, and (c) is to be practiced outside the therapy session. We offer four guidelines to help therapists make successful homework assignments (see Exhibit 3.2).

Guidelines for Making a Successful Homework Assignment

Work Collaboratively

Make certain the patient—not just the therapist—understands the rationale for the homework assignment and agrees to do the assignment. If the patient does not believe the assignment will be useful or if he or she does not agree to do the assignment, it may not happen. To enhance compliance and collaboration, therapists can ask the patient to suggest the homework assignment or to have input into the assignment.

Be Specific and Concrete

Without a concrete and specific plan, patients may be confused about exactly what they are expected to do, which may mean they are less likely to do the homework. A concrete and specific homework plan includes details about when, where, with whom, for how long, and using what materials. These details may seem boring and insignificant, but they can make the difference between a homework assignment that is successfully completed and one that is not. Be sure to allow enough time in the session to work out all these details. We recommend providing a form or an index card for the patient to use when completing the assignment. For example, one of us (J. B. P.) asked a hospital executive who wanted to stop smoking to log each cigarette she smoked during the week. She came back the following week with only a few cigarettes recorded on a stray piece of paper—a "log" she admitted she had completed on the commuter train on the way to the therapy session. After the therapist gave the executive an index card and showed

---

EXHIBIT 3.2

Guidelines for Making a Successful Homework Assignment

- Work collaboratively.
- Be specific and concrete.
- Tie the assignment to the work in session (and thereby to the treatment goals).
- Anticipate obstacles.

her how to slip it under the cellophane of the cigarette pack itself, the executive was able to keep a complete log of every cigarette she smoked at the time she smoked it. She then brought an excellent log to the next therapy session. This simple intervention made a huge difference in the success of her therapy. The Therapy Session Log, described later in this chapter, and the Activity Schedule, Thought Record, Evidence Record, and Positive Data Log forms we provide later in the book are all intended to facilitate homework outside of therapy sessions.

Tie the Assignment to the Work in the Session (and Thereby to the Treatment Goals)

A good homework assignment builds on the work of the session. If the agenda for the session is guided by the treatment goals, as recommended earlier, and the homework comes out of the work of the session, then the homework contributes to progress toward the treatment goals. These connections may seem obvious, but they are not easy to maintain and may not be obvious to patients. We have found that therapists often fail to take the time necessary to explain to patients how the suggested homework assignment is related to what they have been talking about in the therapy session and to their treatment goals. This is particularly true for demanding assignments, such as completing Thought Records or collecting evidence for a Positive Data Log. If patients understand the link between a homework assignment and a treatment goal, they are more likely to carry out the assignment.

Sometimes in the middle of the therapy session and flowing directly from the work of the session, an obvious homework assignment will present itself. We encourage therapists to seize these moments when they occur. Or the therapist can wait until the end of the session to develop a homework assignment based on the work.

Sometimes a therapy session gets stalled. For example, the patient and therapist begin completing a Thought Record (see chap. 5) and are not successful at obtaining any coping thoughts that the patient can use to respond to his or her maladaptive automatic thoughts. In this situation, it is tempting to ask the patient to complete the Thought Record as homework. A moment of consideration, however, suggests that this strategy is not wise. We have learned to use the rule "Do not assign as homework a task the patient was unable to complete in the therapy session."[2]

Two examples of homework assignments tied to the work of the therapy session follow. After a therapy session spent working on the negative automatic thoughts that blocked an unemployed nurse from

---

[2]We thank Rhoda Olkin for this heuristic.

looking in the want ads to search for job opportunities, the nurse agreed to spend 30 minutes on Sunday morning looking in the want ads for job possibilities. He was asked to bring the newspaper with jobs he might apply for circled to his next therapy session. After learning skills in the session to ask her husband to take out the garbage, a wife agreed to make this request of her husband that evening after dinner. As a fallback plan, if she found herself unable to speak up to her husband, she agreed to spend 10 minutes writing down on a Thought Record the thoughts she had that blocked her from talking to him about taking out the garbage.

Anticipate Obstacles

Spend some time during the session anticipating and making contingency plans to handle any obstacles that might prevent the patient from completing the homework task. One way is to ask the patient directly: "Do you see any obstacles that would make it hard for you to carry out the assignment?" Sometimes it is helpful to verify that the patient will have an opportunity to do the homework assignment. For example, the wife who agreed to ask her husband to take out the garbage is not likely to be successful at doing this if her husband will be out of town all week.

Sometimes the patient proposes a homework assignment that appears unrealistic to the therapist. When this happens, use Socratic questioning to examine this issue collaboratively. Sometimes the therapist does not perceive any concrete obstacles but does not feel confident that his or her patient has fully anticipated the obstacles that might arise. In this situation, the therapist can practice the proposed homework assignment with the patient during a session as a way of assessing and troubleshooting potential difficulties. For example, the therapist might work with the patient to role-play calling a friend on the telephone to ask her out to a movie.

Cognitive rehearsal (Beck, 1976) can also be used to identify obstacles to completing homework assignments. In cognitive rehearsal, the patient walks through all the steps involved in completing the task while the therapist listens for potential obstacles. For example, Toni, a depressed unemployed software engineer, agreed as part of her activity scheduling to wash a load of clothes. During a cognitive rehearsal, Toni imagined, out loud, each step of the process. As she imagined reaching for the laundry soap, she remembered that she had run out of soap several weeks ago. Toni and her therapist then discussed how and when she would go to the grocery store to buy laundry soap. Had Toni not rehearsed her homework assignment beforehand, she might have thrown up her hands and gone back to bed when she encountered the empty detergent box.

To anticipate potential obstacles to homework compliance, the therapist can ask the patient "What thoughts might you have that would block you from doing the assignment?" This query might elicit thoughts such as "What's the point? This won't help" or "I'll never be able to do this." The patient and therapist can generate responses to these problematic thoughts that the patient can then use to push through the obstacles. Of course, if the patient has difficulty obtaining responses to these thoughts, the patient may not be ready for the homework assignment in question, and the therapist may wish to back off to a simpler assignment, such as simply monitoring the problem that the patient is not ready to tackle.

Some obstacles can be addressed simply by the way the homework assignment is posed. If the assignment is "Get some job leads from my former boss," the patient has a lower chance of succeeding than if the assignment is "Call my former boss for some job leads." In the first case, the success or failure of the assignment rests in large part on someone else (the former boss), whereas in the second case, it rests entirely in the patient's hands.

SUMMARIZE THE SESSION AND ASK FOR FEEDBACK

At the end of the session, the therapist offers a summary of what happened in the session and requests feedback from the patient. The summary can be brief, such as the following:

> We reviewed your homework and learned you had trouble logging your pleasurable activities because the form I gave you was awkward to use. We decided you will try using the daily calendar page of your Palm Pilot instead, and we programmed a note on each page of next week's calendar to cue you to enter pleasurable activities. We spent most of the session working on your weekend visit with your mother, and we agreed that the weekend will go better if you speak up proactively to initiate plans with her rather than just going along with her plans. We set a homework plan for you to call her tonight to suggest some activities, and we did a role-play of this phone call to prepare for it.

After the summary, the therapist asks the patient for feedback about the session: "Can you give me some feedback about our session today? Was there anything we did that was particularly helpful or anything that was less helpful or not a good use of our time? Was there anything I said that rubbed you the wrong way?" A written scale the patient can use to provide feedback, the Empathy Scale, was devised by David Burns and is available as part of his *Therapist's Toolkit* (1998). Therapists who use this form will discover that there is frequently a disconcertingly large discrepancy between the therapist's and the patient's perceptions of the therapy session. This fact reinforces the importance of the feedback portion of the therapy session. The feedback portion of the therapy session is particularly important when working with individuals who are prone to interpersonal difficulties and misunderstandings because the feedback discussion allows for any misunderstandings to be aired and addressed promptly.

Learning to Conduct a Structured Therapy Session

For the beginning therapist or the experienced therapist who is new to the notion of structured therapy sessions, the prospect of incorporating all of the components of a structured CBT session into his or her daily work is daunting. It is amazingly easy for even the experienced cognitive–behavior therapist to stray from the structure; it is disconcertingly easy to omit setting a formal agenda, to forget to monitor homework assignments scrupulously, or to avoid asking for feedback.

To facilitate learning and consistently using a structured therapy session, we recommend that the therapist use the Therapy Session Log (see Appendix 3A). We designed the form to allow the therapist to focus on only one or two therapy session components at a time. Choose one or two components you would like to try using, become more skilled at using, or use more consistently. Write the names of those components in the "Components" columns on the Therapy Session Log. For each session you conduct, log your patient's initials, indicate whether or not you used the component, and add observations about what made it easy or difficult to use the components, the patient's reaction to the components, and any other useful information. The form reminds you to keep using the components and may yield useful information about what helps and hinders the process. After working for 1 or 2 weeks on one or two components, start a new Therapy Session Log to focus on one or two different components.

Over time with concerted attention and practice, use of the components will become more comfortable and automatic. Note that we recommend that therapists begin to learn and use the components of a structured therapy session even before learning the other technical interventions of the therapy (activity scheduling, using the Thought Record, and schema change) described later in this book. All the structural components described in this chapter—from orienting the patient to the structure of the session to asking for feedback—can be used even by therapists who have not yet learned to carry out the main technical interventions of CBT.

Overcoming Obstacles to Using a Structured Therapy Session

In this section, we discuss common obstacles and strategies for overcoming them that arise when setting the agenda for the therapy session, adhering to the agenda, and assigning homework. We also discuss the problem of homework noncompliance.

SETTING THE AGENDA

Setting an agenda for a therapy session sounds deceptively simple: The patient and therapist agree on what problems will be worked on in the therapy session, the priority order of the items, and perhaps the amount of time dedicated to each. This simple task is much more difficult than it sounds, however. Some patients have great difficulty proposing agenda items; others have difficulty reaching a collaborative agreement with their therapist about what items belong on the agenda; and others avoid or sidestep agenda setting altogether.

Sometimes patients have difficulty offering agenda items because they have had past experiences with psychotherapy in which they were the passive recipients of treatment. These patients might expect therapists to "fix" them, whereas cognitive–behavior therapists expect patients to be equal partners in developing realistic solutions to their problems.

The patient's individualized formulation can yield hypotheses about the origins of agenda-setting difficulties. For example, Noah, a depressed banker, believed that "If I acknowledge my problems, I'll be attacked and criticized." He assiduously avoided agenda setting, fearing that if he acknowledged any problems, he would be vulnerable to attack and criticism by his therapist. He slid by the therapist's request for agenda items by deferring to the therapist's proposed agenda items or by simply plunging into an emotional description of a recent problem. When the therapist noticed Noah's evasion of agenda setting, she asked him about it. They then spent a useful therapy session completing a Thought Record in which Noah listed and developed responses to his automatic thoughts that blocked him from suggesting agenda items for the therapy session. His homework assignment, of course, was to bring two agenda items to the subsequent therapy session.

Vera, a retired teacher, did not offer any agenda items to work on in her therapy sessions and shot down any suggestions her therapist made. Vera's therapist reviewed her formulation and noted that she had been the only child of largely absent parents. She held the belief that "others aren't interested in me," which the therapist hypothesized contributed to Vera's apparent need to describe to the therapist at length her history and accomplishments rather than working on an explicit problem. With Vera's formulation in mind, her therapist suggested that he and she set aside the next few sessions "so I can really get to know you." After her therapist demonstrated his interest in this way, Vera was more open to agenda setting.

A frequent agenda-setting problem is that the check-in portion of the session turns into the therapy session without an explicit agenda being set. Sometimes this problem results from the therapist's assumption that if, for example, Joe plunges into a session talking about the problem he has with his boss and spends the entire session on this issue, the problem with his boss is obviously the main topic Joe wants to take up in that session. This is not necessarily so. Any experienced therapist can offer more than one example of the fallacy of this thinking. In Joe's case, he talked on and on about his boss and then 5 minutes before the end of the session flew into a panic, exclaiming "I don't want to spend the session on my boss. I really need to talk about the fact that I've told my wife I'm going to blow my stack if she lets her parents visit us this weekend!"

Sometimes the check-in part of the session bleeds into the therapy session because the patient or therapist (or both) have poor time-management skills. In this case, the time-management problem in the session can serve as a useful training ground for teaching time-management skills, including how to prioritize problems, how to schedule and protect time, how to set realistic goals, how to manage disruptions, and how to use such time-management devices as timers and calendars. One of us (J. D.) treated a patient who insisted on providing pressured, obsessive, digressive details about any topic she talked about, with the result that the check-in part of the session tended to take 20 minutes or more. The patient's time mismanagement in the session reflected her time mismanagement outside the session. As part of working on this problem, the therapist proposed and the patient agreed to the use of a timer to limit the time spent on the check in. The timer was set first for 3 minutes and then for an additional 2 minutes (to provide a warning that it was time to begin wrapping up). The patient agreed to stop the check in at the end of 5 minutes whether she had finished or not. She gradually learned to self-monitor and self-regulate her behavior.

Another patient was unable to limit her check in to a reasonable time at an early point in the therapy when she was agitated and excited. She and her therapist agreed to omit the check in altogether until a later point in the therapy when her agitation improved and she could function better in the session. Instead of beginning with a check in, the therapist asked the patient to begin her session with a review of the previous session's homework. This strategy provided a limited, highly structured review of what had happened during the previous week. After the review of her homework, the therapist invited the patient to submit agenda items.

Sometimes the therapist avoids agenda setting for his or her own reasons. The therapist may feel tired. Setting a concrete agenda may cause the therapist to feel "on the spot." If a specific problem is tackled, the therapist may feel anxious about the prospect of failing to solve it. An unstructured therapy session does not activate this performance anxiety. To address these issues, therapists can experiment with the sessions in which he or she omits agenda setting or pushes ahead to do it. At the end of each session, the therapist can ask the patient for feedback about the usefulness of the session. We predict that patients will give higher ratings to sessions in which therapists asked for and followed through with an explicit agenda.

ADHERING TO THE AGENDA

Sometimes the patient and therapist set an agenda but have difficulty adhering to it. This can happen if the therapist has unilaterally set the agenda without input from the patient. We find, not surprisingly, that when patients agree passively to agenda items proposed by their therapist that they do not really wish to take up, the therapy session frequently drifts off topic. We cannot stress enough the importance of collaboratively setting the agenda. Collaboration is particularly important for patients who are overly compliant with suggestions given by others (including their therapist). Before placing an item on the agenda that might appear to the therapist as an obvious choice, the therapist can explicitly ask the patient "Is the problem you're having with your wife something you want to work on today?" It is surprising how often the answer to this question is *no*. The therapist can then inquire "Why is that?" or "What do you want to work on instead?"

Difficulties adhering to an agenda after it has been set may also reflect a long-standing compensatory strategy that some patients use to avoid activating a negative schema. For example, patients who have rejection sensitivity may have learned that vague, directionless chitchat is the best defense when interacting with others. Despite the therapist's best efforts, these patients drift off task easily and have trouble maintaining a problem-solving stance in therapy. Patients with perfectionistic or obsessive tendencies may insist on providing excessive details for fear of omitting a vital piece of information that the therapist "must have" to be helpful. Therapists working with these patients never seem to get beyond the check in (or the first agenda item) to do any useful work. We recommend that therapy-interfering behavior such as this be given top priority because unless it is solved, not much else can be accomplished in the therapy. Although it is difficult, it is ideal if the therapist can raise this lack of focus of the therapy session as an agenda item or even suggest that this problem be placed on the patient's problem list.

Summaries (discussed earlier in this chapter) can help the patient and therapist adhere to the therapy session agenda. A summary can be a respectful way to refocus the patient: "You've been telling me how upset you were at work yesterday. We've agreed to work on your relationship with your boss. Should we move back to working on ways you can better cope with your boss?"

Sometimes a deviation from the agreed-on agenda item occurs. As the patient begins talking about one problem, another emerges and the session veers off to focus on the new problem. When this happens, we recommend that the therapist use a summary to ask the patient the following:

> We started talking about the problem with your boss. Now we've moved into a discussion of your conflict with your wife. Would you like to go back to the problem with your boss, or would you like to switch gears and talk about this issue with your wife?

The therapist might (depending in part on the formulation of the case) wish to make a recommendation to the patient about whether to abandon the original agenda item for a new one.

It is not always the patient who has trouble adhering to the therapy agenda. Some therapists have trouble managing therapy time effectively because they lack effective time-management skills or they are rejection sensitive or perfectionistic themselves. These therapists have trouble assertively directing the patient back to the task because they fear that the patient will feel criticized or hurt or that the patient will view them as insensitive or controlling. Therapists with doubts about their competence may defer to the patient and abrogate their responsibility for managing the session time and directing the session. To identify this problem, therapists could audiotape and listen to their therapy sessions and assiduously ask their patients for feedback about the therapy session. Therapists can also use a Thought Record (see chap. 5) to identify and restructure automatic thoughts that may compromise their ability to set and adhere to an agenda.

COMPLETING A HOMEWORK ASSIGNMENT

Homework noncompliance is an important and ubiquitous problem. We cannot discuss it exhaustively here, but we do provide therapists with some suggestions for understanding, preventing, and managing it. The patient's individualized case formulation can yield useful hypotheses about the causes of noncompliance, and a hypothesis, of course, can help the therapist develop strategies to address the problem (Persons, 1989). Using the formulation to understand the patient's behavior can also help the therapist feel less frustrated about noncompliance because, by this view, the noncompliance reflects the patient's central schema and maladaptive behaviors, not just a reluctance to get better or to thwart the therapist. Persons identified three common types of patients who run into trouble with homework: patients who are perfectionistic, those who suffer from a fear of failure, and those who have excessive needs to please others (including the therapist).

Perfectionistic patients may have unrealistic expectations about how a particular homework assignment is to be completed, which may lead them to delay working on the assignment, to try the assignment and experience the result as a failure, or to avoid the assignment altogether. June, a 28-year-old attorney who was depressed and anxious, was given the homework assignment of practicing progressive muscle relaxation daily. June did not do the relaxation practice because when she did try, she worried that she was not doing it correctly. June and her therapist developed adaptive coping responses to her perfectionistic thoughts that helped June get back on track. She was able to persist with her relaxation exercises, which proved to be extremely helpful to her.

For patients who avoid doing homework assignments because they fear they will fail, we encourage the therapist to prepare patients by predicting that this concern might arise as they begin work on the homework assignment and to help patients develop adaptive responses to their problematic automatic thoughts, such as "I don't have to be totally successful at this; I just have to try it." Therapists can also help patients develop a plan for managing homework that is not going well, which might include a telephone call to the therapist to check in, asking family members or friends for help, or reshaping the assignment to something they feel more confident that they can complete successfully. Careful structuring of the assignment can be helpful for a patient who fears failure; for example, an assignment to work 1 hour on the resumé can be easier to complete than an assignment to complete the entire resumé.

Patients who have the need to please others may agree to homework they view as unrealistic or irrelevant because they do not want to disappoint or displease the therapist by giving their true opinion about the assignment. These patients nod their heads and go along for the ride. Therapists can use the formulation to anticipate this problem, asking the people-pleasing patient beforehand about any concerns he or she might have about a proposed homework assignment. Of course, if the therapist asks the overly compliant patient whether the assignment seems useful, the patient may simply assert that it does. A useful follow-up question is the following: "If the assignment did not seem useful to you, would you be able to tell me?" It may also be useful when working with these patients to predict that they may agree in session to something that they will have doubts about later and to develop, even before it arises, strategies for managing this situation. The therapist and patient can agree that when this happens, the patient can change the assignment to one that is more useful and to assertively announce this in the next therapy session. These examples illustrate the therapist's reliance on information about the patient's schema (e.g., "unless I do it perfectly, I'm worthless") to understand and manage homework noncompliance.

Attention to the patient's problem list can also yield information that is useful for the management of homework noncompliance. When the problem list includes such items as "procrastination" or poor job performance because of the patient's inability to meet deadlines, the therapist can anticipate that homework noncompliance will be a problem. A patient who has a history of failing to follow through with commitments he makes to his wife about basic housekeeping responsibilities may also have trouble following through with the tasks of therapy. Therapists can ask patients whether they have a history of starting but not completing tasks, whether they have ever had difficulty completing work assignments, or whether they are known for changing their minds at the last minute. These problems can be sticky ones to address, of course. The therapist can point out the potential noncompliance problem and enlist the patient's commitment to working on it in treatment.

Noncompliance can also result when the patient and therapist do not anticipate obstacles to homework completion. Sometimes a patient and therapist develop a meaningful homework assignment only to discover that the patient lacks the skills necessary to effectively carry out the assignment. A homework assignment that calls for the patient to carry on a conversation at a party for 5 minutes will fail if the patient does not know how to make small talk. Similarly, a homework assignment designed to increase a patient's level of pleasant activities may fail if she does not know how to request that her husband ask for time off from work. Therapists can assess a patient's skill level in two ways: (a)

Have the patient practice, when possible, the assigned homework in session and (b) look for areas in the patient's life where she is already using the skills required by the homework assignment.

Role-plays provide the patient with an opportunity to practice a proposed homework assignment in session. As the role-play proceeds, the therapist observes how the patient, for example, starts a conversation or maintains eye contact. For example, one of us (M. A. T.) was working with George, a depressed young postal worker who was spending his weekends at home in bed. The therapist and George agreed that scheduling pleasant activities (see chap. 4) with friends would probably help improve his mood. However, when George practiced making a telephone call in session, the therapist discovered that George had great trouble starting a conversation and would fall silent or hang up the telephone. The therapist realized that basic skills building was needed, and he taught George how to start a conversation and keep it going. Had the therapist not assessed George's skill level in the homework situation, the assignment would have failed and, even worse, confirmed George's worst beliefs about himself.

Sometimes noncompliance reflects current contingencies that make compliance difficult. A depressed woman is not likely to increase her level of pleasurable activities if her husband berates her when she calls a friend to chat or takes time to enjoy herself at the movies. A single mother with three children may have trouble keeping her therapy appointments or finding time to do her therapy homework unless she can get some child care assistance. Therapists cannot assume that patients will solve all these problems on their own. Instead, therapists can help by teaching patients to anticipate and learn skills to overcome obstacles to successful homework completion.

Summary and Conclusion

In this chapter, we described the eight components of a structured therapy session. Many of the structural elements discussed here (e.g., setting the agenda and asking for feedback) set the stage or clear the way for the fifth component, working the agenda—the heart of the therapy session and the place where the main technical interventions of the therapy are carried out. The primary technical interventions used by the cognitive–behavior therapist during the work the agenda component of the session are discussed in the next three chapters of this book: Activity Scheduling, Using the Thought Record, and Schema Change Methods.

Practice Exercises

These exercises can reinforce what you have learned about using a structured session in CBT. If you are an instructor, use them to stimulate class discussion or to structure sessions in which students can practice the basics of structuring a therapy session.

1. Choose one or two components of the therapy session you would like to practice. Review your list of current patients and choose one who might benefit from the component. Place a note in his or her clinical record to remind you to practice the session component the next time you see the patient. Afterward, ask your patient for feedback. For example, ask your patient how it felt to set an agenda at the beginning of the session and if it was useful.

2. Select a session component and practice using it in a role-play with a colleague or fellow student. First, practice using the component in a role-play designed to go smoothly. Then practice handling one or more of the following problematic situations:
   (a) The patient plunges into the session, and the therapist must interrupt to set an agenda.
   (b) The patient diverges from the planned agenda.
   (c) The patient has not completed his or her homework assignment.
   (d) The patient has no prepared agenda item.

3. In a role-play with a colleague or fellow student, play the role of one of your own patients and ask your colleague to be the therapist and initiate one of the components of a structured therapy session. Focus on one component. Then reverse roles and try again. After you practice each role-play, do the following tasks:
   (a) Evaluate whether the "therapist" followed the guidelines (when setting the agenda and assigning homework).
   (b) Ask the "patient" to give feedback about how it felt to be the recipient of the intervention, if it was helpful, whether there was anything the "therapist" did that felt bad or was not helpful, and whether there was anything the "therapist" could have handled better.

4. List your reservations about using any component of a structured session. For example, list your concerns about setting an agenda, assigning homework, or asking for feedback. After listing your concerns, review the list and then devise a behavioral experiment with a patient or a role-play interaction with a colleague to test whether your concerns are accurate. For example, if you have the thought "my patient will think I'm insensitive and rigid if I

have to ask to set an agenda," then practice agenda setting with a patient or colleague. Then ask your patient or colleague for direct feedback about your concern: "Did you think I was insensitive or rigid?"

5. Use the Therapy Session Log to list, over the course of 1 week, all the homework assignments you give and rate each assignment as to whether it was

- collaborative
- concrete and specific
- tied to the work in the session
- planned with obstacles in mind
- assigned with sufficient time to discuss in the session.

Bring your log to a consultation group with colleagues or fellow students to discuss and problem solve.

6. Typical clinical problems that arise when using a structured therapy session are presented below. Answer the questions provided for each.

(a) *Setting the agenda.* Imagine you are a therapist who is having difficulty setting an agenda. Although you intend to set an agenda each session, you find that you and your patient frequently begin working on a problem without setting an agenda. Generate at least three strategies to address this problem.

(1) Orient your patients to the structure of the session at the very beginning of the session. If you are not doing this, use the Therapy Session Log to help you do it consistently (see Exhibit 3.3 for an example of a completed Therapy Session Log). Before your patient begins talking, say "Let's start today with a brief check in. First, tell me how your week went, and then we'll set an agenda for today. Would that be okay with you?" If that fails, omit the check in and move directly to setting the agenda. Try this with several patients until you become more comfortable with setting an agenda at the beginning of every session.

(2) Make certain that your patients understand the rationale for agenda setting. To drive this point home, say "I want to set an agenda before we get started. An agenda will help us manage the time, so we'll have time to work on what you think is most important today."

(3) You may feel timid about interrupting patients to set an agenda. Practice doing this with a colleague. Ask your colleague to give you feedback about what it felt like to be interrupted. After you interrupt a patient, ask the pa-

EXHIBIT 3.3

A Completed Therapy Session Log

Instructions: Select one or two components of the therapy session (e.g., set the agenda, review homework) on which you would like to focus. Write the components at the top of the two "components" columns on the form. Then, for each patient you see during a week, record the date (in the "date" column) and the patient's initials (in the "initials" column). In the columns corresponding to the components of the therapy session on which you are working, record a score indicating whether you used the component (1) or did not use the component (0). In the "comments" column, note things you did well or poorly or things you learned and would like to remember for the future.

Date	Initials	Components		Comments
		Set the agenda	Review homework	
10/9	C. M.	1	1	Easy; I started by introducing the agenda setting. I put homework on the agenda.
10/9	R. S.	1	1	Not as easy but I started by reminding her about agenda setting and homework review. That helped.
10/10	P. W.	0	1	I reminded him about agenda setting, but he kept talking. Homework was reviewed but not in a structured way.
10/10	J. M.	1	0	I set an agenda but didn't follow it. We got off the topic and never got to homework review.
10/11	D. S.	1	1	I started by reminding her about agenda setting and homework review. She came in with agenda topics and homework ready.

© 1999 San Francisco Bay Area Center for Cognitive Therapy.

tient at the end of the session for feedback about this interruption.

(4) Audiotape several sessions. Listen to the audiotapes to learn more about what is getting in the way of setting an agenda.

(b) *Setting the agenda with one particular patient.* Imagine that you have a patient with whom setting an agenda is a chronic problem. Your patient plunges into the session and ignores your request for an agenda; you find it difficult to interrupt him or her. Generate at least three strategies to address this problem.

(1) Place the agenda-setting problem on the agenda itself. Say to your patient "I've noticed that each week we agree to set an agenda, but it doesn't happen. I'd like to suggest that we put this item on our agenda for today. Would that be all right with you?" Of course, to actually have a chance to say these words, you will need to be prepared to speak before the patient starts talking.

(2) List your thoughts about why you might be having a problem setting an agenda with your patient. For example, you may think "This patient is older than I am, and maybe he'll think I'm being disrespectful or rude if I ask for an agenda. Maybe he'll think I'm being pushy." Then develop adaptive responses to your concerns. Ask a trusted colleague to offer assistance.

(3) Review the individualized case formulation for your patient to develop hypotheses as to why your patient has difficulty setting an agenda. For example, Frank may avoid setting an agenda that commits him to focus on an uncomfortable topic. Or if he feels inadequate about making decisions, he may avoid setting an agenda because he fears that he will choose the wrong topics for the agenda. Work with him to develop hypotheses as to why agenda setting is a problem and to develop solutions to the problem.

(c) *The patient refuses to set an agenda.* Imagine that you have a patient who does not want to set a therapy session agenda, saying "I don't want to set an agenda. I just want to start talking and see what comes up." Generate at least three strategies to address this problem.

(1) Use Socratic questioning to learn more about why your patient does not want to set an agenda. It might also be helpful to list the advantages and disadvantages of setting an agenda. For example, Sarah may believe that a dis-

advantage of agenda setting is that she may make a "bad" choice and waste a session. (An advantage is that she can prioritize and choose a topic to discuss, thus minimizing the likelihood of discussing less relevant topics.) By listing advantages and disadvantages, you can help Sarah directly address her concerns about agenda setting and evaluate whether setting an agenda may be useful.

(2) Propose a behavioral experiment to test your patient's beliefs about agenda setting. For example, Tom might fear that agenda setting will result in a loss of spontaneity, making therapy dull and uninteresting. Ask Tom if he would be willing to try setting and following an agenda for a session and then evaluating the accuracy of his beliefs.

(3) Set up a behavioral experiment to test your patient's hypothesis that agenda setting is not necessary to make progress in treatment. You and your patient can omit agenda setting for a predetermined period of time (e.g., four sessions) and track his progress, using an agreed-on objective measure (e.g., number of fights with wife). Ask your patient to agree that if he makes good progress, you will continue to omit agenda setting, but that if he does not make good progress, he will try agenda setting. The power of this intervention rests in its collaborative and empirical nature and in the fact that the therapist's position is flexible; the therapist is willing to adopt methods that result in treatment progress rather than insisting on using a particular method.

(4) Review your patient's individualized case formulation and generate hypotheses as to why she does not want to set an agenda. For example, Julie may avoid setting an agenda because she avoids any situation she perceives as limiting or confining for fear of losing autonomy. If it is relevant, discuss with your patient your hypothesis that her avoidance of the structure imposed by collaborative agenda setting is an example of how she handles similar situations in other areas of her life.

(d) *The patient who never has time to complete homework.* Your patient always agrees to the homework assignment and seems intent on doing it. But something always comes up, so that the patient cannot do the homework at all or is unable to complete it. Generate at least three strategies to address this problem.

(1) Examine your behavior. Do you ask about your patient's

homework every week? When the patient fails to complete the homework, do you spend time finding out why? If you do not do these things, you may be inadvertently telling your patient that homework is not a priority. Perhaps you are afraid of a negative reaction from your patient (e.g., "She'll get angry or feel criticized if I bring up the homework."). If this is the case, write down some coping responses to address your concern.

(2) Suggest that the patient's homework noncompliance be an item for the agenda. To do this in a soft, supportive, nonpunitive way, the therapist can say "I know that you take your therapy very seriously and that the things we're working on are important to you. But you're having trouble getting your homework done between sessions. I suggest we put on our agenda for today a brief discussion of what came up last week that made it hard for you to do your homework assignment."

(3) Perhaps the homework assignments are unrealistic or you did not help your patient plan for obstacles that arose. If this is the case, spend more time in the session making smaller, more realistic homework assignments or develop a back-up plan for the patient should he or she run into problems with the homework assignment.

(4) If lack of time is an obstacle that interferes with your patient accomplishing other goals, then use activity scheduling to help your patient use his or her time more productively (see chap. 4). Work with your patient to choose a time for completing therapy homework.

Further Readings and Videotapes

Beck, A. T., Rush, A. J., Shaw, B. F., & Emery, G. (1979). *Cognitive therapy of depression.* New York: Guilford Press. Chap. 4, Structure of the therapeutic interview.

Beck, J. S. (1995). *Cognitive therapy: Basics and beyond.* New York: Guilford Press. Chap. 3, Structure of the first therapy session; chap. 4, Session two and beyond: Structure and format.

Burns, D. D. (1985). *The feeling good handbook.* New York: Penguin Books. Chap. 26, Agenda setting: How to make therapy productive when you and your patient feel stuck.

Davidson, J., Persons, J. B., & Tompkins, M. A. (2000). *Cognitive–behavior therapy for depression: Structure of the therapy session* [Videotape]. Washington, DC: American Psychological Association.

Persons, J. B. (1989). *Cognitive therapy in practice: A case formulation approach.* New York: Norton. Chap. 8, Homework.

APPENDIX 3A: THERAPY SESSION LOG

Instructions: Select one or two components of the therapy session (e.g., set the agenda, review homework) on which you would like to focus. Write the components at the top of the two "Components" columns on the form. Then, for each patient you see during a week, record the date (in the "Date" column) and the patient's initials (in the "Initials" column). In the columns corresponding to the components of the therapy session on which you are working, record a score indicating whether you used the component (1) or did not use the component (0). In the "Comments" column, note things you did well or poorly or things you learned and would like to remember for the future.

Date	Initials	Components		Comments

Activity Scheduling 4

As a confirmed melancholic, I can testify that the best and maybe only antidote for melancholia is action. However, like most melancholics, I suffer also from sloth. (Edward Abbey)

ctivity scheduling is a key component of cognitive–behavioral treatment (CBT) for depression. Activity scheduling is deceptively simple: The patient and therapist work together to schedule activities. Nonetheless, activity scheduling is a powerful intervention, and more complicated than it seems at first.

This chapter describes

- theoretical and empirical underpinnings of activity scheduling
- six uses of the Activity Schedule form
- patients for whom activity scheduling interventions are useful
- selecting a focus for activity scheduling
- guidelines for successful activity scheduling
- suggestions for handling typical activity scheduling difficulties
- practice exercises
- further readings and videotapes
- Activity Schedule form.

Underpinnings of Activity Scheduling

THEORETICAL

Activity scheduling is a central component of Beck's (Beck et al., 1979) cognitive therapy for depression. Beck proposed that depressive symptoms consist of mood, behaviors, and cognitions, which are linked to-gether in reciprocal causal relationships. He recommended activity scheduling because it can alleviate negative mood by providing direct evidence to disconfirm depressed patients' negative automatic thoughts and schema, such as their beliefs that they are helpless, unable to func-tion, or unable to enjoy anything. Activity scheduling may also be ef-fective by helping depressed patients recognize that their thinking is distorted and that cognitive errors can lead to decreased activity, moti-vation, and mood.

Activity scheduling is similar to pleasant activity scheduling, a com-ponent of Lewinsohn's (Hoberman & Lewinsohn, 1985) behavior ther-apy for depression. In Lewinsohn's theory, depression results when in-dividuals experience a reduction in positive reinforcers for their actions (or an increase in aversive reinforcement). According to the theory, when individuals receive fewer positive reinforcers for their responses, they begin responding less, experiencing even fewer positive reinforcers, and so on, in a downward spiral. To reverse the cycle, the behavior therapist works with the patient to schedule pleasurable, satisfying ac-tivities. Activity scheduling is also similar to behavioral exposure therapy in that both are proposed to be effective by causing changes in under-lying cognitions, as described in chapter 1.

EMPIRICAL

Activity scheduling is a component of both behavioral and cognitive therapies that have been shown in numerous controlled studies to pro-vide effective treatment for depression (see reviews by the Agency for Health Care Policy and Research, 1993; DeRubeis & Crits-Christoph, 1998; and Persons et al., 1996). An important dismantling study pro-vides direct evidence supporting the value of the activity scheduling component of cognitive therapy. Neil Jacobson, Keith Dobson, and their colleagues (Jacobson et al., 1996) showed that depressed patients who were treated with behavioral activation, an intervention similar to ac-tivity scheduling, benefited as much as patients who received treatment that included behavioral activation, cognitive restructuring, and work on underlying schema. Zeiss et al. (1979) showed that depressed pa-tients benefited as much from scheduling pleasant events as from cog-nitive restructuring or interpersonal skills training, and Rehm, Kaslow, and Rabin (1987) showed that depressed patients treated with behav-ioral interventions did as well as those who received cognitive interven-tions or both cognitive and behavioral interventions.

Uses of the Activity Schedule Form

An Activity Schedule form (see Appendix 4A) can be used to schedule activities. The vertical columns correspond to the days of the week and the horizontal columns divide each day into 1-hour time blocks. We describe many uses of the form in the following sections.

MONITORING

Often the first step in activity scheduling is to collect concrete detailed information about a patient's current activity level; the Activity Schedule form can be used to do this. This process helps patient and therapist identify problematic times or situations and distorted thinking. Depressed patients may have such thoughts as "I don't socialize at all anymore. I never see my friends" or "I'm not getting any work done. I spend all my free time in front of the 'boob tube.'" Patients are often surprised when they compare their completed Activity Schedule to their beliefs about their activities.

Noting that depressed patients are prone to self-criticism, Beck et al. (1979) pointed out to patients that the initial goal of using an Activity Schedule is for them to observe, not to evaluate, how well or how much they are doing. Beck et al. suggested that patients rate the degree of mastery and pleasure for each of their daily activities, using a rough 0 (*no mastery or pleasure*) to 100 (*completely mastery or pleasure*) scale. This intervention can increase the patient's awareness of how activities push mood up or pull it down.

When pleasurable activities or activities that demonstrate a degree of accomplishment are not rated as pleasurable or evoking any sense of mastery, the discrepancies can be discussed; these discrepancies may reflect cognitive distortions and can provide clues about underlying schema. For example, a depressed father attended his son's school play and rated his pleasure as "0." When asked about this, he reported "it doesn't count because I didn't enjoy it as much as I should have. It was a special event for my son, and I should have felt really proud and good, but I didn't. This must mean I'm a bad father."

RECORDING A BEHAVIORAL EXPERIMENT

A behavioral experiment is an activity that is carried out for the purpose of testing out a patient's negative cognition, such as "If I go to the party, no one will talk to me." Burns (1999) developed the "pleasure-predicting method" to help patients set up behavioral experiments to test their predictions (usually negative and distorted) about pleasure. To use the pleasure-predicting method, the therapist asks the patient to rate his or her expected degree of pleasure or satisfaction from a particular activity and then asks the patient to test out the prediction by trying the activity and rating the actual degree of pleasure or satisfaction. Typically, depressed patients learn that they underestimate the degree of satisfaction or pleasure they will experience if they perform the action. For example, Jan planned to go to a movie on Saturday afternoon and have lunch with a friend on Sunday afternoon. She predicted 20% enjoyment from the movie and 30% enjoyment from having lunch. These predictions left her feeling discouraged, and she was tempted to stay home. But she had agreed in therapy to test her predictions, so she followed through with her plans and found that she got 60% enjoyment from the movie and 70% from lunch.

Sometimes the patient's negative predictions come true. When this happens, the therapist and patient can investigate to find out why. Cognitive theory predicts that negative, distorted thoughts are often the culprit. If Jan had left the movie thinking "What a loser I am to have spent Saturday afternoon at the movies just because I promised my therapist I would!" this would probably have detracted from her enjoyment. Cognitive restructuring interventions (chap. 5) can be used to address these maladaptive thoughts.

It is important to set up experiments that are likely to provide useful information. For example, a patient may say "It won't matter if I go to the party because I won't enjoy it as much as I used to enjoy parties." Attending the party to see if she can enjoy it as much as she used to is probably not a useful experiment. If she is depressed, there is a good chance she will not enjoy the party as much as she used to. The better experiment would be to attend the party to see if she gains any pleasure at all or more pleasure than she expected.

The fact that activity scheduling interventions can challenge automatic thoughts and underlying schema may account for the finding by Jacobson et al. (1996) that patients receiving activity scheduling benefited as much as patients who received activity scheduling plus cognitive restructuring and schema change interventions.

INCREASING ACTIVITY LEVEL

Often depressed patients do not engage in any or many activities that would give them satisfaction or provide evidence to disconfirm their negative thoughts. To address this problem, the patient and therapist can work together to plan activities and write them on the Activity

Schedule form. We recommend planning activities that help patients take a step forward from their current activity level. Planning too many new activities can be overwhelming. For one patient, increasing activity level might mean scheduling a few basic tasks, such as preparing dinner or doing laundry, whereas for another it might mean playing volleyball at the gym once or twice a week.

INCREASING PLEASURE OR MASTERY

Some depressed patients experience little satisfaction because they spend most of their time doing things they do not enjoy. After the therapist and the patient have determined that a lack of pleasurable or mastery activities is a problem (use the monitoring intervention to assess this), the Activity Schedule form can be used to plan pleasant, enjoyable events, including things as simple as buying flowers or getting a cup of coffee at a local café on the way home from work.

The individualized case formulation can help the therapist and patient choose therapeutic activities. Sometimes a therapist can even "take advantage" of the patient's schema to activate an immobilized patient. For example, Mrs. Walker was unwilling to agree to undertake any pleasurable activities for her own sake but driven in part by her strong belief that she was a selfish person unless she fulfilled her responsibilities to others, she agreed to follow her therapist's recommendation that she attend her daughter's birthday party. Although it would be preferable for Mrs. Walker to increase her activity level for healthier reasons, it can be helpful, particularly when a patient is very depressed, to make therapeutic use of the patient's vulnerabilities to improve the patient's functioning. Later in treatment, when Mrs. Walker is less depressed, the therapist can use activity scheduling (e.g., a homework assignment to do something purely for her own enjoyment) or other interventions (cognitive restructuring, schema change methods) to address her maladaptive schema.

RECORDING GRADED TASK ASSIGNMENTS

The Activity Schedule form can be used to break large, complex, intimidating tasks into manageable steps. Depressed patients often feel overwhelmed by large tasks. Sometimes they set goals on the basis of their previous level of functioning or on unrealistic, perfectionistic beliefs, such as "unless it's an outstanding achievement, it's worthless." Sometimes patients are unwilling to view an activity that requires a sequence of steps as worthwhile until the end goal is achieved. Graded task assignments can be used to set concrete, realistic goals and to help patients feel a sense of accomplishment about small steps that allow them to move forward to achieve larger goals. For example, an unemployed former executive becomes overwhelmed and immobilized when he thinks about all the work involved in finding a new job. A graded task assignment for him might be to read the job listings in the Sunday newspaper and call one or two of them on Monday; these plans can then be recorded on his Activity Schedule form. The executive is more likely to succeed at this plan than at the vague, intimidating plan of "look for a job this week."

Sometimes patients resist using graded task assignments, saying "I should be able to do so much more" or "I used to do these things without thinking about them, let alone breaking them down into baby steps." A Thought Record form (Appendix 5A) can be used to address this obstacle. Ask your patient whether those thoughts help him or her take action; the patient may be able to recognize that they do not. If your patient has difficulty with this and insists that "I should be able to do it all. I know if I just try harder this week, I'll be able to get these projects done," a behavioral experiment can be planned to test out this belief. The therapist and patient might agree to test the patient's belief (trying harder will get the job done) during the following week, with the understanding that if the patient's method fails, he or she will agree to try the therapist's approach (graded task assignment) the following week.

RECORDING BEHAVIOR PLANS THAT SUPPORT ADAPTIVE THINKING

Many sessions of cognitive therapy focus on attempts to shift the patient's thinking (see chap. 5, Using the Thought Record). To help patients change their thinking, therapists can help patients schedule activities that support and strengthen adaptive cognitions. For example, Sherry viewed herself as ugly, but she was tired of seeing herself that way. She decided she would try to strengthen a nascent view of herself as attractive by purposely behaving "as if" she was attractive. She began buying some new clothes, shaving her legs regularly, and wearing makeup more often; as a result, she began to feel more attractive.

Who Needs Activity Scheduling?

Four types of depressed patients can get particular benefit from activity scheduling: patients who have nothing to do, those who are avoiding doing things they plan, those who have too much to do, and those who are contemplating suicide. Many patients fall into more than one of these categories.

PASSIVE PATIENTS WHO HAVE NOTHING TO DO

Some depressed patients spend large amounts of time doing little or nothing. Beck (Beck et al., 1979) pointed out, and we agree, that until the patient's activity level is adequate, he or she is usually not able to make much use of cognitive interventions. These patients need activity scheduling interventions early in treatment. For example, John had taken a leave of absence from work because he was so depressed. He spent most of his time lying around the house and napping. To increase John's activity level, the therapist could begin by working with John to schedule breakfast with a friend (to help John get out of bed in the morning) or to spend 2 hours on Thursday evening at the social club he joined last year.

PATIENTS WHO ARE PROCRASTINATING, AVOIDING, OR FEELING "STUCK"

These types of patients can use activity scheduling to help them move forward. Activity scheduling makes vague plans more concrete and therefore more likely to be carried out. These patients can use the Activity Schedule form to monitor situations when they procrastinate and to gather data about the sequence of events leading to procrastination behaviors. For example, Judy repeatedly stated that she wanted to improve her social life, but weeks went by without her doing anything about it. She planned social activities on the weekends, but somehow they never happened. Monitoring her time with the Activity Schedule form showed her that she typically waited until late Saturday and Sunday afternoon to tackle important work tasks and errands, leaving her with no time in the evening to socialize. After uncovering this pattern, Judy set a "quitting time" for work and errands on the weekends and pushed herself to make and keep social dates after that time.

Avoidant people often have negative predictions about how uncomfortable they will feel or how unsatisfying the experience will be if they engage in the tasks they are avoiding. A behavioral experiment can be used to test such a belief as "If I go to the gym, I'll feel upset when I see how out of shape I am." The therapist could work with the patient to make a plan to go to the gym on Thursday at 11:00 a.m. for $1/2$ hour and assess how upset she felt afterward.

Activity scheduling for these patients typically involves graded task assignments to help them break down large, challenging tasks into smaller, more realistic ones, thus optimizing their chances of success. A student may procrastinate starting a term paper because she feels that the task is too overwhelming to complete or she does not know where to start. As a result of procrastinating, she feels even more overwhelmed and discouraged. A graded task assignment (e.g., going to the library for 1 hour to find some articles) can help the student take the first step toward completing the term paper.

PATIENTS WHO ARE OVERWHELMED AND HAVE TOO MUCH TO DO

Susan was a single mother who worked full time as an office manager in a stressful workplace, had a long commute to her job, and drove her daughter to a series of afterschool and weekend activities. Her responsibilities often began at 6 a.m. and ended at 11 p.m. She felt overburdened and harried, yet she told herself "I should be able to do all this without feeling stressed. I am making too big a deal out of things." Monitoring provided concrete data (see Exhibit 4.1, Susan's Activity Schedule 1) that showed Susan how overscheduled she was and what unrealistic expectations she had for herself. It also showed her that she did not allow time for pleasure, such as going to the gym, reading, or going out with friends.

Even after she acquired this information, Susan was reluctant to reduce her activity load because she feared "I'll feel worse if I don't get everything done that I want to do." To address this fear, Susan and her therapist set up a behavioral experiment to test her belief. She tried scheduling a lighter workload, allowing time for leisure activities, and she evaluated her mood at the end of each day. The results of this experiment led Susan to take significant steps to reduce her workload by finding some afterschool help with her daughter and arranging carpools with other moms; Susan recorded the results of her work on this issue in a second Activity Schedule (see Exhibit 4.2, Susan's Activity Schedule 2).

PATIENTS STRUGGLING WITH SUICIDAL THOUGHTS AND IMPULSES

Scheduling activities can serve as a behavioral experiment that provides evidence to challenge the hopeless and suicidal patient's beliefs that "I can never enjoy anything anymore," "life is not worth living," and "nothing has meaning." Activity scheduling for the suicidal patient can target increasing activity level, especially activities that bring any increase in pleasure or accomplishment. Activity scheduling is also an antisuicide intervention because the patient and therapist work together to schedule activities that are incompatible with planning and carrying out a suicidal act. It is hard to commit suicide while going for a walk with a friend. Activity scheduling can also serve an assessment function: If the suicidal patient is unable to make or follow through with a simple activity schedule, day treatment or hospitalization may be necessary. A demonstration of the use of activity scheduling for a patient struggling with suicidal thoughts is provided by Persons, Davidson, and Tompkins (2000).

Selecting a Focus for Activity Scheduling

We recommend that the therapist focus activity scheduling on a time period, an activity, or both, with the choice depending on the nature of the patient's problem.

TIME PERIOD

Choose a time of the day or week in which the patient is not using his or her time well.

Evening Hours

If depressed patients have a low mood in the evening after they come home from work, it may be because they have too much unstructured time and they lapse into negative thinking that pulls their mood down. Using the Activity Schedule form to log plans to go to the gym, have dinner with a friend, invite friends over to watch a movie, or read a good book can address this problem. An evening class that meets for several weeks in a row can be particularly useful because if the patient has to schedule the class and pay for it ahead of time, such a one-time commitment can provide numerous busy, pleasant hours.

The Weekend

Many depressed patients feel fine during the week but lousy during the weekend because they have not planned any fun or enjoyable activities —or any activities at all. It can be easy for the depressed person to stay in bed or hibernate at home if no alternative plans have been made. Depending on the patient's level of functioning, activities for a weekend might include doing laundry, going grocery shopping, going out to dinner with a friend, attending a class, or taking a trip out of town.

EXHIBIT 4.1

Susan's Activity Schedule 1

	Monday Date:	Tuesday Date:	Wednesday Date:
7–8 a.m.	Breakfast/dress	Breakfast/dress	Breakfast/dress
8–9 a.m.	Drive to work	Drive to work	Drive to work
9–10 a.m.	Work	Work	Work
10–11 a.m.	↓	↓	° ↓
11 a.m.–12 noon	↓	↓	↓
12 noon–1 p.m.	Take-out food, eat while working	Take out food, eat during meeting	Lunch with Sally
1–2 p.m.	Work	Work	Work
2–3 p.m.	↓	↓	↓
3–4 p.m.	↓	↓	↓
4–5 p.m.	↓	↓	↓
5–6 p.m.	Drive home	Drive home	Drive home
6–7 p.m.	Take Jill to dance class/ eat	Pick up Jill, make dinner	Take Jill to dance class/ eat
Evening (after 7 p.m.)	Get Jill, help her w/ homework, prepare for meeting	Clean up, help Jill w/ homework, TV	Get Jill, help her w/ homework, prepare for meeting

Thursday Date:	Friday Date:	Saturday Date:	Sunday Date:
Breakfast/dress	Breakfast/dress	Breakfast, clean	Sleep
Drive to work	Drive to work	Take Jill to dance, errands	↓
Work	Work	Grocery shop	Breakfast, morning paper
↓	↓	Put away groceries, get Jill	Take Jill to her game
↓	↓	Take Jill and a friend to the mall	Watch game
Take out food, eat while working	Pizza in conference room	Laundry, clean	↓
Work	Work	Lunch, clean	↓
↓	↓	Laundry, clean	Lunch
↓	↓	Errands	Take Jill to Karen's
↓	↓	↓	Shop for work clothes
Drive home	½ hr at TGIF party	Get Jill, start dinner	↓
Pick up Jill, eat	Drive home, make dinner, give Jill a ride to a show	Dinner, dishes	Pick up Jill, make dinner
Clean up, help Jill w/ homework, talk to parents, TV	Eat, watch TV, pick up Jill	Watch TV	Help Jill w/home-work, prepare for work

EXHIBIT 4.2

Susan's Activity Schedule 2

	Monday Date:	Tuesday Date:	Wednesday Date:
7–8 a.m.	Breakfast/dress	Breakfast/dress	Breakfast/dress
8–9 a.m.	Drive to work	Drive to work	Drive to work
9–10 a.m.	Work	Work	Work
10–11 a.m.	↓	↓	↓
11 a.m.–12 noon	↓	↓	↓
12 noon–1 p.m.	Take-out food, EAT W/ PEOPLE IN OFFICE	Take out food, eat during meeting	Lunch with Sally
1–2 p.m.	Work	Work	Work
2–3 p.m.	↓	↓	↓
3–4 p.m.	↓	↓	↓
4–5 p.m.	LEAVE EARLY, DRIVE HOME	LEAVE EARLY, WALK W/ SALLY	↓
5–6 p.m.	Drive home, READ BOOK	Drive home	Drive home
6–7 p.m.	Take Jill to dance class/ eat/GYM	Pick up Jill, make dinner	Take Jill to dance class/ eat/GYM
Evening (after 7 p.m.)	GYM, get Jill, help her w/homework, prepare for meeting	Clean up, help Jill w/ homework, CALL FRIENDS	GYM, get Jill, help her w/homework, prepare for meeting

Note. Entries in all caps denote leisure activities Susan added to her schedule during her session.

Thursday Date:	Friday Date:	Saturday Date:	Sunday Date:
Breakfast/dress	Breakfast/dress	Breakfast, clean	Sleep
Drive to work	Drive to work	Take Jill to dance, GYM	↓
Work	Work	GYM	Breakfast, read morning paper
↓	↓	Shower, get Jill	Take Jill to her game
↓	↓	Shopping	Watch game
Take out food, READ BOOK DURING LUNCH	Pizza in conference room	Shopping	↓
Work	Work	Lunch, clean	↓
↓	↓	Errands	Lunch
↓	↓	↓	Take Jill to Karen's
LEAVE EARLY, WALK W/SALLY	↓	↓	HIKE WITH JIM
Drive home	HAPPY HOUR	Start dinner, TALK W/SALLY	↓
Pick up Jill, eat, READ BOOK	DINNER W/FRIENDS	Dinner, dishes	↓
READ, DATE WITH JIM	GO OUT W/ FRIENDS, pick up Jill	TV	Help Jill w/home-work, prepare for work

One or Two Complete Days

Some depressed patients have difficulty with daily functioning and planning. The therapist can help these patients plan 1 or 2 complete days and model for them how to make a realistic and useful plan for the day. In the session, the therapist could walk the patient through 1 complete day, beginning with the time the patient plans to get out of bed and ending with the time the patient plans to go to bed. In between, the patient and therapist schedule eating breakfast, getting ready for work, getting to work on time, eating lunch, leaving work on time, doing something after work, eating dinner, talking to a friend on the phone, and watching an enjoyable TV show, for example. The therapist can suggest that the patient record these plans on an Activity Schedule form and note which plans were kept and which were not.

Interval of Time Between Therapy Sessions

Planning for the interval between therapy sessions is a good focus of an Activity Schedule because it allows the therapist and patient to focus on a concrete, limited block of time that can then be reviewed in the next therapy session. Depending on the patient's needs and level of functioning, this interval might be 1 day, several days, or 1 week. If a patient is actively suicidal or immobilized, the patient's Activity Schedule would most likely cover only 1 or 2 days and may include one or more telephone check ins with the therapist. For higher functioning patients, the Activity Schedule can cover a longer time period.

A Complete Week of Activities

The Activity Schedule itself, of course, comprises 1 complete week. Reviewing a patient's schedule for 1 complete week gives a good sense of the ebb and flow of his or her activities over the workdays, weekends, and evenings.

ACTIVITY

Activities of Daily Living

These activities include getting up, brushing one's teeth, getting to work on time, and so on. Depressed patients sometimes fail or struggle to complete these basic tasks. If this is the case, the therapist can focus the patient's activity scheduling interventions on them before more complex tasks are attempted.

Particular Work or School Tasks

Depressed patients sometimes have difficulty completing work or school tasks. For example, Walter got up every day planning to work on his dissertation but inevitably found himself writing personal letters, reading the newspaper, reading and writing email, eating, or masturbating. He was continually surprised to find that at the end of a busy day, he had accomplished little or no work on his dissertation. To solve this problem, he and his therapist developed an Activity Schedule that called for him to get up every weekday morning, get dressed, eat breakfast, leave the house by 9 a.m., and go to the library. He stayed there until 3 p.m. While at the library, he set himself the task of writing 4 manuscript pages before he allowed himself to do anything else related to his work, including reading. This complex and demanding Activity Schedule evolved gradually over many weeks of therapy and led to a remarkable increase in Walter's dissertation-writing behavior.

Pleasurable Activities

Fred had a demanding and highly stressful job as a software engineer for a high-tech firm. He worked long hours yet found that he was always behind on his work. He told himself that he did not deserve to have any fun until he was caught up on his work. But because he never got caught up, he never scheduled anything fun. Fred felt trapped but could not see his way out. After a discussion with his therapist, Fred admitted that the prospect of completely catching up on his work was in fact a fantasy; it was never going to happen. He reluctantly agreed to schedule one fun activity a week whether his work was done or not. He found that when he forced himself to go bowling, he forgot about the work on his desk and enjoyed himself. He was also surprised to find that when he scheduled a bowling date in the evening, he worked more efficiently during the day because he knew he could not "dilly dally" all day and then stay late in the office to make up for it. As a result, Fred found that scheduling fun things to do in the evening actually increased his work productivity rather than decreasing it, as he had feared.

Socializing

Often depressed patients become isolated and withdrawn, telling themselves "Why bother? I won't enjoy myself anymore. No one wants to be with me when I'm depressed anyway. I'll just bring my friends down." Although these thoughts have a grain of truth, they are probably also distorted. The isolated, withdrawn patient can test them out by scheduling social behavioral experiments.

Therapy Homework

The Activity Schedule form can be used to record a patient's therapy homework plan and to specify concrete details of the plan (when, where, for how long, with whom). For example, a depressed single man can use the Activity Schedule form to record his homework assignments: "Call Beth at 6 p.m. tonight. If she's not there, leave a message telling her she can reach me at work between 10 a.m. and 4 p.m. tomorrow. Call Jane on Sunday morning between 10 a.m. and 12 noon."

Guidelines for Successful Activity Scheduling

To carry out a successful activity scheduling intervention, the therapist can follow these guidelines (see Exhibit 4.3).

PROVIDE A RATIONALE

The therapist can use Socratic questioning (a dialogue designed to help the patient think about things in a new way) to make sure the patient understands why activity scheduling is worth doing. If activity scheduling seems trivial or not helpful to the patient, she is unlikely to work hard to follow through with it. Do not assume your patient understands the rationale for the intervention; take the time to assess your patient's understanding of activity scheduling and her willingness to try it.

Various rationales for the use of activity scheduling can be presented, depending on the patient. Some patients accept a simple statement from their therapist that until they resume a reasonably normal level of activities, they are unlikely to overcome their depression. Others who are depressed about their poor functioning at work or withdrawal from family and friends are receptive to the use of activity scheduling to address the particular problem behaviors they are concerned about. One rationale patients often accept readily is from the behavioral ex-

EXHIBIT 4.3

Guidelines for Successful Activity Scheduling

- Provide a rationale.
- Use Socratic questioning to elicit activity scheduling suggestions from the patient.
- Start where the patient is, not where the patient thinks he or she should be.
- Be specific and concrete: where, when, with whom, and for how long?
- Plan ahead for potential obstacles.

periment. If the patient proposes the following: "There's no point in my going to that party—I won't enjoy it," the therapist can respond with "Would you be willing to do an experiment? Would you be willing to go to the party for 1 hour or 2 to test out your prediction?"

A shared case formulation can provide a strong rationale for activity scheduling. For example, John and his therapist developed a working hypothesis that when John was faced with difficult work tasks, his self-schema of being incapable and incompetent was activated, triggering avoidance behaviors. John understood how his schema, thoughts, behaviors, and moods were related and that he needed to push against his tendency to avoid them. This understanding provided a compelling rationale for the use of activity scheduling.

USE SOCRATIC QUESTIONING TO ELICIT ACTIVITY SCHEDULING SUGGESTIONS FROM THE PATIENT

Activity scheduling is much more likely to succeed if the therapist sets up the interaction, so that the patient is telling the therapist what activities or time periods to schedule rather than the other way around. Most people do not like to be told what to do; they are more committed to following through with plans they develop than with plans dictated by another. In addition, if therapists simply tell patients what to do, they may recommend activities patients do not enjoy or do not want to do under any circumstances. Socratic questioning also serves as an invaluable assessment. By using Socratic questioning to elicit the patient's ideas about activities, the therapist can observe the patient's distorted thinking in action. Socratic questioning can elicit the patient's belief that nothing is worth doing or the patient's tendency to schedule too much to do and feel overwhelmed. This information can be used both to develop a better activity schedule and to teach patients about the thinking errors that are preventing them from doing this for themselves.

From our experience as therapists, we have learned it is important not to sell the patient short; do not assume he or she has no ideas at all until you check it out. To elicit activity suggestions from the patient, the therapist can say such statements as the following: "I've learned that you feel better when you spend time with people, but lately you have been isolating yourself. We agreed that a good plan is to work on becoming more socially active again. What ideas do you have about what you could do this week?" If the patient is unable to offer suggestions, the therapist can offer some options and ask the patient to choose among them. The therapist might say "You told me that you and Elena used to get together every Thursday after work. Is that something you'd like to start doing again? Or you could make a lunch date with one of your coworkers or invite one of your friends to a movie. Do any of these ideas sound good to you?" It is not uncommon for patients to offer their own ideas after they hear some examples that pique their interest—or are way off target.

START WHERE THE PATIENT IS, NOT WHERE THE PATIENT THINKS HE OR SHE SHOULD BE

Often depressed patients are immobilized and unable to get out of bed but expect themselves to spend hours working on their dissertation or clean the house from top to bottom. It is important that the therapist not buy into the patient's unrealistic expectations about what he or she should be able to do. To ascertain what is realistic, the therapist can carefully assess the patient's current level of functioning. The therapist can ask the patient to record on the Activity Schedule form how he or she spends every hour for 1 or 2 days or a complete week. For example, Anne wanted to be more active, so she could accomplish more and feel better about herself. The therapist learned that Anne wanted to join a gym and work out in the mornings before work, enroll in two or three classes to make progress on completing her degree, take on more projects at work (she was self-employed), and buy tickets to shows and plan dinner dates and other social events with friends at least 3 nights each week. She was eager to take on all these new activities right away, saying "Other people do all these things; I can too." Using the guideline "Start where the patient is," the therapist worked with Anne to examine whether her plan to tackle all these new activities at once was realistic.

The therapist suggested that Anne monitor her daily activities to assess whether her plan was realistic. Anne did this and brought a completed Activity Schedule form to her therapy session the next week. She had hoped to prove that she could tackle all the changes she wanted to make, but the concrete evidence on her Activity Schedule form showed her that her thinking was not realistic. She had repeatedly slept late, which meant that she started and ended work late. When she came home, she was often tired. Despite her intention to make headway on a needlework project, she typically watched TV and went to bed, sometimes even skipping dinner. Once the discrepancy between Anne's actual level of functioning and her goals became clear to her, she used activity scheduling to set small, realistic goals. As her functioning improved, when she made small changes, she tackled more ambitious goals.

BE SPECIFIC AND CONCRETE: WHERE, WHEN, WITH WHOM, AND FOR HOW LONG?

It is essential that the therapist specify exactly what activity will be carried out, where, when, with whom, how, and for how long when making an activity schedule. A specific plan might call for the patient to spend 15 minutes filing papers at her desk immediately after returning home from her therapy session. In contrast, a vague plan would be to work at her desk sometime during the week. A specific plan would be to call Dan tonight and ask him to go to dinner one night next week. A vague plan would be to call a friend and make a date.

Specific plans are easier to carry out than vague plans, especially for depressed people. Specific plans are also more rewarding because it is clear when they have been completed. If the plan is vague, the patient may not feel confident he or she has done what was expected. To make things clear and concrete, the therapist and patient can write down the agreed-on plan on the Activity Schedule form. If possible, keep a copy and send one home with your patient. Ask your patient to bring this Activity Schedule to the next therapy session and review it with you.

PLAN AHEAD FOR POTENTIAL OBSTACLES

Work with patients to anticipate and make a plan to handle obstacles and problems that might arise. Often the therapist can anticipate obstacles that the patient does not. If the patient has not exercised for 3 months and plans to run every day next week, the therapist can use Socratic questioning to point out to the patient that such a plan is probably unrealistic. A failure at such an ambitious plan will be a setback, whereas a success at a modest plan will be a step forward. If the patient has a plan to call a friend to go to the movies, the therapist can work with the patient to make a backup plan in case the friend is not available.

The therapist needs to keep in mind that activity plans made during the session can seem easier and more manageable to the patient than when the patient is at home alone. To address this problem, the therapist can ask direct questions, such as "Imagine it is Wednesday evening after work. How hard, on a scale of 0 (*totally easy*) to 100 (*impossible*) will it be to leave the office at 5:00 p.m. and go to the gym for 1 hour?" If the patient gives a high number, more work is needed on the activity plan before the patient leaves the session. To address unanticipated obstacles that might arise after the patient leaves the session, especially if the patient is depressed and unlikely to be able to manage any setbacks, the therapist can schedule a telephone check in at a specific time or ask the patient to call if he is unable to complete the planned activity. A telephone check in allows the therapist to intervene right away rather than letting another week of immobilization pass.

The therapist can walk his patient through the proposed plan to evaluate whether it is realistic. The therapist can use Socratic questioning to point out problems he notices: "Okay, let's imagine it's 7:00 a.m. Monday morning. You just got up. What needs to happen for you to be at the gym by 7:30 a.m. and at work by 9:00 a.m.?" As the therapist walks the patient through the plan, the patient will see that the plan is not realistic and will be receptive to the therapist's help in modifying it. This step-by-step strategy not only helps the patient make a more realistic plan but also teaches the patient a method for doing this on his own.

To assess obstacles to the activity schedule, the therapist can also ask about these directly: "Can you see any obstacles that might get in the way of getting up at 10:00 a.m. on Sunday morning and going to a café to read the paper?"

Suggestions for Handling Typical Activity Scheduling Difficulties

THE PATIENT DOES NOT BELIEVE ACTIVITY SCHEDULING WILL BE USEFUL

If the patient believes activity scheduling is a waste of time, we recommend that the therapist use Socratic questioning or a Thought Record form (see chap. 5) to find out why the patient believes this intervention is not useful. In this way, the therapist obtains a "miniformulation" that explains a particular piece of behavior or thinking, namely, the patient's reluctance to try activity scheduling. A full understanding of the patient's reluctance likely leads directly to ideas for interventions to address the problem.

Some patients believe that the intervention is too simplistic to help. Examining this thinking (see chap. 5) can help patients see that this assumption is not very adaptive because it prevents them from trying something that might make a difference for them. A behavioral experiment can help with this problem too. For example, Marcy was reluctant to break her work on a term paper into small pieces (i.e., graded tasks), insisting that she needed to carve out a large block of time to sit down and "just do it." Marcy agreed to do an experiment to test her hypothesis. Marcy agreed that she would try her method during the coming week. If her method did not work, in her next therapy session she would try breaking the project into small pieces and scheduling a piece to do each day. A behavioral experiment is most useful when patients believe their therapists are truly open to the results of the experiment, so it is important that therapists maintain a genuine scientific stance when their patients agree to behavioral experiments.

Some patients are blocked by automatic thoughts, such as "I don't want to schedule activities because I never follow through with plans and then I feel worse." The therapist can use Socratic questioning to help the patients see that the solution the patient has adopted (avoid making any plans) is not likely to be adaptive over the long haul—or even over the short one. The therapist could suggest using graded task assignments to set up activities that the patient can successfully complete.

Monitoring can be a useful way to help patients learn whether activity scheduling is useful to them. Instead of insisting that patients schedule activities, therapists could suggest that they use an Activity Schedule form to log their activities throughout the day and to assign mood ratings (0 [*depressed*]–10 [*happy*]) for each activity. In this way, patients can gather evidence about the usefulness of activity scheduling (i.e., whether the patient feels better when active).

THE PATIENT SAYS "I'LL TRY ACTIVITY SCHEDULING, BUT NOTHING REALLY INTERESTS ME."

To handle this attitude, the therapist can view this response from the depressed patient as a distorted cognition, not a statement of fact. The therapist can apply Socratic questioning to an idea or two from the patient about things she would have a small chance of enjoying or would be willing to try to test the hypothesis that nothing gives her any pleasure or enjoyment. The process of eliciting suggestions from the patient can also be used to teach patients how negative their thinking is.

When the patient is unable to offer suggestions for items to put on the Activity Schedule form, the therapist can ask the patient how she spent her time before she became depressed. Patients may have enjoyed bowling, going to bookstores, spending time with friends, exercising, or cooking. These activities provide a good starting point for activity scheduling. Exercise, if it was important to the patient, is a particularly valuable activity because there is evidence in the literature that exercise is an effective treatment for depression (Simons, McGowan, Epstein, & Kupfer, 1985).

Sometimes when the therapist suggests reinstating a previously pleasurable activity, the patient protests: "I don't do those things now because I know I wouldn't enjoy them." The therapist could use "pleasure predicting," another behavioral experiment designed to test to what degree a patient will enjoy an activity. In this intervention, patients agree to try an activity that they believe will provide them with little or no pleasure and they rate their pleasure using a 0 (*no pleasure*) to 10 (*complete pleasure*) scale before they do the activity. Patients try the activity and rate their actual pleasure. Usually patients find that the activity was more pleasurable than they predicted, demonstrating to them the tendency of depressed individuals to minimize the potential pleasure of an activity. The fact that as part of the intervention the patient must engage in pleasurable activities is an added bonus.

The therapist can also directly suggest activities to the depressed patient. Activities of daily living (e.g., getting out of bed, preparing meals, bathing, getting dressed in the morning) are obvious choices if the patient is not completing them routinely. The therapist can also suggest such pleasurable activities as going to a movie, going to the park, and calling a friend; these suggestions, of course, can be drawn from the information that the therapist gleans about the patient's interests.

Burns (1999) suggested a strategy for attacking "do-nothingism" that we find helpful. We teach our patients about do-nothingism using the following sample dialogue:

> When we aren't depressed, we often decide whether to do a certain thing (e.g., go see *Titanic*) by asking ourselves "Do I feel like doing this?" Imagine you are depressed. If you ask yourself "Do I feel like doing a certain thing, what answer will you get?" ("no"). What this means is that, when you are depressed, you cannot decide whether to do a certain thing by asking yourself if you feel like doing it. When you're depressed, you don't feel like doing anything. When you're depressed, you need to start to do some things, whether you feel like doing them or not. You'll feel like doing them later.

THE PATIENT FAILS TO COMPLETE THE ACTIVITY SCHEDULE FORM

At times, the therapist and patient may agree that the patient will try certain activities, but then the patient does not follow through with them. Such failures may be due to poor collaboration between the therapist and patient when deciding on what activities to schedule. The therapist may fail to make the scheduled activities concrete and specific enough, or the patient's fears of failure or criticism may interfere.

Some patients are able to introspect about why they did not complete the activity that was scheduled as homework (e.g., "My mother needed me to help her move, so I cancelled my movie plans."). Other patients appear to have no idea about why they did not follow through with the scheduled activity. In this situation, we recommend that the therapist walk the patient through the period before and after the activity that was to be completed. For example, "Let's go back to Monday morning at 7:00 a.m. Your plan was to leave for the gym. What actually happened when you woke up that morning? How were you feeling? What thoughts were you having? What was the first thing you did?" In this way, perhaps the therapist and patient can identify events or feelings about which the patient is unaware but which nonetheless prevented him or her from completing the scheduled activity. Once the problem is identified, the therapist can work with the patient to develop a plan to solve it.

Homework noncompliance is a common and important problem. We offer other strategies for overcoming obstacles to completing homework assignments in chapter 3 (Structure of the Therapy Session).

Summary and Conclusion

This chapter described activity scheduling, an intervention directed at the behavioral element of the mood–behavior–cognitions triad of depressive symptoms. Cognitive theory predicts that behavioral change produces cognitive and mood change. In the next chapter, we focus on the use of the Thought Record form to attack the cognitive component of depressive symptoms directly.

Practice Exercises

These exercises are intended for clinicians and students to practice what has been covered in this chapter. Instructors can use them to stimulate class discussion and experiential learning.

1. Try activity scheduling yourself. Complete an Activity Schedule form for 1 day or 1 week, or use it to schedule any of your own problematic times or activities. One of the best ways to learn about activity scheduling is firsthand.
2. Role-play activity scheduling with a colleague or fellow student. Play the role of one of your own patients for whom activity scheduling might be useful (see the section titled Who Needs Activity Scheduling?). Then reverse roles and try again. As you practice each role-play, carry out the following steps:
   ▪ Use the Activity Schedule form.
   ▪ Count how many of the five Guidelines for Successful Activity Scheduling (see Exhibit 4.3) you used in your role-play.

■ Evaluate your effectiveness by asking your role-play partner for feedback: What did it feel like to be the recipient of activity scheduling? What was helpful? What was not helpful?

3. Review your list of current patients and choose one or two who might benefit from activity scheduling (review the section titled Who Needs Activity Scheduling?). Place an Activity Schedule form in the clinical record of your patient to remind you to try the intervention one of the next times you see the patient.

4. Read each of the following three vignettes (Joe, Mary, Mike). For each vignette, answer the following four questions (answers are provided in the Answer Key that follows).

(a) What could activity scheduling help the patient accomplish?

(b) What are some good initial foci of activity scheduling for the patient?

(c) What obstacles might you predict?

(d) Suggest some interventions that would help overcome these obstacles.

JOE

Joe is a 30-year-old unemployed, single man who lives alone. His primary treatment goals are to improve his social skills so he can find a girlfriend and to get a job. Currently he is spending most of his time at home in bed sleeping or watching TV. He has agreed to do volunteer work for a local community agency 5 mornings a week but has been going to work only once or twice a week. When he thinks about getting ready to go to his volunteer job, his thoughts are "I'm too tired. I'm not up for it today. It won't matter if I miss today. I'll go tomorrow. I'll get an earlier start and feel better tomorrow." He has difficulty settling down to work in therapy, insisting that he knows he will feel less depressed if he can "just find a girlfriend and a job."

MARY

Mary is a 40-year-old married woman with three children. She works as an administrator for a large organization. She is president of the PTA at her children's school and volunteers for several local charities, often organizing large fundraising events. Six months ago, her mother had a stroke and now needs quite a bit of care. Although her siblings live nearby, Mary has been taking most of the responsibility for her mother's care, stating that she is the most "organized and together" of all her siblings and that her siblings have always depended on her to be the strong one. Mary has been feeling overwhelmed, overburdened, fatigued, and sad and is unable to enjoy the things she once enjoyed. She reports feeling guilty and inadequate for "not doing a good enough job with anybody," including her mother, children, husband, coworkers, and friends. Since assuming primary care for her mother, she has discontinued many of her social and pleasurable activities, including getting together with friends, taking walks, and going to the gym. When she considers planning one of these events, she has such thoughts as "I won't enjoy it. I'm too tired. I don't have the time." When Mary thinks about cutting back on some of her responsibilities she has assumed, she feels guilty and thinks that "I shouldn't have to let anything go; I need to do it all."

MIKE

Mike is a 26-year-old unmarried graduate student who states that a major cause of his depression is that he cannot make any progress on his dissertation. He is keeping up with his course work and teaching, but he finds himself avoiding working on his dissertation. When he thinks about his dissertation, he has such thoughts as "It will be too hard. I won't be able to do it. I don't know where to start. I don't have enough time to accomplish anything significant. I'm too tired. I'm not ready. I'll work on it tomorrow." He wakes up each day with a plan to spend the day working on his dissertation, but then he begins to find other things to do, such as clean his apartment, make phone calls, and play computer games. As a result, he finds that the day "just slipped away." He is feeling increasingly discouraged. He spends less time with his friends than he previously did, feeling he does not have the time to socialize because he needs to work on his dissertation. He is having trouble sleeping and difficulty concentrating, and he is not enjoying much of anything.

Answer Key

We offer several answers to each of the questions. You may have additional answers.

JOE

(a) *What could activity scheduling help the patient accomplish?* Activity scheduling could help Joe get out of bed in the morning, get dressed, and get to his volunteer job. These are things he needs to accomplish if he is to reach his goals of getting a girlfriend and a job.

(b) *What are some good initial foci of activity scheduling for the patient?* A good initial focus of activity scheduling is to ask Joe to simply monitor his daily activities—to just write down on the Activity Schedule form how he spends every hour of every day between therapy sessions. This assignment will help Joe attend to the details of how he is actually spending his time. Another good initial focus for Joe is to schedule times when he will plan to carry out basic activities of his day: getting up in the morning, getting dressed, and getting to his volunteer job. It might also be a good idea to schedule a social event because Joe has a goal to improve his social functioning. Joe's therapist worked with him to schedule some of these activities on his Activity Schedule form. Joe's Activity Schedule (see Exhibit 4.4) begins with the therapy session in which the activity scheduling intervention occurs and ends with another therapy session a few days later. Because Joe is functioning at such a low level, we recommend scheduling only a few relatively brief activities, a telephone check in each day, and a second therapy session that week to review his progress.

(c) *What obstacles might you predict?* Joe's problem is that he is thinking far ahead about ambitious goals he wishes to accomplish (get a girlfriend, get a job), but he is not focused on day-to-day functioning. He might not accept the rationale for scheduling activities, such as getting up and getting dressed. He might insist that he would function at a high level if he just had a paid job he liked, or he might maintain that he knows what he needs to do to get to his volunteer job, namely, "just do it." He may want to focus his treatment on social skills development instead of activity scheduling, believing that if he felt more confident socially, he could achieve his goals. If he does agree to activity scheduling, he may want to schedule activities that are unrealistic, given his current functioning level. Even if he makes realistic plans, Joe may fail to carry them out.

(d) *Suggest some interventions that would help overcome these obstacles.* Work with Joe to set up a behavioral experiment to test his hypothesis that he does not need activity scheduling (Joe believes that he needs to "just do it"). To test Joe's hypothesis, he can suspend his activity scheduling for 1 week and try the just-do-it strategy. He can collect data to evaluate how successful his strategy is. Before the experiment begins, work with Joe to establish a clear, concrete measure of success. In Joe's case, he agreed that the measure of success would be the number of times that week he went to his volunteer job; he set a goal to go three times during the week. Before the experiment began, the therapist asked Joe to agree that if the just-do-it strategy failed, he would try activity scheduling. This method is fail safe: If Joe's strategy works, everybody wins; if Joe's strategy fails, he and his therapist have a clear plan about what they will try next (i.e., activity scheduling).

Use Socratic questioning to teach Joe that overly ambitious goals are difficult to achieve and that failure leads to demoralization and reduced effort. For example, the therapist asks Joe, "Suppose we set the goal that next week you will look for a job. What specific activities does this involve? On a scale of 1 (*easy*) to 100 (*extremely difficult*), how hard do these activities seem? How likely are you to carry out the plan? How will you feel if you make the plan and do not carry it out? Now suppose we set the goal that next week you will go to your volunteer job twice. How hard does that sound? How likely are you to carry out the plan? How will you feel if you do not carry it out? How will you feel if you carry it out?"

Use cognitive restructuring (see chap. 5) to elicit and teach Joe to respond to the negative automatic thoughts that are sabotaging his efforts to follow through with his activity scheduling plans. If Joe wishes to work on social goals rather than vocational ones, the therapist can use activity scheduling to schedule specific social events and interactions. It does not matter too much what Joe does; the main goal is to increase his level of activity.

MARY

(a) *What could activity scheduling help the patient accomplish?* Mary is clearly overwhelmed with too many things to do. Activity scheduling could help Mary set more realistic and balanced goals that include more time for herself and pleasurable activities and less time taking on responsibilities that others could assume.

(b) *What are some good initial foci of activity scheduling for the patient?* A good first activity scheduling intervention is to ask Mary to monitor her current activities; that is, ask her to simply write down on an Activity Schedule form how she spends her time between one therapy session and the next. This exercise can be used to teach her how demanding her current schedule is and how it contributes to her depressed mood. Then ask Mary to examine her schedule to look for burdensome activities she

EXHIBIT 4.4

Joe's Activity Schedule

	Monday Date:	Tuesday Date:	Wednesday Date:
7–8 a.m.			
8–9 a.m.			
9–10 a.m.			Get up, get dressed
10–11 a.m.			Volunteer job
11 a.m.–12 noon		Therapy session with Joan	↓
12 noon–1 p.m.			Call Joan to check in
1–2 p.m.			
2–3 p.m.			
3–4 p.m.			
4–5 p.m.		Call Heather to make plans for later in the week	
5–6 p.m.			
6–7 p.m.			
Evening (after 7 p.m.)		Go to bed at midnight	

Thursday Date:	Friday Date:	Saturday Date:	Sunday Date:
Get up, get dressed			
Volunteer job	Therapy session with Joan		
↓			
Call Joan to check in			

EXHIBIT 4.5

Mary's Activity Schedule

	Monday Date:	Tuesday Date:	Wednesday Date:
7–8 a.m.			
8–9 a.m.			
9–10 a.m.			
10–11 a.m.			
11 a.m.–12 noon			
12 noon–1 p.m.			
1–2 p.m.			
2–3 p.m.			
3–4 p.m.			
4–5 p.m.			
5–6 p.m.			
6–7 p.m.			
Evening (after 7 p.m.)			

Thursday Date:	Friday Date:	Saturday Date:	Sunday Date:
		Call sister about Mom's medical appt.	
Lunch with Susan			
Call sister to ask her to take mom to doctor and dentist; shopping			

could consider letting go and pleasurable activities she could add. For example, Mary's Activity Schedule showed she was not doing any activities for pleasure. Her siblings live nearby but are not helping care for her mother. The therapist could work with Mary to plan two things: a pleasurable event for herself and telephone calls to her sisters to ask them to take their mother to her next medical appointment (see Exhibit 4.5).

(c) *What obstacles might you predict?* Mary's guilt and her belief that she is not doing enough for everybody may make it difficult for her to decrease her responsibilities and take more time for herself. She may worry that she will feel worse if she does not keep to her current schedule because it may feel like she has let others down. In fact, she may even believe that she ought to schedule even more caretaking responsibilities. Mary may also feel so depressed and burdened that asking her to make any changes in her schedule, even increasing enjoyable activities or dropping burdensome ones, may feel overwhelming.

(d) *Suggest some interventions that would help overcome these obstacles.* Work with Mary to set up a behavioral experiment to test her belief that she will feel guilty if she decreases some of her responsibilities and spends more time on herself. If she does experience guilt, use cognitive restructuring to help her cope with the negative thoughts underlying the guilt. Use cognitive restructuring (see chap. 5) to address Mary's reluctance to make changes in her schedule. As part of this exercise, the therapist can suggest to Mary that if she takes better care of herself, she will be better able to help others. She will also set a good model for her own daughter, who is learning from her mother that it is more important to care for others than for oneself. Do a role-play in the session to assess whether Mary has skill deficits that block her from asking others assertively for help. If this is the case, provide Mary with some assertiveness training.

MIKE

(a) *What could activity scheduling help the patient accomplish?* Activity scheduling could help Mike make progress on his dissertation, spend his time more productively and enjoyably, and decrease his symptoms of depression.

(b) *What are some good initial foci of activity scheduling for the patient?* Monitoring his current daily activities would help Mike see more clearly the discrepancy between what he does and what he plans to do. One of Mike's main problems is that he avoids dissertation writing until late in the day, but then he finds that the day is gone. He is also expecting himself to spend the entire day writing; this goal is too ambitious and scary, so he avoids it altogether and accomplishes nothing, making it even more difficult to accomplish anything the next day, setting up a downward spiral of demoralization.

Work with Mike (using graded task assignments) to schedule a small block of time (1 hour) or a small writing goal (1 page) for him to shoot for on a daily basis, first thing in the morning. Establishing a reward (e.g., lunch with a friend) after accomplishing the task can be helpful as well. Many dissertation writers find they are more successful if they get up and go out of the house to a library or other place that promotes writing behaviors and reduces distractions. Mike's Activity Schedule is provided in Exhibit 4.6.

(c) *What obstacles might you predict?* Mike might see activity scheduling as too trivial or simplistic. He may have trouble letting go of beliefs that he should be able to spend whole days working on his dissertation, that he will never finish unless he does, and that he is failing if he only schedules 1 page or 1 hour of work at a time. He might have difficulty knowing what part of the dissertation to tackle first.

(d) *Suggest some interventions that would help overcome these obstacles.* Work with Mike to develop a behavioral experiment to test the hypothesis that activity scheduling is too trivial and simplistic to be helpful. Ask Mike if he would be willing to try it for 1 week to see if it helps. Use Socratic questioning and cognitive restructuring (see chap. 5) to challenge the thoughts that interfere with his willingness to try activity scheduling or that interfere with the dissertation writing itself. For example, it is important to challenge Mike's belief that unless he plans to spend entire days working on his dissertation, he will never complete it. One tack to take here is to ask Mike how productive this strategy has been to date.

Help Mike break his dissertation project into small, manageable tasks and write one or two of them on his Activity Schedule form. To do this, you may need to get into a discussion of the details of the dissertation itself. Recommend that at the end of each day's work, Mike write down a small, manageable plan for the next day. This strategy can help him overcome the daily obstacle of not knowing where to start. A telephone or email check in with you may help him stay on track.

Mike's Activity Schedule

	Monday Date:	Tuesday Date:	Wednesday Date:
7–8 a.m.			
8–9 a.m.			
9–10 a.m.			Get up, get dressed, and go to the library
10–11 a.m.			1 hr work on dissertation
11 a.m.–12 noon			Call Joan to follow up
12 noon–1 p.m.			Lunch with Susan
1–2 p.m.			
2–3 p.m.			
3–4 p.m.		Therapy	
4–5 p.m.			
5–6 p.m.			
6–7 p.m.			
Evening (after 7 p.m.)			

© 1999 San Francisco Bay Area Center for Cognitive Therapy.

Thursday Date:	Friday Date:	Saturday Date:	Sunday Date:
Get up, get dressed, and go to the library			
1 hr work on dissertation			
Call Joan to follow up			

Further Readings and Videotapes

Beck, A. T., Rush, A. J., Shaw, B. F., & Emery, G. (1979). *Cognitive therapy of depression.* New York: Guilford. Chap. 7, Application of behavioral techniques.

Beck, J. S. (1995). *Cognitive therapy: Basics and beyond.* New York: Guilford Press. Chap. 12, Additional cognitive and behavioral techniques.

Burns, D. D. (1999). *Feeling good: The new mood therapy.* New York: Morrow. Chap. 5, Do-nothingism: How to beat it.

Leahy, R. (1996). *Cognitive therapy: Basic principles and applications.* Northvale, NJ: Aronson. Chap. 5, Behavioral interventions.

Lewinsohn, P. M., Muñoz, R. F., Youngren, M. A., & Zeiss, A. M. (1978). *Control your depression.* Englewood Cliffs, NJ: Prentice-Hall. Chap. 7, Pleasant activities.

Persons, J. B. (1989). *Cognitive therapy in practice: A case formulation approach.* New York: Norton. Chap. 4, Behavioral interventions.

Persons, J. B., Davidson, J., & Tompkins, M. A. (2000). *Cognitive–behavior therapy for depression: Activity scheduling* [Videotape]. Washington, DC: American Psychological Association.

APPENDIX 4A: ACTIVITY SCHEDULE

	Monday Date:	Tuesday Date:	Wednesday Date:
7–8 a.m.			
8–9 a.m.			
9–10 a.m.			
10–11 a.m.			
11 a.m.–12 noon			
12 noon–1 p.m.			
1–2 p.m.			
2–3 p.m.			
3–4 p.m.			
4–5 p.m.			
5–6 p.m.			
6–7 p.m.			
Evening (after 7 p.m.)			

Thursday Date:	Friday Date:	Saturday Date:	Sunday Date:

Using the
Thought Record

5

What disturbs men's minds is not events but their judgments on events. (Epictetus)

This chapter focuses on the Thought Record, a tool used to help patients identify and make changes in negative, unrealistic, maladaptive modes of thinking. In this chapter, we present

- theoretical and empirical underpinnings of the Thought Record
- two uses of the Thought Record
- when to use a Thought Record
- guidelines for using the Thought Record successfully
- selecting a situation on which to focus a Thought Record
- overcoming obstacles to using the Thought Record
- practice exercises
- further readings and videotapes
- Thought Record and Evidence Record forms.

Underpinnings of the Thought Record

THEORETICAL

In his cognitive theory, Beck (1976; Beck et al., 1979) proposed that when maladaptive schemas are activated by negative life events, they give rise to symptoms of depression, which are made up of negative automatic thoughts, maladaptive behaviors, and depressed mood. The term *automatic* is used to describe the negative thoughts because they arise without effort or intention and often even without awareness. Beck proposed that changes in automatic thoughts lead to changes in the mood and behavioral components of depression and in underlying schema. These propositions provide the theoretical underpinning for the interventions directed at changing automatic thoughts that are described in this chapter.

The Thought Record is a tool the therapist can use in the process of teaching patients to identify and change the automatic thoughts that drive their negative moods and maladaptive behaviors. Note that the columns of the Thought Record (see Appendix 5A) mirror the elements of Beck's (1976; Beck et al., 1979) cognitive theory. The "situation" column of the Thought Record is used to describe the particular external event that is activating the underlying schema (not shown on the Thought Record) and giving rise to the problematic "behaviors," "emotions," and "thoughts." Our Thought Record (Appendix 5A) differs from other thought records (e.g., the Daily Record of Dysfunctional Thoughts; Beck et al., 1979) by including a "behavior" column that is used to record the behavioral component of the individual's reaction to the problematic situation. We include a column for noting depressive behaviors because Beck proposed that depressive symptoms are made up of thoughts, emotions, and behaviors. The therapist's job is to help the depressed patient obtain more reasonable, rational, realistic, and adaptive cognitive and behavioral coping "Responses" to the situation.

EMPIRICAL

Empirical support for the value of the Thought Record in working with depressed patients comes from the randomized controlled trials (RCTs) demonstrating that cognitive–behavior therapy (CBT) is effective in treating depression (Craighead et al., 1998; DeRubeis & Crits-Christoph, 1998). Cognitive restructuring, using a form similar to the Thought Record, is an important component of CBT for depression. Of course, CBT includes other components as well, so the RCTs do not provide compelling evidence that cognitive restructuring interventions themselves are a necessary or sufficient component of effective treatment for depression.

More direct evidence that cognitive interventions alleviate depressive symptoms is provided by studies in which researchers examined outcomes of depressed patients treated with cognitive interventions alone (insofar as this is possible). Several studies of this sort show that cognitive interventions are effective in alleviating depression and that outcomes of patients receiving cognitive interventions do not differ from those of patients receiving behavioral or social skills interventions

(Fleming & Thornton, 1980; Rehm, Kaslow, & Rabin, 1987; Zeiss et al., 1979).

The positive outcomes from studies of cognitive interventions suggest that cognitive interventions are sufficient to alleviate symptoms of depression. Are cognitive interventions necessary to effectively treat depression? Results of a dismantling study by Jacobson et al. (1996) suggest they are not. These researchers showed that depressed patients who were treated with behavioral interventions alone did as well as those who were treated with behavioral interventions plus cognitive restructuring. Of course, as Hollon et al. (1987) and Whisman (1999) pointed out, the fact that cognitive interventions are not necessary to produce recovery does not disprove the hypothesis that recovery occurs through cognitive change. (It is possible that behavioral interventions "work their magic" by producing cognitive change.)

More evidence of the value of cognitive interventions in treating depression comes from a study of changes occurring within therapy sessions. If depressed patients, during a session of cognitive therapy, experience a reduction in the degree of belief in their distorted automatic thoughts, do they also experience an improvement in their mood? Cognitive theory, of course, predicts that they will. To answer this question, Persons et al. (1988) collected data during 17 therapy sessions in which the Thought Record was used to help patients restructure their negative automatic thoughts about an upsetting situation. Patients rated on a 0 to 100 scale the strength of their negative mood (0 = *no negative mood* to 100 = *intense negative mood*) and the degree of belief in their negative automatic thoughts (0 = *no belief* to 100 = *complete belief*) at the beginning and end of the therapy session. When a multiple regression analysis was conducted, the investigators found that as predicted by cognitive theory, mood change during the session was a function of cognitive change during the session. Longer term benefits of the use of the Thought Record were demonstrated by Neimeyer and Feixas (1990), who showed that depressed patients who were more skillful at completing the Thought Record were less depressed 6 months after group CBT than patients who were less skillful.

These findings suggest that cognitive restructuring using the Thought Record can help patients recover from depression. Of course, the findings generalize only to samples similar to those studied. They also do not provide the clinician with the answer to the question "Will the depressed patient who is in my office right now benefit from the use of the Thought Record?" To answer this question, the clinician can monitor the patient's mood during the session to find out if using the Thought Record in the process of cognitive restructuring produces a mood shift. To do this, the clinician first asks the patient to describe a particular situation that is upsetting to him or her and then to rate the intensity of the emotional distress the patient is experiencing at that moment in the therapy session. After spending some time in the session on cognitive restructuring (using methods described later in this chapter), the therapist then asks the patient to rerate his or her negative mood. Other methods for monitoring the effects of the use of the Thought Record include monitoring the patient's depressive symptoms to see if they change following the intervention, observing whether the intervention helps the patient behave more adaptively, and asking the patient for feedback about whether the intervention is helpful.

Two Uses of the Thought Record

In this chapter, we teach cognitive interventions using the Thought Record form. When carrying out Thought Record interventions in a formal, structured way, the therapist can provide Thought Record forms, pens and pencils, and a table or clipboards. Both patient and therapist write on the forms. Cognitive interventions can also be carried out without using the Thought Record form. Nearly all of the interventions described in this chapter can be carried out in a less structured or even an informal, conversational way that does not entail the use of the Thought Record form. We emphasize the use of the Thought Record form because it provides a clear, structured approach to therapy, which appears to be useful to depressed patients (see Shaw et al., 1999).

The Thought Record can be used in two primary ways. The first is to teach the model that negative thoughts occurring in specific situations cause negative mood states and maladaptive behaviors. The second is to promote change.

TEACH THE COGNITIVE MODEL

The cognitive model gives patients a framework for understanding why they feel and behave the way they do; this can be reassuring to patients who are disturbed by what they perceive as inexplicable, "out of the blue" reactions. An understanding of the model is also useful because when patients understand the relationships among their thoughts, moods, and behaviors, the rationale for making cognitive and behavioral changes becomes clear. The Thought Record can be used to teach the cognitive model in general terms by focusing on a particular problematic situation the patient is experiencing or by identifying themes that emerge over the course of repeated Thought Records.

General Terms

The therapist can introduce the cognitive model by saying the following:

> A situation is a situation. It's how you think about or interpret the situation that determines how you feel. Can you imagine a situation in which different people might have very different thoughts and feelings? Do you see how those different feelings and thoughts might lead to different behaviors?

Sometimes the patient can think of an example right away—perhaps a situation in which the patient and a friend had different thoughts and emotional reactions to the same movie. If the patient generates an example, the therapist can then use a Thought Record to show the patient how each person's reactions are linked to his or her thoughts about the event.

If the patient has difficulty providing an example, the therapist can describe one, choosing a situation the patient is likely to have experienced, such as (for many patients) attending an office party. The therapist can propose the following:

> Think about all the people at this party. Imagine a woman who is new to the company who is having such thoughts as "Nobody will like me. I'm such a loser." How do you think she's feeling? How might she behave? Now imagine another person at the same party who is thinking "I'm so glad it's Friday. I can't wait to party!" How do you think she is feeling? Behaving? Imagine a man at the same party who is thinking "If I say anything, I'll sound stupid and look like a jerk." How do you think he feels? What might he be doing?

Patients are often capable of describing the feelings and behaviors these partygoers might have in response to their thoughts. Another illustrative teaching example is the situation of hearing a scratching noise at one's window, which can elicit several emotional reactions (pleasure, anticipation, fear) and behaviors (playful movements, dialing 911) depending on the cognitions of the person in the situation ("My girlfriend is playing peek-a-boo," "A burglar is trying to get in.").

Understand a Personal Problematic Situation

The therapist can also teach the cognitive model to a patient by working through a Thought Record that addresses a situation that is problematic for that patient. To begin the process, the therapist asks the patient to describe a recent upsetting situation, negative mood, or problematic behavior. This can be a situation that the patient found easy to understand or a confusing one, as in the case of John, who told his therapist he had been feeling "lousy" lately but did not know why. He suspected that he felt bad because after many months of postponing the decision, he and his brother had finally decided to put their father into a nursing home. But John could not understand why he felt so bad and insisted "I shouldn't feel bad about this. My brother and I discussed it a long time, we shared the decision, and I know it was the only reasonable thing to do." The therapist used a Thought Record to help John understand his emotional reactions in this painful situation. As his Thought Record (see Exhibit 5.1) illustrates, John identified a long stream of thoughts about his decision, including that he was reneging on a promise he had made to his father years ago that he would never place him in a nursing home and that he (John) was selfish for placing his father in a nursing home rather than caring for him at home. After his therapist helped John elicit these thoughts and write them on a Thought Record, John understood why he felt so lousy and why he had delayed making the decision for so long; he felt less distressed and uncomfortable about the situation.

Identify a Theme

Over the course of repeated Thought Records, the patient and therapist often identify specific automatic thoughts (e.g., "I'm not good enough") and themes (e.g., concern about making mistakes or about being criticized by others) that recur in diverse situations. These recurring thoughts and themes probably reflect underlying schemas (see chap. 2). When patients (and therapists) see that the Thought Record yields information about schemas (as demonstrated in the video by Persons, Tompkins, & Davidson, 2000) that appear to play a role in numerous diverse problems, they gain confidence in the therapy's potential to address problems at a deeper level, not just the superficial (or situation-specific) one.

PROMOTE CHANGE

A major goal of cognitive therapy is to help patients change their thinking to feel better and function better. In this section, we describe several interventions the therapist can carry out with a Thought Record to help patients do this. We also describe the use of the Evidence Record.

To help patients restructure or reframe their view of problem situations, therapists can ask patients any or all of the following questions about their negative automatic thoughts. These questions are also listed in Exhibit 5.2, Questions That Promote Cognitive Restructuring.

Are These Thoughts Helpful?

June is a college freshman. She is accustomed to excelling in her school-work, but she finds the academic rigor at college to be more challenging

John's Thought Record

Date	Situation (event, memory, attempt to do something, etc.)	Behaviors	Emotions	Thoughts	Responses
	Making the final decision to put my father in a nursing home	Procrastinating on making the decision	Lousy Guilty	I'm doing the wrong thing. I'm going back on my word. Years ago, I promised him I would never do this. If I was stronger and less selfish, I would take care of him myself at home. He'll be lonely and miserable and become depressed. He'll waste away.	

© 1999 San Francisco Bay Area Center for Cognitive Therapy.

EXHIBIT 5.2

Questions That Promote Cognitive Restructuring

Are these thoughts helpful? Use the following questions to explore this further: "Do these thoughts help you feel better? Do they help you behave more adaptively? Do they help your self-esteem? Do they help you interact successfully with others?"

Do these thoughts contain cognitive distortions? To answer this question, review the list of cognitive distortions (see Exhibit 5.3, Cognitive Distortions Defined) and list the distortions that appear in each automatic thought. Use the information about the distortions to aid in generating responses to the thoughts. For example, the thought "He hates me" is "mind reading." Identifying this distortion leads to the following response: "I can't be sure he hates me. I'm assuming he does, but I don't really know."

Are these thoughts consistent with the evidence? Use the Evidence Record to list concrete, specific events or facts that support an automatic thought. After doing this, write a balanced view that integrates both types of evidence. On the basis of this balanced view and of evidence that does not support the automatic thought, write a short list of responses to the negative automatic thought for use the next time it arises.

Are there alternative explanations? Consider whether there are other possible explanations for an upsetting situation. For example, an auto repairman who is upset about an irate customer can ask himself the following: "The fact that this man is angry with me might mean I'm a bad repairman. What else could it mean?"

What would one say to a friend in this situation? Asking this question encourages one to be more generous and evenhanded in one's views. For example, the car repairman can ask himself the following: "If this angry customer were angry at my friend Joe and he were upset, what would I say to Joe to help him handle the situation?"

How did one learn to think this way? An understanding of the origins of a thought or line of thinking can help generate responses to it. For example, "I learned to believe the world was full of unending burdens and obligations because my mother believed this. But I don't have to accept her view of the world."

than she had anticipated. She felt devastated when she earned a *B–* on a recent midterm chemistry exam, and she began avoiding doing her chemistry reading and homework. When she completed a Thought Record about the midterm exam, June identified her automatic thoughts: "I really blew it," "I should be able to get *A*s," "I'm going to fail the final exam," "I'm going to fail out of college," and "I'm not as smart as everybody else here." June's therapist used a series of Socratic questions to teach June that her thoughts about her midterm exam were making a difficult and demanding situation worse. The therapist then asked June, "When you have these thoughts, how do you feel? When you feel like that, is it harder or easier to do your chemistry homework?" June quickly saw that her thinking about the problem was exacerbating her distress.

To help June generate some coping responses, the therapist asked June "Is there another way of thinking about this situation that would help you feel better and function better?" With her therapist's help, June developed (and wrote on her Thought Record) several responses to her automatic thoughts, including the following: "This catastrophic thinking doesn't help me. Even though I did really well in high school, it's going to take some time to adjust to college. If I work hard, I can do it. In the past, when I had setbacks and worked hard, I was successful." When working with patients to evaluate the usefulness of their automatic thoughts, the therapist can ask any or all of four questions: "Do these thoughts help you feel better? Do they help you behave more adaptively? Do they help your self-esteem? Do they help you interact successfully with others?"

Do These Thoughts Contain Cognitive Distortions?

To help patients shift to more reasonable, realistic modes of thinking, Aaron Beck (Beck et al., 1979), David Burns (1999), and others have identified and named the typical cognitive distortions reported by depressed patients. When teaching patients about cognitive distortions, we recommend giving them a list of thinking errors (see Exhibit 5.3, Cognitive Distortions Defined) they can use as a guide. Often patients feel better after simply identifying the distortions in their thinking, and a list of thinking errors helps them do this.

For example, Quint, a salesman, sat down at his desk in the morning to do some work; he spent an hour shuffling papers without accomplishing anything. He began feeling depressed and discouraged, so he pulled out a Thought Record and listed his automatic thoughts:

> I'm always disorganized. I can't even find the form I need. I'll never be able to get this job done. I might as well give up. I'm a failure as a businessman. If I can't get this job done, people will think I'm incompetent, and no one will hire me again.

As a first step to responding to these thoughts, Quint reviewed the list of thinking errors and wrote down, next to each automatic thought, the thinking errors he noted (see Exhibit 5.4). For example, he identified several distortions in his thought "I'm always disorganized" (overgeneralization, focus on the negative, all-or-nothing thinking). The simple process of identifying thinking errors helped Quint to realize that his thinking was "out of line" and that his situation was not as dire as he had feared.

Depressed individuals usually find the process of identifying errors in their thinking to be reassuring and helpful. However, a few are disturbed by it because they conclude that "There must *really* be something wrong with me if my thinking is so distorted!" To address this reaction, the therapist may find it helpful to let patients know that everybody has distorted thoughts when their mood is depressed. The therapist can also

EXHIBIT 5.3

Cognitive Distortions Defined

Overgeneralization. The error of concluding the general from the specific. For example, "my wife didn't smile and say hello when she came home last night. She must be unhappy." Or "he was really nice to me today. This means he's a wonderful person, and I can trust him completely."

Focus on the negative ("doom and gloom"). The distortion of selectively attending to negative information; this is the "glass-half-empty" view of the world. For example, Jane focuses on the 5 items she missed on a 100-item exam and feels like a failure.

Disqualifying the positive. The fallacy of ignoring or devaluing positive evidence, events, and information. Jane, who agonizes about the 5 items she missed and ignores the 95 items she got right, is disqualifying the positive. Another example is the woman who when evaluating her performance as a mother refuses to include the fact that she gets her kids to school on time everyday as evidence that she's a good mother because "I'm *supposed* to do that."

Predicting the future. The error of predicting the future on the basis of the present. This is often a problem because the view of the present is distorted, so the view of the future then becomes distorted as well. For example, "the first couple I treated broke up; this means I'll never be a successful couples therapist." Or "that date didn't go well; I'll never find a life partner."

Emotional reasoning. The fallacy of inferring facts about the world from emotional experiences. For example, a person who is afraid of elevators concludes on the basis of his fear reaction when he gets in an elevator that elevators are dangerous. Another example is a depressed patient who concludes from his feelings of hopelessness about recovery from his illness that he *is* hopeless and *will* never get better.

All-or-nothing thinking (also termed "dichotomous thinking"). The error of viewing things in "black and white" terms, ignoring the "grays." For example, "Joe didn't return my call promptly; he's a totally unreliable person." Or "I got a mediocre grade on my first case conceptualization writeup; I fail at everything I try."

Personalization. The mistake of drawing a conclusion about oneself from an event or situation that might have other meanings. For example, "Jack didn't return my call; this means he doesn't like me." Or "the fact that Susan turned me down for a date means I'm a loser."

"Should" statements. The error of translating one's wishes and preferences into moral imperatives for oneself and others. For example, "she should be on time for meetings with me. If she's not, she's not a responsible professional person." "People should drive courteously. If they don't, they shouldn't be allowed to drive." Or "I should always be on time."

Catastrophizing. The error of drawing conclusions, usually about the future, that involve exaggerated horrendous outcomes. For example, "I overdrew my checking account; this means my credit rating will be ruined." Or "I failed that exam; that means I'll fail out of graduate school."

Labeling. The fallacy of drawing general conclusions about a person or situation, often using a negative or inflammatory term, on the basis of one or two specifics about that person or situation. For example, "my supervisor was curt with me today; this means he's a jerk." Or "my patient didn't do his homework last week; this means he is not motivated to get better."

Mind reading. The error of making inferences about another person's thoughts or feelings without collecting direct information from the person in question. For example, "my boss frowned at me in the hall today; this means he's thinking of firing me." Or "my patient was late to therapy today; he thinks that the therapy is not helping him."

EXHIBIT 5.4

Quint's Thought Record

Date	Situation (event, memory, attempt to do something, etc.)	Behaviors	Emotions	Thoughts	Responses
Monday morning	Sit down at my desk to start working	Shuffled papers for 1 hr	Discouraged Depressed	I'm always disorganized. I can't even find the form I need. I'll never be able to get this job done. I might as well give up. I'm incompetent and a failure as a businessman.	[Overgeneralization, all-or-nothing thinking, focus on the negative] The fact that I can't find this one form doesn't mean I'm *always* disorganized. I usually find the forms I need. [Catastrophizing, predicting the future] There's no reason to believe that I *never* will get this job done just because I'm having trouble getting started. [Overgeneralizing] Just because I'm having trouble getting started, it doesn't mean I'm incompetent or a failure as a businessman.

remind patients that although identifying thinking errors can be disturbing, it can also be helpful: "If you identify distorted thinking, you can learn to correct it. If these thoughts go unnoticed and you react to them as if they were true, can you see how you will feel worse?"

The process of identifying thinking errors is a first step to generating responses to them. For example, Quint's observation that the thought "I'm always disorganized" is all-or-nothing thinking helped him generate his response: "The fact that I can't find this one form doesn't mean I'm always disorganized. I usually find the forms I need" (see Quint's Thought Record, Exhibit 5.4).

Are These Thoughts Consistent With the Evidence?

Depressed patients have many automatic thoughts that are simply not consistent with objective reality. This notion, of course, is the key concept underpinning cognitive therapy. Some of the most important methods of cognitive therapy target this problem; we describe several of them here (see also A. T. Beck et al., 1979; J. S. Beck, 1995; and Greenberger & Padesky, 1995). The therapist can introduce the general concept that depressed people have irrational, distorted thinking by using the methods described in Teach the Cognitive Model. Then the therapist can propose the following: "Let's take a look at some of the thoughts on your Thought Record to see whether they reflect objective reality. Let's pick one of your thoughts and ask, 'What evidence supports this thought?' We can also ask, 'Is there evidence that does not support or contradicts the thought?'" When June, the college freshman, examined her prediction "I'm going to fail out of college," she had to acknowledge that she was getting As and Bs in all of her classes and that little or no objective evidence supported her prediction that she would fail.

An Evidence Record, depicted in Appendix 5B, can be used to examine in detail the evidence supporting and not supporting a negative thought that is particularly disturbing to a patient, such as June's thought "I'm going to fail out of college" or Quint's thought "I am a bad businessman." At the top of the Evidence Record, the patient writes the negative thought that he or she would like to work on. Below that in the column on the left, he or she lists "Evidence supporting my thought" and in the column on the right "Evidence not supporting my thought." *Evidence* consists of concrete, objective events or facts that support (e.g., "I turned in my English paper 2 days late") or do not support the thought ("I got an A in English last term"). Feelings, perceptions, or assumptions (e.g., "I feel like I don't belong at this school") are not concrete evidence and do not belong on the Evidence Record. A demonstration of the use of the Evidence Record is provided by Davidson et al. (2000).

Quint's Evidence Record evaluating his thought "I'm a failure as a businessman" appears in Exhibit 5.5. Quint found it easy to list evidence supporting his thought, but at first he needed help from his therapist to list evidence that did not support his thought. As he continued thinking about evidence that did not support his thought, he found that the process became easier. When he stood back and evaluated all the evidence supporting and not supporting his negative thought, it was difficult to ignore the conclusion that his belief was not supported by the evidence.

After using the Evidence Record to examine the validity of a particular distorted thought, the therapist can help the patient develop adaptive responses to the thought to place in the "Response" column of the Thought Record, saying "Let's take a look at the thought you are working on: 'I'm a failure as a businessman.' What have you learned here today that you can use to respond to this thought when it comes up again?" The therapist is looking for an answer such as the following: "I reviewed the evidence and concluded that this idea seems true, but it isn't." Another excellent strategy is to suggest that the patient summarize the evidence in both columns of the Evidence Record to create a balanced, comprehensive response:

> Overall, the evidence shows I'm doing well at my job. This has been a difficult year for my company, and I lost that one big account, but I got more accounts this year than most of my coworkers. I got some negative feedback from one client, but I have many positive reviews from several other clients. My last work evaluation was positive.

If the patient does not volunteer any good coping responses, the therapist can offer some suggestions and work with the patient until he or she arrives at some appropriate items for the "Response" column of the Thought Record. The patient may find it helpful to write the coping responses on an index card for ready use the next time the problematic thought arises. The process of examining the evidence may also lead to behavioral coping responses or action plans in addition to cognitive responses. For example, if Quint's "I'm a bad businessman" thought tends to come up in the morning when he first sits down to work, an Activity Schedule (see chap. 4) can be used to help him function better at that time.

It is not unusual for patients to use an Evidence Record to examine thoughts that are probably schema (e.g., "I'm incompetent."). When this happens, the Evidence Record is similar to the Positive Data Log (see chap. 6, Schema Change Methods). The difference between the Evidence Record and the Positive Data Log is that the Evidence Record lists evidence that both supports and refutes a maladaptive negative thought, whereas the Positive Data Log lists only evidence supporting a positive alternative to the negative automatic thought (e.g., "I am a competent

EXHIBIT 5.5

Quint's Evidence Record

Thought: I'm a failure as a businessman.

Evidence supporting my thought	Evidence not supporting my thought
I didn't get that last account. They chose to go with another company.	I got more accounts this year than almost all of my coworkers.
My boss told me he got some negative feedback about me from a client.	My last work review was positive.
My sales were the same this year as they were last year, meaning I showed no improvement.	I got negative feedback from one client and positive feedback from five or six.
	This was a difficult year for the company. My sales were the same this year, but that's better than my coworkers are doing.

and capable person"). The Evidence Record tends to be particularly useful early in treatment, when patients need to evaluate the validity of their negative automatic thoughts. The Positive Data Log is useful later in treatment, after the patient and therapist have identified core schema and after the patient clearly understands that the negative schema are irrational and dysfunctional and he or she is ready to work on strengthening alternative, more positive schema.

Are There Alternative Explanations?

Jill's boyfriend did not call her when he had said he would. She felt upset and hurt, thinking "His not calling proves that he doesn't really care about me. He's probably out with his friends and flirting with other women." To generate some responses for her Thought Record, Jill asked herself whether there were other possible explanations (an important client he had to entertain that evening) for her boyfriend's failure to call that evening than his not caring about her.

What Could One Say to a Friend in This Situation?

When patients have difficulty proposing adaptive responses to automatic thoughts, the therapist can ask, "Suppose your friend's boyfriend didn't call at the time he said he would. What would you tell your friend that would help her cope with the situation?" Patients can often suggest good coping responses for others when they cannot generate them for themselves. After the patient generates some coping responses, the therapist can then ask "Would it help you to say those things to yourself?"

How Did One Learn to Think This Way?

Understanding the origins of their automatic thoughts can sometimes help patients develop responses to them. For example, when his therapist asked him how he learned that making a mistake meant he was a failure, Josh recalled after some questioning from the therapist numerous upsetting childhood incidents in which Josh's father flew into a rage and berated Josh harshly when he made a minor mistake. This insight led Josh to a response he wrote on his Thought Record: "I tell myself I'm a failure in this situation because my father did; he taught me to think that way. But I'm not a failure. I'm an adult now, and I can learn to stop telling myself I'm a failure when I make a mistake."

When to Use a Thought Record

The Thought Record can be used at almost any point in therapy and can be introduced as early as the initial session. A Thought Record can be used when collecting information for a case formulation, when helping patients change their thinking, and when trying to understand and address difficulties that arise in the therapeutic process.

GATHERING INFORMATION FOR THE CASE FORMULATION

The Thought Record can be used to collect information about the cognitive, emotional, and behavioral components of problems on the problem list (see chap. 2, Individualized Case Formulation and Treatment Planning). In fact, a Thought Record that captures the mood, behavioral, and cognitive components of the patient's reaction to a particular situation can be seen as a "miniformulation" that guides interventions to help the patient manage that situation. The process of collecting repeated Thought Records often reveals problems that belong on the problem list, and recurrent themes in the automatic thoughts often suggest schema hypotheses. The Thought Record can also be used to carry out a more structured intervention, namely, the downward arrow technique (see chap. 2) used to generate schema hypotheses.

COGNITIVE CHANGE IS NEEDED

If the problem list describes problems in terms of cognitive, behavioral, and mood components, it points to cognitive components of problems that can be addressed using a Thought Record. For example, a depressed patient who is avoiding calling friends because of her fear of rejection can benefit from working with her therapist on a Thought Record that tackles the situation: "Consider calling Spenser to make plans to go jogging." The depressed patient who is worried about work because of a fear of failure can benefit from doing a Thought Record focused on the situation: "Anticipate getting Alexx's feedback about my grant proposal on Monday."

A PROBLEM OCCURS IN THE THERAPEUTIC PROCESS

The Thought Record can be extremely useful in helping patient and therapist understand and manage difficulties that arise in the therapy itself. When patients are reluctant to try an intervention the therapist recommends, a Thought Record can be used to identify and address this resistance. For example, Julia was depressed and was spending most of the day at home watching TV or napping. She was unemployed but was not looking for a job, and she was avoiding her friends. Julia's therapist recommended that Julia use an Activity Schedule form to plan a few pleasant and productive alternatives to lying in bed all day, but Julia dragged her heels and insisted she felt too bad to do anything. By working through a Thought Record with her therapist, Julia learned that when she was in bed during the day, she had a chain of pessimistic thoughts ("I'm a real loser. I can't do anything. No one will want to spend time with me") that worsened her mood and sapped her energy. Julia also learned that when she gave into her thoughts and stayed in bed all day, she reinforced her view of herself as a loser and felt even worse. After she grasped these concepts, Julia agreed to take some steps to increase her activity level.

Glitches in the therapeutic alliance can also be addressed using a Thought Record. For example, when John's therapist was 5 minutes late for his therapy session (situation), John felt angry and upset (emotions). When his therapist noticed that John was withdrawn and distant (behaviors) and inquired about it, John admitted he was upset and explained why. After spending some time empathizing and providing support, John's therapist suggested they use a Thought Record to learn more about what was particularly upsetting to John about this situation and to help him with it. John agreed; he listed several automatic thoughts on his Thought Record: "Jackie doesn't care about me. She just wants to collect her fee." With some help from his therapist, John was able to develop some responses to these thoughts:

> The fact that Jackie was late doesn't mean she doesn't care about me. I'm personalizing. She explained she had a flat tire; that doesn't have anything to do with me. During the year I have worked with her, Jackie has never been late before, and I know she works hard for me. She seems concerned about my feelings in this situation, and that indicates her caring for me.

The Thought Record can also be used to address patients' negative feelings about or doubts about therapy, such as the following: "No other therapy has helped me, so this one probably won't either," "This therapist looks too young to help me," or "Cognitive therapy seems cold, intellectual, and superficial. My problems are deeper than that." After a Thought Record revealed George's doubts that cognitive therapy would be helpful, his therapist recommended a behavioral experiment to test George's hypothesis that the therapy would not help. George agreed to work hard in his therapy for six sessions and to log his mood and school attendance daily, so he could evaluate whether the therapy helped him feel less depressed and improve his school attendance. His therapist explained that although a complete recovery from depression would not be expected after six sessions, some improvement would be expected within that time if the therapy was helpful to him. George and his therapist agreed that if no improvement was apparent after the six sessions, George would seek a consultation with a pharmacotherapist and accept a referral to another therapist.

Guidelines for Using the Thought Record Successfully

To make effective use of the Thought Record, therapists can follow two general guidelines (see Exhibit 5.6).

USE SOCRATIC QUESTIONING

Socratic questioning is questioning that helps the patient think about something in a new way (Padesky, 1993b). Socratic questioning is more useful than lecturing because most people are not receptive to others' ideas about how they "should" think about things; instead they want help arriving at a view of the situation that would be useful to them (Beck et al., 1979). Socratic questioning is also valuable because it allows the therapist to model skills the patient can use in situations other than the one currently being tackled. By modeling the therapist, the patient can learn to ask himself or herself such Socratic questions as "What thoughts am I having in this situation? How do these thoughts make me feel?" "Is there another way to think about this situation that would help me feel better and function better?"

FOCUS ON A CONCRETE, SPECIFIC SITUATION

A Thought Record focused on a concrete, specific situation ("Joe didn't return my phone call yesterday") is likely to be more helpful than a Thought Record focused on a general or abstract situation ("People don't treat me with respect."). If patients focus on an actual concrete event,

---

EXHIBIT 5.6

Guidelines for Using the Thought Record Successfully

- Use Socratic questioning.
- Focus on a concrete, specific situation.

they are more likely to remember and even begin to experience again the thoughts and feelings they experienced in that situation as they work on it. Without this information and without the emotional charge that seems to arise from a focus on a specific situation, the Thought Record can become a purely intellectual exercise. General discussions not tied to a specific situation tend to become dry, sterile, intellectual debates that are devoid of emotional charge and, in our experience, rarely productive. To transform a general situation such as "feeling sad this week" into a more specific situation, the therapist could ask the following questions: "Was there a time this week when you felt especially sad? When was it? What was the situation exactly?"

Selecting a Situation

Cognitive theory proposes that when schema are activated, they produce negative mood, maladaptive behavior, and distorted thinking. Therefore, the presence of a negative mood state or a maladaptive behavior are cues pointing to the presence of distorted thinking that can be identified and addressed with a Thought Record. To select a useful situation on which to focus a Thought Record, therapists can choose a situation in which the patient experiences a negative mood state or a maladaptive behavior (or both).

NEGATIVE MOOD

Although depressed patients are not always aware of their negative thoughts or the situation that triggered them, they usually notice when they are feeling distressed and can report this to the therapist. A situation in which a person experiences a negative mood state of any sort (e.g., upset, depressed, angry, frustrated, panicky, anxious) is likely to entail distorted thinking as well and is thus an ideal candidate for therapeutic work using a Thought Record. For example, Sharon reported she began feeling inadequate and worthless the evening before her therapy session when her son asked for her help with his algebra homework.

MALADAPTIVE BEHAVIORS

Maladaptive behaviors or urges to engage in maladaptive behaviors are another excellent focus for a Thought Record. Maladaptive behaviors include procrastination, taking a sick day from work when not sick, chronically canceling or saying *no* to social engagements, overeating, abusing drugs or alcohol, spending hours on the telephone, going to bed in the middle of the day, watching too much TV, canceling appointments with therapists and other doctors, and making excessive appointments with therapists and other doctors.

Problematic behaviors can be easier to identify than thoughts because they are more concrete and visible. However, maladaptive behaviors can be difficult to identify because it is not always immediately apparent to patients (or therapists) that they are maladaptive. For example, the patient who schedules numerous appointments with doctors may be motivated by appropriate wishes to care for her health or by an irrational fear that she has a significant illness that her doctors have failed to detect. A Thought Record can be helpful in assessing whether a particular behavior is maladaptive by identifying the thoughts driving the behavior; if they are distorted, this suggests that the behaviors are maladaptive.

A Thought Record can also help patients counter behaviors that they know are maladaptive. For example, Elena worked with her therapist to overcome her resistance to calling her parents. Elena knew that calling her parents weekly was a good idea for several reasons. She was socially anxious and isolated; a weekly call to her parents would be a good exposure task for her. In addition, her parents were getting older, and Elena wanted to improve her relationship with them in the time they had left. She had made a New Year's resolution to do this every Sunday. But when she met with her therapist on February 15, she had still not made a single Sunday phone call. She and her therapist used a Thought Record to identify and respond to the thoughts she was having that prevented her from picking up the telephone to make the call. This intervention led to an action plan in the response column of her Thought Record to "call parents on Sunday at 10 a.m." With this assistance and structure, Elena was able to make the call.

Overcoming Obstacles to Using the Thought Record

With practice, therapists can learn to use Thought Records with ease in a variety of situations for a variety of purposes. However, obstacles to the use of the Thought Record do arise. We describe several that occur frequently and suggest some solutions to them.

DIFFICULTY ELICITING AUTOMATIC THOUGHTS

When they are asked to identify automatic thoughts, patients may state "I don't know what thoughts I had in that situation" or "I didn't have any thoughts; I just had feelings." One strategy that helps patients elicit automatic thoughts is to re-create the problematic situation by asking the patient to describe every aspect of the situation (who, where, when, etc.) in vivid detail. If the re-creation is effective, the patient will re-experience some of the feelings and thoughts the patient had in the situation, and the therapist can help the patient capture them on a Thought Record.

Another helpful strategy is for therapists to ask patients to tell them more about their feelings. Often patients label as feelings what are in fact thoughts. For example, a depressed person may say "I felt like a loser" or "I felt like I never do anything right." When these thoughts emerge, the therapist can ask for other, related thoughts and feelings, and the patient is likely to be able to report some.

The therapist may wish to "prime the pump" of the patient's automatic thoughts by suggesting thoughts that the therapist predicts the patient might have in the situation. The schema hypotheses in the case formulation can serve as a guide to the therapist when making these predictions. For example, Jane's therapist hypothesized that Jane's self-schema included a view of herself as not as good as others. In the therapy session, Jane and her therapist worked on a Thought Record focused on an evening when Jane felt particularly depressed; she had stayed home and watched TV instead of going to a dinner party. When asked to report her automatic thoughts at the moment she decided to stay home, Jane insisted that "I wasn't thinking anything. I just felt depressed and tired, and I wanted to stay home." After other strategies for eliciting thoughts failed, her therapist proposed the following: "Is it possible that you were having such thoughts as 'I don't belong at that dinner party. All those people have high-powered professional jobs, and I don't.'" Even if these proposals are off base, they may prompt Jane to remember what she was thinking.

THOUGHT RECORDS ARE NOT HELPFUL

Some patients do not find the Thought Record helpful. The immobilized individual who is spending most of his or her time in bed may not be able to grasp and use cognitive interventions. Behavioral interventions, including activity scheduling (see chap. 4), are often better initial interventions for such a person.

People who worry obsessively may not find the Thought Record helpful because it may fuel, rather than alleviate, obsessive thinking. People who worry or doubt sometimes use the Thought Record to list all their concerns in excessive, exhaustive detail. Or when using the Evidence Record, such people may engage in what one of our patients called "mental ping pong," namely, listing every piece of evidence supporting and not supporting each maladaptive thought without developing a balanced summary that summarizes them. The therapist can help these patients develop adaptive responses that allow them to disengage from the obsessive thoughts, such as the following: "This thinking doesn't help me. It only causes me to obsess and doubt. What can I do instead?" These and other strategies described by Jeffrey Schwartz in his book *Brain Lock* (1996) can be helpful for the obsessive thinker. If the obsessive patient does work on a Thought Record, we recommend that he or she set a time limit (e.g., 15 minutes) for completing it.

When patients (especially depressed patients, who tend to jump to negative conclusions) complain that they do not find the Thought Record helpful, the therapist can use Socratic questioning to obtain a detailed understanding of why the intervention was not helpful. To assist in assessing whether the Thought Record is helpful to the patient, the therapist can ask the patient to rate the intensity of his or her negative mood on a 0 (*least intense*) to 10 (*most intense*) scale before and after completing the Thought Record.

Therapists cannot assume that the Thought Record is the wrong intervention until they have obtained detailed information about the patient's experience with the intervention. Review the completed Thought Record carefully with the patient. The therapist may discover that the patient had difficulty eliciting automatic thoughts, did not understand the columns on the Thought Record, or was unable to develop helpful responses to maladaptive thoughts. The patient may have wanted to use an Evidence Record but could not decide which automatic thought to use. When these problems are uncovered, it is often easy to help patients solve them. If the patient has difficulty generating believable adaptive responses, the therapist can review the patient's responses to help him or her strengthen them. Sometimes patients who complain that the Thought Record is not helpful have unrealistic expectations about how they should feel after using the Thought Record. Therapists can even use a Thought Record to uncover and reframe maladaptive beliefs about the Thought Record itself.

THE PATIENT FAILS TO USE THE THOUGHT RECORD OUTSIDE THE SESSION

Patients who learn the skill of completing a Thought Record obtain a problem-solving method they can use for the rest of their life. Thus, learning to use a Thought Record outside the therapy session is a valuable skill. However, we have found it to be a difficult skill to impart; therefore, we offer some suggestions here to assist the therapist in making successful Thought Record homework assignments.

First, it is important to work with the patient to complete a Thought Record during a session before assigning one as homework. Before patients can practice using Thought Records successfully outside the session, they need to learn how to use them in the session. Some patients have many questions and become confused when learning to describe the cognitive, emotional, and behavioral components of a situation. Frequent questions include "What's the difference between a thought and a feeling?" "How much should I write?" and "What goes in the Response column?" By completing a Thought Record during the session, the therapist can answer these questions as they arise. Additionally, when the therapist uses the Thought Record effectively to help a patient solve a distressing problem in the therapy session, the patient is motivated to learn to use the method outside the session.

Second, make the homework assignment specific and concrete. As we emphasized in chapter 3 (Structure of the Therapy Session), therapy homework assignments are more likely to be completed if the details of the assignment are specific and concrete. After a patient has learned to use a Thought Record in the session, it is easy to assume that the patient can now use a Thought Record whenever a negative mood state or problematic behavior arises. The therapist may also assume that Thought Record homework assignments cannot be specified in detail because it is difficult to predict the occurrence of problematic situations. However, these assumptions can lead to homework noncompliance because they leave the patient with such questions as "How many Thought Records should I complete? My negative moods occur several times a day; am I supposed to do a Thought Record about each one? How much time should I spend on a Thought Record? What strategy should I use to respond to my negative thoughts?" If these questions are left unanswered, patients may feel so confused or overwhelmed about the prospect of filling in a Thought Record that they abandon any effort to do the task at all. The following is a good example of such a patient's summary of a concrete and specific Thought Record homework assignment:

> This week I will complete two Thought Records, one on Tuesday and one on Friday during my afternoon break. I'll spend no more than 15 minutes on each. I'll choose one situation for each Thought Record that focuses on when I felt especially discouraged at work. I'll write down my automatic thoughts, mood, and behaviors, and then I'll bring the Thought Records to my therapy session, so I can go over them with my therapist.

Third, it is important that the therapist anticipate and make plans to overcome obstacles to completing Thought Records outside the therapy session. A common obstacle is a patient's fear that others will see the Thought Records. The therapist can work with the patient to find a safe place to keep Thought Records, perhaps at home in a locked desk or in a backpack or briefcase where others do not generally look. If problematic situations often occur at work, keeping Thought Records in a purse or briefcase helps ensure that coworkers will not see them. If Thought Records are too cumbersome to carry, patients can write notes in their daily planner or on scrap paper until they can come home in the evening and complete an entire Thought Record.

Fourth, investigate whether patients' maladaptive schema may be interfering with homework compliance. For example, a patient with the self-schema of "I'm inadequate" may believe that he must perform perfectly at all times. His automatic thought that "I need to do a perfect Thought Record, or my therapist will think I'm hopeless" may block him from attempting a Thought Record at all. To identify and assist with this problem, the therapist can fill in a Thought Record during the session to address the situation in which the patient considered doing a Thought Record outside the session but then avoided doing so. Other methods for handling homework noncompliance are described in chapter 3 (Structure of the Therapy Session).

Summary and Conclusion

In this chapter, we presented interventions intended to produce change in negative automatic thoughts. We showed methods and guidelines for using the Thought Record and the Evidence Record to teach the cognitive model and to promote cognitive change. We described strategies for identifying automatic thoughts and developing adaptive, balanced responses to them. We highlighted one strategy in particular, "examine the evidence," which involves collecting concrete evidence to evaluate the patient's distorted thoughts. In the next chapter, we describe interventions intended to produce change in underlying schema.

Practice Exercises

These exercises allow clinicians and students to practice the interventions presented in this chapter. Instructors can use them to stimulate class discussion and experiential learning.

1. Complete a Thought Record and an Evidence Record yourself to examine a recent problem you encountered.
    (a) To use a Thought Record, focus on a negative mood or problematic behavior in a particular situation, and write down

your emotion, behavior, and thoughts in the situation. Rate the intensity of the mood that emerges as you recall the situation on a 0 (*least intense*) to 10 (*most intense*) scale. Then spend about 20 minutes using some of the strategies described in the section entitled "Promote Change" to generate some more adaptive responses to the situation. Rerate your mood after doing this exercise. If you do not achieve an improvement in your mood, ask a trusted friend or colleague for some pointers or put the Thought Record aside and come back to it in a day or two to see if you can be more successful.

(b) To use the Evidence Record, choose a belief about yourself or another (e.g., "I am a competent therapist" or "My boss is critical") and make a list of evidence supporting and not supporting this belief. After listing the evidence, write a balanced summary of the evidence that integrates the evidence supporting and not supporting your belief.

2. With a fellow student or colleague, role-play using a Thought Record and an Evidence Record with a hypothetical depressed patient. Use one of the vignettes provided below or play the role of one of your own patients. Then reverse the roles and try again. As you practice each role-play, follow these steps:

(a) Use the forms for the Thought Record and the Evidence Record.

(b) Follow the guidelines for using the Thought Record.

(c) Evaluate your effectiveness by asking your role-play partner for feedback: "What did it feel like to be the recipient of my intervention? What was helpful? What was not helpful?"

3. Review your list of current patients and choose one or two who might benefit from a Thought Record or Evidence Record. Place a Thought Record or Evidence Record in that patient's clinical chart to remind you to try the intervention the next time you see the patient. After trying the intervention, ask your patient for feedback about its helpfulness.

4. Read each of the following vignettes and answer the accompanying questions (answers follow in the answer key below).

SAM

Sam is a 35-year-old unmarried man who lives alone and is self-employed as a computer consultant. He is looking for a part-time salaried job to provide a more stable income. After his recent breakup with his girlfriend, he is dating some new women and trying to go out more with his friends. Sam came to his therapy session stating that he had had a horrible weekend. He felt depressed and stayed home all weekend, canceling plans he had made with his friends. As the weekend progressed, he felt worse. He had been feeling much better the week before. He stated that he could not understand why he got so depressed this weekend. He reported that because he felt so depressed again, it made him feel hopeless about ever getting better.

1. What could a Thought Record help Sam accomplish in this therapy session?
2. How can the therapist obtain information that would allow him or her to focus the Thought Record on a particular situation?
3. When choosing a situation for the Thought Record in the session, Sam told the therapist that he began feeling depressed on Friday afternoon after he received a rejection letter from a company where he had applied for a job. Sam had believed he was well qualified for the job he sought, and he had expected to be offered the position. After receiving the letter, Sam cancelled his evening plans and stayed home. What automatic thoughts might Sam have had after receiving the letter? Complete the "situation," "behaviors," "emotions," and "thoughts," columns of Sam's Thought Record.
4. What cognitive distortions might you help Sam identify, and what adaptive responses to those thoughts might you develop together? Complete the "responses" column of Sam's Thought Record.

JOHN, JANE, AND SALLY

Imagine that these three individuals, John, Jane, and Sally, each receive the following initial evaluation from their supervisor:

> Overall rating: Satisfactory. Comment: You are doing a fine job. I am pleased with your performance and with how quickly you are learning the requirements for this position. An area for improvement: I suggest you work on responding to customers' requests in a more timely manner. Action: I recommend continued employment.

Imagine three different emotional, behavioral, and cognitive responses to this evaluation. Compose three Thought Records, one for each individual.

JIM

Jim is a 50-year-old married salesman who lives with his wife. He has worked for 20 years for the same company. Although he earns a good living, he is not keeping pace with some of the new employees. His children have moved out of the house to get married or go to college.

Jim has stopped going to the weekly meetings of his antique car club because in the evening when the meetings are scheduled, he feels too tired to go. He realizes he is depressed and seeks treatment. During his initial assessment, he reports feeling optimistic about learning tools he can use to treat his depression, especially using Thought Records to identify distorted thoughts.

Jim came to his second therapy session stating that he felt discouraged. He tried using a Thought Record, but he felt down almost all the time, so he could not pinpoint any specific situations that upset him. He stated that he was worried that he might be too depressed for this technique to work for him.

1. How might the therapist respond to Jim's difficulty using the Thought Record?
2. Jim complains that when he feels bad he does not know what thoughts he is having. How can the therapist help Jim identify his automatic thoughts?
3. How can the therapist ensure that Jim will be more successful the next time he tries to complete a Thought Record outside the session?
4. If Jim completed an Evidence Record to assess his belief of "I have failed as a father," what evidence supporting and not supporting this belief might appear on his form?
5. On the basis of what was learned from his Evidence Record, what responses might be generated for the "responses" column of his Thought Record?

Answer Key

We offer several answers to each of the questions posed above. You may be able to suggest additional answers that we have not provided.

SAM

1. *What could a Thought Record help Sam accomplish in this therapy session?* A Thought Record could help Sam understand why his mood worsened over the weekend and why he felt worse this week than last week. He could identify situations that were related to his depressed mood and learn how his thoughts caused his mood to drop and caused him to cancel his plans with his friends. He could also develop cognitive and behavioral responses that would help him feel and function better.

2. *How can the therapist obtain information that would allow him to focus the Thought Record on a particular situation?* To help Sam identify a specific problematic situation, the therapist can use Socratic questioning to help him locate changes in mood or problematic behaviors. The therapist might ask him "When did you start to feel more depressed? Did anything happen that day?" The therapist might reconstruct the events leading up to Sam's noticing he was feeling depressed. Or the therapist might ask him for more information about a problematic behavior, for example, Sam's decision to cancel his plans with his friends.

3. *What automatic thoughts might Sam have had after receiving the letter? Complete the "situation," "behaviors," "emotions," and "thoughts," columns of Sam's Thought Record.* See Exhibit 5.7, Sam's Thought Record.

4. *What cognitive distortions might you help Sam identify, and what adaptive responses to those thoughts might you develop together? Complete the "responses" column of Sam's Thought Record.* See Exhibit 5.7, Sam's Thought Record.

JOHN, JANE, AND SALLY

Imagine three different emotional, behavioral, and cognitive responses to this evaluation. Compose three Thought Records, one for each individual. See Exhibit 5.8, the Thought Record for John, Jane, and Sally.

JIM

1. *How might the therapist respond to Jim's difficulty using the Thought Record?* Jim is having difficulty identifying specific situations that can be tackled in a Thought Record. Because Jim feels depressed almost all the time, he believes that no specific situations are problematic for him. However, Jim's view that he feels depressed all the time is probably not completely true. To help Jim identify situations in which he feels particularly bad, use Socratic questioning to help him locate changes in mood or problematic behaviors. The therapist can ask, "Were there times this week when you felt especially depressed? Were there times when you felt a little better than usual? Were there any behaviors you noticed this week that you didn't like?" For example, Jim may have had problems with overeating or not spending time on his usual hobbies. Another strategy is to walk Jim through 1 day or through 1 week. Sometimes the therapist can identify a problematic situation the patient does not perceive.

In Jim's case, because he felt upset about not finding a situation on which to focus a Thought Record, the therapist might work with him on a Thought Record during his session by focusing on the situation "I can't find a situation on which to focus a Thought Record." See Exhibit 5.9 for his completed Thought Record.

2. *Jim complains that when he feels bad he does not know what thoughts he is having. How can the therapist help Jim identify his automatic thoughts?* To help a patient identify automatic thoughts, focus on a particular problematic situation. Jim and his therapist focused on an evening he was at home watching TV when he began feeling sad and discouraged.

   To help Jim identify his thoughts in the situation, work with Jim to re-create the situation. Help Jim imagine that he is at home watching TV: Describe the details of where he was sitting, what the room looked like and felt like, what program he was watching, who was saying what, and so on. The process of re-creating the situation may re-evoke the feelings and thoughts Jim was having at the time. Often patients who are just learning this method have difficulty differentiating between feelings and thoughts. If he is asked about his feelings, Jim may reply, "I was feeling like a failure." The therapist can point out that this is a thought and belongs in the thought column. The therapist can also offer some options, asking Jim, for example, "Were you thinking, 'I'm not as good a father as Bill Cosby'"? After re-evoking the situation and asking a number of questions about it, the therapist and Jim together completed his Thought Record (see Exhibit 5.9) describing Jim's emotional upset in response to getting a phone call from his daughter while watching a TV show about a close, warm family.

3. *How can the therapist ensure that Jim will be more successful the next time he tries to complete a Thought Record outside the session?* To help Jim succeed with his therapy homework, develop a concrete, specific plan that is realistic for him. A concrete plan specifies, for example, how many Thought Records Jim is expected to complete. We suggest that Jim be asked to complete one or two and that he spend no more than 15 minutes on each. Jim also needs some help choosing a situation on which to focus his Thought Record. To help him pinpoint a specific situation, the therapist can advise Jim to focus his Thought Record on a situation in which he notices a negative mood (e.g., sad, depressed, angry, irritated) or a problematic behavior (e.g., overeating, oversleeping, losing his temper), perhaps giving some examples of each. The therapist can suggest that if he gets stuck again, Jim can

EXHIBIT 5.7

Sam's Thought Record

Date	Situation (event, memory, attempt to do something, etc.)	Behaviors	Emotions
4/7	Received rejection letter on Friday afternoon.	Canceled plans with friends. Stayed home and watched TV. Didn't make dinner.	Depressed Hopeless

Thoughts	Responses
If I can't get this job, I'll never qualify for any job.	I can apply for other jobs and sooner or later I will get a job. It just may take some time. One job does not predict all future job possibilities. I've been rejected for jobs in the past, but I've always been hired eventually.
I'll never get a job I like.	Most jobs have had aspects that I like, so when I do get a job, I'll probably like it or aspects of it.
If they didn't hire me, it means they didn't like me because I know I was qualified.	There might be other reasons why they didn't hire me. It doesn't mean it was because they didn't like who I am as a person. Maybe another candidate had more computer skills. Maybe they had someone in mind to hire, and I never really had a chance. Maybe they thought I was overqualified and wouldn't stay very long. It's not possible to be liked by everybody, and I'd rather work somewhere where my boss and I like each other.
No one will ever hire me. I'm such a failure.	Just because I failed to get this job doesn't mean that I am a failure as a person. I know people who haven't gotten every job they applied for, and I know they're not failures. It just means I failed at getting this job.
I fail at everything I try.	Just because I failed to get this job doesn't mean I always fail at everything I try. I have had some successes including getting other jobs and winning some awards at school.
I'll never have enough money to live a decent life.	I have no evidence that I'll never have enough money to live a decent life. I've always been able to make money. I want to make more money, and that's why I'm applying for jobs.
Why bother dating? No one will be interested in someone like me who doesn't have much money and can't get a good job.	I've had girlfriends before when I had less money. Some women have been interested in me. It seems difficult now because I just broke up with my girlfriend and I'm worried about money.

John, Jane, and Sally's Thought Record

Date	Situation (event, memory, attempt to do something, etc.)	Behaviors	Emotions
	John, Jane and Sally each got the following initial 3 month written evaluation from their supervisor: Overall rating: Satisfactory. Comment: You are doing a fine job. I am pleased with your performance and with how quickly you are learning the requirements for this position. An area for improvement: I suggest you continue to work on responding to customers' requests in a more timely manner. Action: I recommend continued employment.	JOHN Go home, have some beers, skip dinner, go to bed JANE Go home, call my friends to tell them the good news SALLY Call and make an appointment to talk with the supervisor, leave work for a while to "cool off"	Sad, depressed, discouraged, hopeless Happy, pleased, excited Angry, frustrated

© 1999 San Francisco Bay Area Center for Cognitive Therapy.

Thoughts	Responses
"Satisfactory" is a bad rating. It's like getting a C in school. I can never do better than average. I thought I was doing really well, but I guess I'm not that great. I'm too slow. I'm probably going to get fired soon if I don't start to do better.	
I'm so relieved! I didn't think I was doing very well, but I passed my first 3-month evaluation. My supervisor thinks that I'm doing well. She only pointed out one area in which I could improve. She thinks I'm a quick learner. I really love this job.	
Who does she think she is? I'm working so hard for her and all I get is "satisfactory." She's pleased with how quickly I am learning? Is that the best she can do? That's insulting. That's just a polite way of saying she is trying to find something to compliment me on. Big deal. I do so much better than people who've been there for years. How dare she say I need to respond to customer's requests more quickly? No one ever recognizes my abilities. People don't appreciate me. I always get cheated.	

EXHIBIT 5.9

Jim's Thought Record

Date	Situation (event, memory, attempt to do something, etc.)	Behaviors	Emotions
Friday in session	I can't find a situation for a Thought Record.	Tell my therapist I'm discouraged. No Thought Record to bring in.	Discouraged, depressed, hopeless
Wednesday evening	Watching a TV program about a family that was close and then received a phone call from my daughter in college. She wants me to bring her some clothes she left at home. I try to have more of a conversation with her, but she hurries to get off the phone.	Kept watching TV longer than intended.	Sad, down, depressed

Thoughts	Responses
I should be able to find many situations for a Thought Record. If I can't even find one situation, then I'm a hopeless case. I must be too depressed for these techniques to work for me. My therapist must think I'm hopeless if I can't even complete one Thought Record. I'm never going to feel any better.	I'm overgeneralizing, predicting the future, catastrophizing, mind reading, and using "should" statements. This is the first time I've tried using a Thought Record. There's no reason why I should be able to succeed at this my first time out. Just because I had trouble finding a situation, it doesn't mean I'm a hopeless case or too depressed for this to work. I did well to come back and tell my therapist why I couldn't complete a Thought Record, and I learned how even this could be a situation to use for a Thought Record. My therapist is helping me learn to do this. That's why I came here. She didn't say I'm hopeless. She said this happens to a lot of people. I'm feeling better already as I do this.
I miss spending time with my kids. There really is something wrong with me. My kids don't like me. My kids aren't close to me. We're not much of a family. I can't even be a good father. I've failed as a father.	I feel lonely now that my children are older and two of them live outside of the house. It's true that my children aren't as interested in spending as much time talking to me as they used to, but that's appropriate for their ages. It doesn't mean I've failed as a father. I miss the days when they were younger, and we all spent more time together. They are doing well, and my wife and I have done a pretty good job raising them. Life isn't always like TV. Maybe my wife and I should talk about doing more things together now that the kids are older.

EXHIBIT 5.10

Jim's Evidence Record

Thought: I have failed as a father.

Evidence supporting my thought	Evidence not supporting my thought
My daughter in college usually only calls when she needs something. She hangs up quickly when we talk on the phone.	I've always provided for all three of my children. They've had a nice home. All of my children have had or will have the opportunity to go to college.
My youngest daughter comes home and goes to her room. She doesn't spend much time with me anymore. She's angry with me most of the time and says I don't understand her.	I've provided my daughter with enough money to be able to attend college. My daughter is doing well and likes college. She has many friends and wants to spend time with them rather than talk to me. That's age appropriate.
My son has lost his past two jobs. He didn't complete college. I see him only twice a month.	When she came home for the holidays, we had a nice talk. She asked for my advice on classes to take next semester.
	My other daughter is a healthy teenager with typical teenage problems. She sat with me on the couch and watched TV the other night when she was feeling sad. She has a picture of me in her room.
	I supported my son in trying college and in changing his mind and deciding to leave college and try to work for a while. I help him out financially when he is in trouble. I listen to him when he is frustrated. When he does come over for dinner, we always play some basketball together.

complete another Thought Record focused on the situation of not being able to find a situation for a Thought Record.

4. *If Jim completed an Evidence Record to assess the belief of "I have failed as a father," what evidence supporting and not supporting this belief might appear on the Form?* See Jim's Evidence Record (Exhibit 5.10).

5. *On the basis of what was learned in his Evidence Record, what responses might be generated for the "Responses" column of his Thought Record?* See the part of Jim's Thought Record (Exhibit 5.9) focusing on the phone call from his daughter at college.

Further Reading and Videotapes

Beck, A. T., Rush, A. J., Shaw, B. F., & Emery, G. (1979). *Cognitive therapy of depression.* New York: Guilford Press. Chap. 8, Cognitive techniques.

Beck, J. S. (1995). *Cognitive therapy: Basics and beyond.* New York: Guilford Press. Chap. 6, Identifying automatic thoughts; chap. 7, Identifying emotions; chap. 8, Evaluating automatic thoughts.

Burns, D. D. (1999). *Feeling good: The new mood therapy.* New York: Morrow.

Davidson, J., Persons, J. B., & Tompkins, M. A. (2000). *Cognitive–behavior therapy for depression: Using the thought record* [Videotape]. Washington, DC: American Psychological Association.

Freeman, A., Pretzer, J., Fleming, B., & Simon, K. M. (1990). *Clinical applications of cognitive therapy.* New York: Plenum Press. Chap. 1, Cognitive therapy in the real world; chap. 3, Cognitive and behavioral interventions; chap. 4, The treatment of depression.

Greenberger, D., & Padesky, C. A. (1995). *Mind over mood: A cognitive therapy treatment manual for clients.* New York: Guilford Press. Chap. 2, It's the thought that counts; chap. 3, Identifying and rating moods; chap. 4, Situations, moods, and thoughts; chap. 5, Automatic thoughts; chap. 6, Where's the evidence?; chap. 7, Alternative or balanced thinking.

Leahy, R. (1996). *Cognitive therapy: Basic principles and applications.* Northvale, NJ: Aronson. Chap. 6, Cognitive interventions.

Padesky, C. (1996a). *Guided discovery using Socratic dialogue* [Videotape]. Oakland, CA: New Harbinger.

Padesky, C. (1996b). *Testing automatic thoughts with thought records* [Videotape]. Oakland, CA: New Harbinger.

Persons, J. B. (1989). *Cognitive therapy in practice: A case formulation approach.* New York: Norton. Chap. 6, Dysfunctional thinking; chap. 7, Changing dysfunctional thinking.

APPENDIX 5A: THOUGHT RECORD

Date	Situation (event, memory, attempt to do something, etc.)	Behaviors	Emotions

Thoughts	Responses

APPENDIX 5B: EVIDENCE RECORD

Thought: _____

Evidence supporting my thought	Evidence not supporting my thought

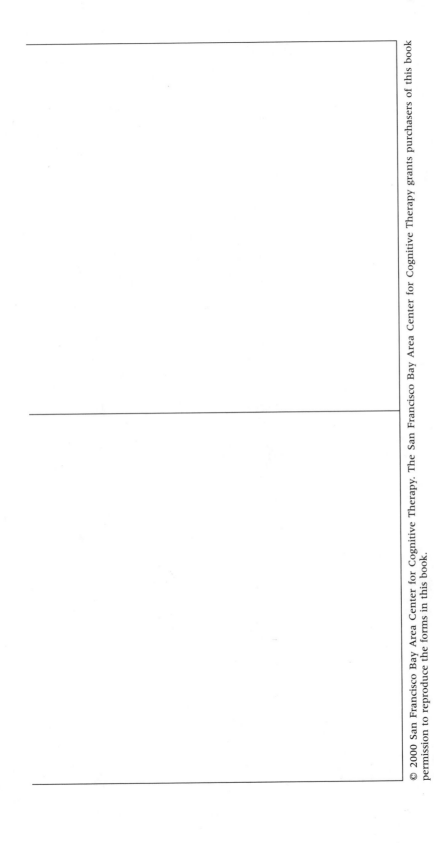

Schema Change Methods | 6

Nothing is so firmly believed as that which we least know. (Michel de Montaigne)

chema change methods are strategies designed to restructure the maladaptive core beliefs (schema) presumed responsible for many of a depressed person's problematic moods and behaviors. In this chapter, we teach the use of the Positive Data Log, one of the simplest schema change methods.

In this chapter, we present the following:

- theoretical and empirical underpinnings for the use of schema change methods
- the Positive Data Log and three observations about schema that support its use
- guidelines for setting up and reviewing a Positive Data Log
- strategies for overcoming common obstacles to the use of the Positive Data Log
- practice exercises
- further readings on schema change methods
- Positive Data Log form.

Underpinnings for Schema Change Methods

THEORETICAL

Schema are deep cognitive structures that enable an individual to interpret his or her experiences in a meaningful way (Beck, 1976). In cognitive theory (see Figure 1.2), depressed patients have distorted, negative schema (e.g., "I am inept"), which when activated by life events, give rise to negative automatic thoughts (e.g., "I can't do this"), problematic moods (e.g., depression, helplessness), and maladaptive behaviors (e.g., procrastination). According to cognitive theory, if a patient experiences a symptom remission but retains pathological schema, he or she is vulnerable to a relapse or recurrence of the depressive symptoms. Therefore, it is important to work in therapy to change negative, pathological schema.

Beck (1976) described four types of schemas: views of self, others, the world, and the future. He proposed that depressed patients hold negative, distorted views of themselves (e.g., worthless, useless, a loser, bad, defective, unlovable, second rate, a piece of garbage), others (e.g., uncaring, attacking, critical, rejecting), the world (e.g., burdensome, dark and unforgiving, bleak, ungratifying, punishing), and the future (e.g., hopeless, unrewarding, futile). Clinically, it may not be necessary (or possible) to work on all of the patient's maladaptive schema; in therapeutic work, it will probably be necessary to focus on the one or two that cause the most problems for the patient. Most often, in our experience, these are the views of self and others.

EMPIRICAL

Several studies show that depressed patients treated with cognitive therapy are less likely to relapse than are patients treated with acute pharmacotherapy (Blackburn et al., 1986; Evans et al., 1992; Simons et al., 1986). Because cognitive therapy includes interventions (e.g., the Positive Data Log) designed to produce schema change and pharmacotherapy does not, this finding is consistent with and supportive of the view that working with depressed patients to change their schema can reduce their risk of relapse.

This evidence, however, is indirect because the early researchers studying relapse in cognitive therapy and pharmacotherapy did not examine schema change directly; therefore, we cannot be confident that it is schema change that accounts for the difference in relapse rate between cognitive therapy and pharmacotherapy. More direct evidence that cognitive therapy produces schema change and pharmacotherapy does not was recently produced by Zindel Segal et al. (1992). They measured schema change in patients treated with cognitive therapy or pharmacotherapy and showed that cognitive therapy, not pharmacotherapy, appears to produce schema change and that schema change during treatment reduces the rate of subsequent relapse.

Thus, we do have some evidence that cognitive therapy produces schema change and reduces relapse. However, we do not have good evidence that the schema change interventions themselves are the active ingredient of the therapy resulting in schema change. In fact, some data to the contrary come from a dismantling study of cognitive therapy conducted by Jacobson et al. (1996). These investigators showed that depressed patients who received schema change interventions did not have better outcome or fewer relapses than patients treated with cognitive therapy who did not receive schema change interventions. This finding suggests that the behavioral and cognitive interventions these patients received were sufficient to accomplish schema change. We await the results of additional studies of the question of whether schema change interventions themselves operate as theoretically specified.

Notwithstanding the current lack of specific evidence of the value of schema change interventions, we recommend that therapists consider using these interventions. We have found in our clinical experience that structured schema change methods, such as the Positive Data Log, play a useful role in increasing the patient's awareness of his or her particular schema vulnerability in a way that the Thought Record does not. Thought Records cast a wider net because they are not necessarily focused on a particular schema. Schema change methods, in contrast, help patients work intensively in a focused way on their core vulnerability, a core vulnerability that cognitive theory suggests underlies distorted thinking, behavior, and emotional responses in a range of situations.

Schema Change Methods

Several schema change methods have been developed, including the historical test of schema (Young, 1999), continuum methods (Padesky, 1994), the core belief worksheet (J. S. Beck, 1995), and the Positive Data Log (Padesky, 1994). After brief descriptions of the first three methods, we describe the Positive Data Log in detail.

HISTORICAL TEST OF SCHEMA

This test, developed by Jeffrey Young (1999), assumes that because schema are formed in response to life experiences over a lifetime, they can be restructured through a systematic and realistic review of the evidence from these experiences that supports the negative schema and evidence that does not support it. To carry out a historical test of schema, the patient and therapist first identify a particular negative schema. They then compile a list of events (evidence) that confirm and disconfirm the schema for discrete age periods of the patient's life. Age periods usually cover 2–4 years. Because patients are less likely to judge themselves harshly during the infancy and toddler period, Young recommended starting there to increase the likelihood that the patient will be able to generate disconfirming evidence of a negative schema. Each review of an age range concludes with a summary of the data. The summary is a direct challenge to a negative schema and is intended to provide a more balanced and flexible view.

For example, David held the belief that he was "fatally flawed" and that he had been this way from birth. He and his therapist agreed to test this schema with a review of his history. David's therapist asked him to interview his mother and school friends and to read through childhood artifacts (his baby book, school yearbooks, letters from friends) to collect evidence to test his negative schema. A section of David's historical review of schema is shown in Exhibit 6.1.

Over eight therapy sessions, David and his therapist completed and reviewed his historical test of schema worksheets for eight different periods in his life. These periods were divided by natural life events, such as David starting a new school or job, or by events that David viewed as particularly important, such as his first date or his mother's first psychiatric hospitalization. At the end of this process, David (with the help of his therapist) wrote an overall summary of his life that reflected a more balanced self-schema:

> I have health and emotional problems that have made things hard for me at times. In spite of these problems, I've accomplished a lot; most people wouldn't even know that I have struggled. If I were really fatally flawed, I would be much worse off than I am. In fact, many people would see my professional accomplishments and my persistence in overcoming my difficulties as strengths.

CONTINUUM METHODS

A negative schema and its alternative are absolute and opposite beliefs. These views of self, others, the world, and the future can be conceptualized as occupying the poles of a continuum in which the larger middle territory reflects more balanced, realistic, and therefore rational evaluations of self, others, the world, and the future. The goal of schema change methods is to help patients shift their evaluations from the extremes to the middle ground to reduce absolutistic thinking. Padesky (1994) developed several continuum methods for this purpose: charting on the adaptive continuum, constructing criteria continua, two-dimensional charting of continua, and using a two-dimensional continuum graph to illustrate interdependent schema beliefs. Due to space limitations, we present only the process of constructing criteria continua here.

EXHIBIT 6.1

David's Historical Review of Schema: Age 6–9 Years

Instructions: For each period in your life, list the evidence supporting and not supporting your maladaptive schema. Be as concrete and specific as possible. Then review the evidence supporting and not supporting the maladaptive schema; write a brief summary of what the evidence suggests. Remember, perceptions, assumptions, and feelings are not evidence. For example, feeling "weird" in middle school is not real evidence supporting Bob's view of himself as weird. Instead, Bob needs to write down the facts supporting the assumption that he was a weird child. For example, did his teachers place Bob in special classes? Did his teachers call him weird? Are there any school or medical records documenting his weirdness?

Maladaptive schema	"I'm fatally flawed."
Age range	6–9 years

Evidence supporting maladaptive schema	Evidence not supporting maladaptive schema
"I couldn't play football because of my asthma." "My mom sent me to stay with my father."	"I joined the swim team and did okay." "I wasn't hospitalized during this period." "I had several 'jock' friends." "I kissed a girl (Barbara) for the first time." "My mom was hospitalized because she was having a really tough time; that's why I went to live with my father."

Summary	"Between the ages of 6–9 years, I had some health problems, but it didn't hold me back much. I was sent to live with my father during this period, but that had more to do with my mom's problems than with me."

The therapist begins this continuum method by asking the patient to rate him- or herself (or others) on a desired schema continuum. For example, George was socially anxious and avoidant. He held the belief that "I'm not interesting to anyone." George's desired alternative schema was "I'm interesting to people." When asked to rate himself on a continuum of "I'm interesting to people," he rated himself 10% and marked this on the desired schema continuum with an *X*. Because schema are stated in abstract and global terms, patients generally rate themselves in extreme terms (i.e., near 0%). However, they tend to rate themselves in realistic terms when asked about the concrete and specific evidence supporting their schema. This discrepancy between global and specific judgments underpins the effectiveness of the criteria continua intervention.

George and his therapist then identified various criteria George could use to judge a person as being of interest to people. George could do this easily. But if he had trouble with this, the therapist could ask about specific, concrete domains of his life (e.g., work, friendships, family relationships, interests, mood). The therapist might say to George, "What do you think work life would be like for someone who had 100% of this quality of 'not being interesting to anyone'? What do you think work life would be like for someone who had none (0%) of this quality?"

It is very important to define the endpoints of the criteria continua in absolute terms. That is, 0% is defined as the complete absence of a quality or experience, and 100% is defined as the perfect achievement of these same qualities. At times, patients define criteria endpoints (0% and 100%) that are not absolute or black–white but rather are somewhere in between. For example, when asked about the dating experiences of someone who was 0% of "I'm interesting to people," George stated that the person might have dated a few women. Having "dated a few women" is not a continua endpoint and cannot be used to anchor this criteria continuum. Through Socratic questioning from his therapist, George was able to see that a person with the complete absence of this quality or experience (i.e., 0%) would never have dated or have asked anyone out.

After George and his therapist completed constructing all his schema continua, his therapist asked him to place an *X* on each continuum according to how George rated himself. George's criteria continua appear in Exhibit 6.2. George was then asked for his impressions. He told his therapist that on the basis of this evidence, perhaps people were more interested in him than he thought.

THE CORE BELIEF WORKSHEET

Judy Beck (1995) developed a core belief worksheet, which can be used to restructure maladaptive schema. In the top part of the worksheet, the patient and therapist write out the old maladaptive core belief (e.g., "I'm fatally flawed") and a new adaptive core belief (e.g., "I'm okay") in the therapy session. As homework, the patient collects two types of evidence and writes it in the bottom part of the worksheet: evidence that contradicts the old core belief and supports the new core belief (e.g., "I was invited to Jim and Cindy's home for Thanksgiving dinner") and evidence that supports the old core belief with a reframe (e.g., "I invited Joyce to Jim and Cindy's home for Thanksgiving, but she said she

---

EXHIBIT 6.2

George's Self-Ratings on a Global Continuum and Criteria Continua

Interesting to people

|X

0%   100%

Love life

| X

Never dated, never even asked   Dating all the time, never
a woman out on a date   been turned down

Work

| X

Never invited to parties given   Always invited to parties given by
by coworkers   coworkers, always first to be asked

Friendships

| X

Never becomes friends with   Easily becomes friends with
anyone   anyone he wants, at any time

Appearance

| X

So ugly that he's shunned by   Gets comments all the time
everyone   about how good looking he is

---

couldn't make it. This was disappointing, but it doesn't mean that I'm fatally flawed. I waited too late, and Joyce had other plans.").

Notice that Judy Beck's (1995) core belief worksheet and the Evidence Record we present in chapter 5 as a method for restructuring automatic thoughts, are similar. This similarity of methods used to address automatic thoughts and core schema reflects the fact that automatic thoughts derive from schema and, in fact, often match (Persons, 1989). Sometimes patients' schema emerge as automatic thoughts (e.g., "I'm a worthless piece of garbage!"), so it makes sense that similar methods can be used to treat both.

In summary, according to cognitive theory, if patients experience symptom remission but retain their pathological schema, they are vulnerable to a relapse or to a recurrence of depressive symptoms. Therefore, it is important to work in therapy to change negative, pathological schema. To that end, we presented brief descriptions of several schema change methods that can be used to restructure, in a systematic way, the underlying negative, pathological schema; we now focus in detail on a final method, the Positive Data Log.

THE POSITIVE DATA LOG

A Positive Data Log is a log of evidence in support of an individual's positive or balancing schema. The use of the Positive Data Log as a schema change strategy is based on three observations about schema.

Activated in Many Situations

A person who believes that "I'm incompetent" can experience maladaptive emotional, behavioral, and cognitive reactions in multiple situations when this schema is activated. For example, a business executive's incompetence schema can be activated at work when a colleague does not return his telephone call promptly, in heavy traffic when an impatient driver honks at him, and at home after a shopping trip when he discovers the expensive shirt he just bought does not fit properly.

Include Positive and Negative Information

We know from the information-processing literature that schema are multidimensional and contain both positive and negative information (Segal, 1988). Whether the positive or negative aspect of a schema is activated appears to depend on many factors, including the nature of the situation and the valence of the individual's mood state (Bower, 1981; Persons & Miranda, 1992). Thus, the executive who feels incompetent in the situations described above can feel highly competent when he receives a promotion from his boss or a compliment from a colleague. Padesky (1993a) called the schema that oppose the negative schema *balancing schema*. According to cognitive theory, problems arise both when negative schema are too strong or activated too often and when balancing or positive schema are too weak or activated too infrequently (Beck, 1976).

Determine What One Notices, Attends to, and Remembers

A large experimental literature demonstrates the way one's schema guide and select the information one takes in and remembers (Williams et al., 1988). Depressed individuals remember fewer and less specific positive autobiographical memories and more specific negative memories; they have a bias to attend to negative information (Williams, 1992). These deficits are certainly present in depressed individuals, and there is some evidence that they persist in vulnerable individuals even when they recover from depression (Gotlib & Krasnoperova, 1998).

The Positive Data Log capitalizes on all three of these ideas. The Positive Data Log teaches a patient to notice the multiple situations in which schema are activated, helps the patient strengthen the positive or balancing schema, and helps the patient notice and overcome schema-driven biases in processing information.

Prior to setting up the Positive Data Log, the therapist and patient must identify a maladaptive schema that contributes to maintaining the patient's depressive symptoms and associated problematic behaviors. Thought Records are also helpful here (see chap. 5). In particular, the downward arrow technique (see chap. 2) can be used to generate schema hypotheses. It is important that the patient agree with the wording and content of the maladaptive schema statement and that the schema is salient to his or her clinical problems and treatment goals.

We offer several guidelines (see Exhibit 6.3) to assist the therapist in setting up a Positive Data Log (see also Tompkins, Persons, & Davidson, 2000).

Guidelines for Setting Up a Positive Data Log

Provide a Rationale

Keeping a Positive Data Log is a difficult task because as the information-processing literature shows, individuals often fail to perceive or remember information that contradicts their negative schema. For this reason, it is essential to provide your patient with a convincing rationale for doing the hard work necessary to keep a Positive Data Log. We recommend that the therapist use an idea suggested by Christine Padesky (1993a): the concept of the schema as a "self-prejudice." Prejudice is a useful metaphor for how individuals maintain a problematic schema or belief in the face of contradictory evidence. We recommend that therapists use guided discovery to elicit experiences that the patient has had with prejudice. This may include situations in which the patient had a conversation or encounter with someone who did not share his or her view or in which the patient observed a prejudiced individual. Careful questioning by the therapist helps the patient understand how mal-

---

EXHIBIT 6.3

Guidelines for Setting Up a Positive Data Log

- Provide a rationale.
- Identify balancing schema.
- Start the Positive Data Log during a session.
- Instruct patients to enter evidence on the Positive Data Log as soon as possible.

adaptive schema are maintained through discounting, distorting, minimizing, or ignoring evidence that disconfirms the maladaptive schema.

Identify Balancing Schema

Because the patient will be asked to record evidence in support of his or her positive or balancing schema on the Positive Data Log, it is important that the balancing schema be stated in clear and specific terms. Use the patient's words for greater impact. For example, one of our patients, an accountant, used a Positive Data Log to collect data to support her belief that "I'm on the A team." The A-team and B-team metaphor was her own highly personal way of capturing her negative (B team) and balancing (A team) views of herself. Another patient, a Hispanic biochemist with the self-schema of "I'm a piece of trash," showed little emotion when his therapist described how his abusive father had ridiculed him and told him repeatedly that he was a useless piece of trash. Only after his therapist suggested that he write his schema in Spanish, the language his father spoke to him, did the patient show any feeling when he worked on his maladaptive schema.

Start the Positive Data Log During a Session

Spend time starting the Positive Data Log and demonstrating how to use the Positive Data Log form during a session. When the accountant described above had difficulty finding evidence that she was on the A team, the therapist was able to suggest several entries based on her awareness of what was going on in the patient's life. For example, the therapist was able to point out to the accountant that she had recently been assertive with a coworker and that this might be viewed as A-team behavior. Starting the Positive Data Log during a session also enables the therapist to teach the patient how to correctly record evidence on the Positive Data Log. Evidence should be concrete, specific, and based on what is observed rather than what is perceived or understood.

Teaching patients to view events in concrete and objective terms builds on what they learned when using Thought Records in earlier sessions to examine their thinking. Depressed individuals are prone to view events in vague and impressionistic terms; this tendency contributes to their cognitive distortions. For example, a patient recording evidence in support of her adaptive self-schema of "I'm competent" might write "I felt better after my meeting with Bob" on her Positive Data Log. This piece of evidence is vague, and it describes a feeling, not an event. We recommend that the patient act as an observer of his or her behavior and record instead what happened in the situation. Thus, a better description of this evidence might be "Bob congratulated me for getting the marketing proposal in on time."

Instruct Patients to Enter Evidence on the Positive Data Log as Soon as Possible

Explain to patients that it is important that they enter evidence on the Positive Data Log as soon as they observe it. If they wait until the end of the day—or even a hour or two—to enter evidence, the evidence may be lost because the depressed patient may forget, minimize, or discount it. Some patients complain that recording evidence immediately is inconvenient or embarrassing or that they cannot keep track of the Positive Data Log form. Rather than insisting that patients use the Positive Data Log form, the therapist can discuss with them other ways they could record observations conveniently. For example, they could use a small pocket notebook, their calendar, or their Palm Pilot. Remember that depressed patients surrender easily to challenges or frustrations. Taking the time to develop a method of recording that the patient can complete easily in a variety of situations increases the likelihood that the patient will complete his or her log.

Once the therapist and patient have developed a system for recording evidence on the Positive Data Log form, they next must create a process for consistently reviewing the Positive Data Log over the next weeks or months of treatment. We offer guidelines (see Exhibit 6.4) to help the therapist review the patient's Positive Data Log form in the session.

Guidelines for Reviewing a Positive Data Log

Be Sure to Review the Positive Data Log

It is important to remember to review the Positive Data Log to encourage compliance and to get as much benefit from the intervention as possible. It is easy for both patient and therapist to give up when the patient has difficulty completing the log. We recommend that the therapist and patient agree up front to include a review of the Positive Data Log on every therapy session agenda. At first, the review of the Positive Data Log may take a substantial portion of the therapy session, but over

---

EXHIBIT 6.4

Guidelines for Reviewing a Positive Data Log

- Be sure to review the Positive Data Log.
- Reward small steps.
- Remember that depressed individuals are biased to ignore, minimize, and forget information that supports their balancing schema.
- Watch for opportunities during the session to add items to the Positive Data Log.

time, the review can be accomplished in a few minutes. As in the case of other homework assignments, follow through is key. Therapists who do not consistently review the Positive Data Log in every session run the risk of giving their patients the message that the intervention is not important. It is unusual for a patient to continue an intervention when the therapist has abandoned it.

To reinforce the use of the Positive Data Log, therapists can ask their patients to write a brief summary of the evidence on their Positive Data Log for the week. For example, Jason, who is collecting evidence to support his balancing belief that "I'm likeable," summarizes the evidence on his Positive Data Log for the week with the following:

> I received several calls from friends this week asking me to join them for the holidays. This felt good, and I know they didn't need to do this. My boss and a new customer both told me they liked my telephone voice. I've never thought about this before, but now I remember that in the past other people have said this about me as well. Six strangers smiled at me on my walk to work this week. I smiled back and even gave a little wave to an attractive woman.

Jason's therapist asked him to write these summaries in his therapy notebook, so that he could periodically review them with his therapist during his sessions or on his own outside his sessions when his mood dipped or when he felt like giving up on the Positive Data Log because he believed it was not helping.

When setting up a Positive Data Log, we recommend that therapists explain to patients that this intervention will continue for many weeks and perhaps months of therapy. Patients who understand that schema change work is an ongoing process will be more likely to work on their Positive Data Log persistently over time. In fact, we recommend to patients that they continue their Positive Data Log after therapy has ended. It can be a useful relapse prevention tool, particularly for patients who are experiencing ongoing stressors (e.g., health problems, divorce proceedings) that trigger their maladaptive schema. Therapists can include a review of a patient's Positive Data Logs (or summaries of the logs) as part of scheduled booster sessions.

As the therapy progresses, the therapist may observe that patients add more evidence to their Positive Data Logs without help from their therapist. An increase in the number of spontaneous entries in a patient's Positive Data Log suggests that schema change is occurring. As their balancing schema develop and strengthen, patients depend less on their therapist to help them to add evidence to their Positive Data Log.

There are other indices of schema change. Patients who are strengthening their balancing schema may also find it easier to generate adaptive responses to their negative automatic thoughts when doing Thought Records. When therapists observe this in session, we recommend that they call this to their patient's attention. We recommend that therapists check with their patients to see whether they are finding it easier to challenge negative automatic thoughts outside their sessions as well. Finally, therapists may see an improvement in the patient's scores on measures of treatment outcome, such as the Beck Depression Inventory. We have found it helpful to ask patients to plot the number of Positive Data Log entries each week on graph paper. Clear feedback such as this helps to remind the patient (and the therapist) that schema change is occurring and encourages the patient (and the therapist) to continue using the Positive Data Log.

Reward Small Steps

Therapists need to praise their patients for their efforts to accomplish the difficult task of keeping their log. Depressed patients are adept at punishing themselves but have difficulty praising and rewarding themselves. In the early phase of the Positive Data Log intervention, patients may find only a single piece of evidence in support of their balancing schema; they may minimize or discount even that. It is important for the therapist to praise patients' efforts to enter evidence on their Positive Data Log forms and remind them that schema change (and the Positive Data Log) is a long-term project. Because it took patients many years to develop their negative schema, it will take them some time to change it.

The therapist needs to help patients be realistic about the process of schema change and predict that they may experience a few "bumps" along the way. It is common for patients to come to their session one week with little or nothing on their Positive Data Log, after entering many pieces of evidence the week before. Often this occurs because some life event has triggered the patient's negative schema, temporarily blocking his or her ability to see evidence in support of a balancing schema. Predicting these bumps and learning from them can help patients stay on track and may encourage them to work a little harder to find evidence that is difficult to see when their schema are activated but easy to see when they are not.

Remember That Depressed Individuals Are Biased to Ignore, Minimize, and Forget Information That Supports Their Balancing Schema

A depressed person's negative schema guide his or her processing of information in such a way as to block receipt of information that supports balancing schema. Point this type of distortion out whenever you see it and teach patients to do this for themselves. A Thought Record can be used to structure this type of therapeutic work (see chap. 5). For example, George held the self-schema "I'm incompetent" and came to his therapy session reporting that he had not found any evidence to enter on his Positive Data Log that week. The therapist pointed out to George that he could place on his log as evidence in support of his balancing schema "I'm competent" that he arrived for his therapy session on time. George discounted this evidence quickly by telling his therapist that being punctual was the minimum he expected of himself and was not really evidence of his competency. Using a Thought Record, George and his therapist identified other automatic thoughts that served to discount this and similar evidence. They then evaluated whether these thoughts were helpful and reasonable. With careful inquiry, the therapist was able to help George see that being prompt is a fundamental attribute of competency and one that many people do not have.

Watch for Opportunities During the Session to Add Items to the Positive Data Log

Patients may not see evidence in support of their balancing schema when the therapist can see it clearly. Therapists should assume that patients have overlooked evidence in support of their balancing schema. They should treat all discussions and all information they obtain about the patient as opportunities to add to the patient's Positive Data Log.

When therapists hear something that might be evidence in support of their patient's balancing schema, consider asking the patient "Did you put that on your Positive Data Log?" If the answer is *no*, ask the patient to get out his or her log and add the item at that time. We recommend that therapists use probe questions (see Exhibit 6.5) to elicit evidence in support of a balancing schema, as in the following interaction.

Therapist: "Joyce, if people at work thought you were "likeable," how might they interact with you?"

Patient: "Well, I guess they might come up to my desk to chitchat."

T: "Yes, if you were likeable, people might come up to your desk to say hello and chat. Anything else?"

P: "I guess people might call me to ask me to do things with them, like go to a movie or something."

T: "Yes, anything else?"

P: "I guess if I was really likeable, people would smile or wave at me when I walked down the street. Even strangers might smile at me if I was really likeable."

EXHIBIT 6.5

Probe Questions

Use the following questions to probe for possible evidence in support of your patient's alternative schema.

▪ "Walk me through your day. Let's see if we can find something that you may have missed."
▪ "Tell me about the interactions you've had with people this week. Let's see if we can find something that you may have missed."
▪ "If people thought you were _____ [use an alternative schema], how might they interact with you? Did anything like that happen to you this week?"
▪ "If you really believed you were _____ [use an alternative schema], what might you be doing or saying? Did you do or say anything like that this week?"
▪ "Can you think of someone who has a lot of this quality we've called _____? [use an alternative schema] What do they do or say that makes you think they're _____ [use the same alternative schema]? Did you do or say anything like that this week?"
▪ "Can you think of people who view themselves as _____ [use an alternative schema]? What do they do or say that makes you think they have this view of themselves? [wait for the patient to generate some items] Did you do anything like that this week?"

T: "Yes. Now did anything like that happen this week?"

P: "No, not really."

T: "So, no one came up to your desk at work to chitchat. Is that right?"

P: "Well, yes, of course people came up to my desk to talk to me. My office is near the break room, and people walk by all the time."

T: "Did these people chitchat with you?"

P: "Well, people came to my desk to talk business, but there wasn't any chitchat."

T: "So no one came into your office to say 'hi.' Is that right?"

P: "Well, I guess people did. Yes, Janice came by to show me the pictures of her son's birthday party. That was nice. Janice is a sweetheart."

T: "So Janice came into your office to chitchat. Anyone else?"

P: "Well, now that you mention it—but this isn't really chitchat—Susan came into my office later that day. She was upset because her best employee just quit, and she wanted to talk about it."

T: "So let me see. Janice came into your office to chat about her son's birthday party, and Susan sought you out to discuss a situation she was upset about. Is that right?"

P: "Yes."

T: "Well, how about these examples. Aren't these pieces of evidence that you're likeable?"

P: "Well, I guess so. But does this really mean that I'm likeable? They don't seem that important to me."

T: "I understand that these pieces of evidence don't seem important to you, but they don't mean that you're not likeable. Is that right?"

P: "Well, yes I guess so. They don't disprove I'm likeable."

T: "Right. How about in this case we add them to your Positive Data Log? If later, we decide that they don't belong on your log, we can always take them off. Would that be all right?"

P: "Sure. I'm willing to do that."

Obstacles to Implementing the
Positive Data Log

Schema change can take weeks or even months of tedious and difficult work. We describe several obstacles that can arise when implementing Positive Data Logs and offer some solutions to them.

DIFFICULTY ENTERING EVIDENCE ON THE POSITIVE DATA LOG

Early in the schema change work, patients are likely to come to their therapy session complaining that they did not find any or much evidence to add to their Positive Data Log. We recommend that therapists point out to the patient that this is a common problem in the early phase of schema change. If the patient is wanting to give up on the log, it may help to review with the patient the rationale for the Positive Data Log.

Explaining that schema are rigid and longstanding may help patients understand the difficulty they are having and work against the tendency of depressed patients to become discouraged easily and give up.

It may also be useful for therapists to review patients' schema hypotheses and discuss these with them to ensure that the schema that are the focus of the Positive Data Log are relevant and salient to the patient's presenting problems. Patients have little reason to comply with the Positive Data Log if they do not believe that strengthening a specific balancing schema will have a significant impact on their depression and associated problems.

When patients have difficulty identifying items for their Positive Data Log, it can be helpful for their therapists to direct them to monitor a particular area of their lives in which it is easier for them to see evidence supporting their balancing schema. For example, Joyce, who held the negative self-schema "I'm worthless," had trouble finding evidence supporting her balancing self-schema "I'm worthwhile." Joyce felt particularly worthless in the area of relationships with friends, family, and men. However, she was a successful patent attorney and could more easily see that she was successful in her profession and that other attorneys respected her work. Joyce and her therapist agreed to begin focusing her data collection on her professional life before focusing on her personal life.

Therapists can use the probe questions provided in Exhibit 6.5 to help patients identify potential evidence for their Positive Data Log that otherwise might be overlooked. We recommend that therapists teach their patients to ask themselves these questions as they review their day. Patients can write the probe questions on an index card or in their appointment book so that they can quickly review them at any time during their day.

At times, patients may report that they were able to find evidence for their Positive Data Log but failed to enter it on the form. We recommend that therapists ask their patients about any reservations they may have about their Positive Data Log or about problems that may have arisen as they tried to add items to their Positive Data Log. Often such inquiry leads to adjustments to the intervention that better meet the patient's needs. For example, Sarah, a busy telecommunications executive, felt awkward entering evidence on her Positive Data Log form at work. She feared colleagues or customers would ask her about it, and she did not feel she could assertively tell them that it was private. Instead, Sarah and her therapist decided that it would work better for her to enter evidence in her appointment book. Sarah felt that she could do this during meetings or business lunches (situations that routinely activated her negative schema) without attracting attention. Later, she would transfer the entries onto her Positive Data Log form.

Depressed patients frequently are ambivalent about a piece of evidence and cannot decide whether to enter it in their Positive Data Log. We recommend that therapists ask their patients to use a "question mark" to sidestep this obstacle. Therapists can discuss with their patients the importance of adding *all* evidence to their Positive Data Logs, no matter how small or insignificant they think it is. Therapists can explain that disqualifying the positive (see Exhibit 5.3 for a list of cognitive distortions), a common feature of depression, frequently gets in the way of adding evidence to Positive Data Logs. To overcome these problems, therapists can ask patients to place *all* evidence on their Positive Data Logs and then to place a question mark next to the evidence they have doubts about. The question mark can reflect the patient's uncertainty that the evidence supports a balancing schema or that it is important enough to add to the log. In this way, all the evidence gets onto the patient's Positive Data Log and can be reviewed during the next session.

Contracts may help patients who are having difficulty complying with the Positive Data Log intervention. The treatment agreement we ask our patients to read and sign clearly states that homework is a key component of cognitive–behavior therapy and that they are expected to complete the homework assignments that they have agreed to do. However, it sometimes helps to ask patients to sign a separate contract that explicitly describes the Positive Data Log (i.e., why it is important that Positive Data Logs be completed and what is expected of the patient and therapist when using the Positive Data Log). A contract for a specific intervention, such as the Positive Data Log, emphasizes to the patient the importance of completing what has been agreed on. Patients who have difficulty completing a Positive Data Log for themselves sometimes are able to complete one for their therapist, particularly when this expectation is spelled out in a written contract. In addition, because contracts are tangible evidence of what was agreed on, it is more difficult for patients to say that they forgot, did not understand the assignment, or did not agree to do it. We recommend that therapists refer to the contract when discussing with their patients why they are not following through with what they have agreed to do.

Finally, we cannot emphasize enough the importance of therapists' revisiting a patient's individualized case formulation (see chap. 2) when problems with the Positive Data Log (or other interventions) arise. Perfectionistic patients or those with an excessive fear of rejection or need to please others may have great difficulty complying with the Positive Data Log intervention. A patient with a self-schema of "I'm worthless" and an other schema of "People are harsh and critical" may hesitate to add evidence that shows that she is worthwhile to her Positive Data Log. She may fear that her therapist will look at the evidence and say, "You think a friend calling to invite you to a movie is evidence you're worthwhile? That's ridiculous. Your friend just feels sorry for you." The case formulation helps the therapist predict such potential problems and to intervene appropriately. For example, to handle this problem, the therapist might do a Thought Record with the patient to get these automatic thoughts out on the table and address them.

DISCOUNT OR MINIMIZE POSSIBLE POSITIVE DATA LOG EVIDENCE

The act of reviewing the Positive Data Log may itself trigger patients' maladaptive schema, leading them to discount or minimize any evidence their therapist might offer. When patients come to their session and report that "nothing really happened this week that proves I'm competent," the therapist should not assume this statement is true. We recommend that therapists take the stance that evidence in support of the balancing healthier schema is there, even when the patient believes it is not. Patients argue, complain, and protest when their therapist insists evidence is there and that it is just a matter of finding it. We recommend that therapists walk their patients through their day or week to help them find evidence in support of their balancing schema. Again, the probe questions (see Exhibit 6.5) are helpful here. Schema change work at times can be tedious and frustrating for the patient and therapist. However, if patients could see what their therapist sees, then they would not need schema change work.

When therapists point out to their patients a potential piece of evidence for their Positive Data Log, patients often respond with "that isn't really important; it's too small to really matter." For example, when Alice's therapist pointed out to her that her daughter's choice to spend the evening with her rather than with her friends might mean that she is a lovable person, Alice discounted this piece of evidence by saying, "Well, for God's sake, she's my daughter! Of course she loves me. She has to." In such cases, therapists can use the question mark intervention discussed earlier or encourage the patient to view the evidence from a different perspective. The therapist could say to the patient "Suppose a friend of yours also believed that he is unlovable, and he was working on his Positive Data Log. If his daughter chose to spend time with her dad rather than with her friends, would you think this evidence belonged on your friend's Positive Data Log?" If the answer to that question is *yes,* the therapist could then say "If it belongs on your friend's Positive Data Log, don't you think it belongs on yours?"

Treating the Positive Data Log as an experiment can also help overcome a patient's tendency to discount small pieces of evidence. When therapists encounter resistance to a piece of evidence, we recommend that they ask their patients whether they would be willing to add the evidence to their Positive Data Log, even if they believe it is too small and insignificant to be worth adding. This intervention is similar to the question mark intervention.

Therapists can even ask their patients to rate the strength of their belief (0–100%) that a piece of evidence is suitable for their Positive Data Log. In this way, patients are encouraged to include evidence on their Positive Data Log, even if they are not 100% certain that it is appropriate. The therapist then monitors the outcome, perhaps with a daily mood log that patients can use to rate their mood (on a scale from 1 to 10) to see if adding small items to the Positive Data Log improves the patient's mood. If the results of this experiment show that adding all evidence, even evidence that the patient views as insignificant, improves a patient's mood, then the therapist may be able to convince the patient that it is important to add both large and small evidence to the Positive Data Log.

Finally, Thought Records (see chap. 5) can be used to examine and restructure automatic thoughts that may block a patient's ability to use the Positive Data Log intervention effectively. For example, Kevin, who held the self-schema of "I'm a piece of garbage" resisted adding small items (a friend calling him to say hello) to his Positive Data Log. Kevin's Thought Record showed the automatic thought of "I don't deserve credit for the small things I do." Kevin and his therapist used several strategies to evaluate and restructure this maladaptive thought, which enabled Kevin to agree that it was important to add this evidence about his friend's phone call and other similar small pieces of evidence to his Positive Data Log.

Summary and Conclusion

In this chapter, we presented several schema change methods that are used to restructure the negative, pathological schema that when activated by life events are thought to give rise to depressive symptoms. In particular, we focused on the Positive Data Log and presented guidelines for implementing this schema change method. Although we focused on specific schema change methods, we assume that schema change can occur as a result of other interventions as well, such as activity scheduling and using Thought Records. In the next chapter, we focus our attention on a clinical case in which the use of the key components of cognitive-behavior therapy for depression to treat over time a depressed young woman is illustrated.

Practice Exercises

These exercises can reinforce what you have learned by reading about the Positive Data Log. If you are an instructor, use them to stimulate class discussion or to structure sessions in which students can practice the basics of setting up and reviewing a Positive Data Log.

1. Try keeping a Positive Data Log yourself. Complete a Positive Data Log (see Appendix 6A) for 1 week. For example, therapists at times have doubts about their competence and their ability to help their patients. You might use a Positive Data Log to record behaviors that support your view of yourself as a competent therapist. Record the times when you set a therapy session agenda with a patient, when you consulted with a colleague on a difficult case, or when you completed all your progress notes before you left for the day.

2. Team up with a colleague or fellow student to role-play setting up and reviewing a Positive Data Log with a patient. Play the role of one of your own patients for whom a Positive Data Log might be useful. Then play the role of the therapist working with that patient and try again. Evaluate your effectiveness by asking your role-play partner for feedback. As the patient (or the therapist), consider the following:
   (a) What did it feel like to set up and review a Positive Data Log?
   (b) What was helpful about this intervention?
   (c) What was not helpful?

3. Review your list of current patients and choose one or two who might benefit from a Positive Data Log. Place a Positive Data Log form in the clinical record of that patient to remind yourself to try the intervention the next time you see the patient.

4. Read the following case vignettes (Jane, Gus, and Susan), and answer the questions that follow each vignette (answers to these questions are provided in the Answer Key that follows).

JANE

Jane is a 43-year-old divorced White female pharmaceutical company sales representative who lives alone. Jane sought treatment because she wants to be married but is not dating and is stuck in an emotional entanglement with a man (Jack) with whom she has been involved for many years. She and Jack have a history of an intense, conflictual (including physical fights) relationship. Jane states she would never marry Jack, but she does not want to break off with him for fear of ending up alone and for fear that she would lose access to the dog they share. Jane is successful professionally, although she knows she needs to increase her ability to confront interpersonal difficulties assertively, especially when subordinates do not measure up to her expectations. She has a small group of girlfriends with whom she tends to be overaccommodating and unassertive. Jane is bright and attractive, has good social skills, and does not abuse drugs or alcohol. She meets diagnostic criteria for major depression and social phobia.

An assessment indicates that Jane holds the following self-schema: "I'm unlovable, unlikable," "I'm stupid," and "I'm defective, not up to par with others." Her schema about others include "others aren't interested in me, don't take me seriously." These beliefs contribute to her tendency to be unassertive and overaccommodating, which lead to infrequent but powerful, frightening, and humiliating angry outbursts that strengthen her beliefs that she is defective and unlovable and that others do not want to be with her.

(a) What are some possible balancing or positive schema that could be addressed using a Positive Data Log?
(b) In what sphere of Jane's life would you first focus the Positive Data Log and why?
(c) What types of evidence from the work arena would be appropriate entries on Jane's log of "I'm likable"?
(d) On the basis of Jane's schema of "I'm not likable," what types of automatic thoughts might get in the way of adding entries to her Positive Data Log?

GUS

Gus is a 47-year-old single White male who lives with his girlfriend Karen of 20 years. Gus is self-employed as a real estate assessor. He takes jobs when they come his way, but he does not put much concerted effort into finding consistent work. As a result, Gus has an erratic income and depends on his girlfriend to pay the rent and living expenses. Gus seeks treatment because he is unhappy with his girlfriend and uncertain about whether to break off the relationship. He is frustrated and unhappy with his job but not clear what he would do if he made a job change. Karen is Gus's only serious long-term relationship. The relationship has not been sexual for 10 years, but Gus does not discuss this with Karen. Gus does not break off the relationship because he is afraid he will never find anyone else and he is financially dependent on Karen. Gus's unassertiveness with Karen tends to lead to increasing frustration and sometimes to verbally abusive outbursts.

After repeated urgings by his therapist, Gus finally spoke with Karen about trying couple therapy to address his unhappiness with their relationship. They now meet weekly with a couple therapist. However, Gus is not satisfied with the progress of the couple therapy but will not discuss this. Also Gus does not fully participate in the agenda-setting part of the couple therapy. Instead, he defers to Karen and uses the couple therapy session the way she would like him to. Gus has few friends and spends most of his time watching TV or managing his small stock portfolio that does generate a small income. Gus is bright and amiable and does not abuse alcohol or drugs. He has a long history of unsuccessful treatment for depression.

Gus holds the self-schema of "I have nothing to offer." His other-schema include "others are not interested in me; others are better than I am." These beliefs contribute to his tendency to be unassertive, over-accommodating, and passive with Karen, his friends, family members, therapists, and coworkers. Over time, he becomes dissatisfied and resentful, which he manages by avoiding potential conflicts. Gus's beliefs also prevent him from taking on greater challenges at work and asking for appropriate compensation. Because of this, Gus is underemployed and chronically dissatisfied with his work and personal relationships, further strengthening his belief that he is unimportant and that he has nothing to offer.

(a) What alternative or balancing schema could the therapist work on with Gus?

(b) With which balancing schema might the therapist begin?

(c) Suppose Gus comes to his therapy session reporting that he did not put anything on his Positive Data Log. What might the therapist do?

SUSAN

Susan is a housewife who lives with her husband and three children; she works part time as a technical writer and does some volunteer work for her church; as part of this work she writes brochures and other materials. Her negative self-view includes the following beliefs: "I'm no good," "I'm incompetent," "I'm a fraud; others may think I'm good and competent, but I'm really not." To help Susan develop a self-concept of "I am truly good [or competent], her therapist suggested that she begin a Positive Data Log that focused on one area of her functioning in which she felt relatively good but continued to have many doubts, namely, her writing. Susan agreed, and she is using a Positive Data Log to collect data to support her adaptive self-schema of "I'm a good writer."

(a) Suppose that Susan came to her therapy session with nothing on her Positive Data Log and the therapist learned that one reason Susan did not get any feedback about her writing is that she did not do any writing during that week. How might the therapist handle this?

(b) Suppose that when the therapist questioned her about the fact that she had not entered anything on her Positive Data Log, Susan reluctantly admitted that several members of the congregation gave her positive feedback about a letter she wrote. However, she insisted that this item did not belong on the Positive Data Log, saying that her letter was simply a revision of a letter by another volunteer and insisting, "Sure, my letter was better than the other one, but the other letter was terrible. If that letter was an *F*, mine was a *C*. And the positive feedback I got was from people who don't know anything about writing." What strategies can the therapist use to address Susan's tendency to discount evidence that she is a good writer?

(c) Suppose Susan came to her therapy session saying, "I think we should talk about the Positive Data Log next week. Nothing came up this week that I could put on the log, but I'll keep working on it." How might the therapist handle this?

Answer Key

We offer several answers to the questions posed above. You may be able to suggest additional answers that we have not provided. Do not hesitate to be creative!

JANE

(a) *What are some possible balancing or positive schema that could be addressed using a Positive Data Log?* Positive balancing schema include "I'm lovable," "I'm a likable, appealing person," "I'm OK (not defective)," "I'm intelligent," and "Others find me interesting, want to be with me, value me."

(b) *In what sphere of Jane's life would you focus the Positive Data Log and why?* To get the log started, focus on a sphere in which Jane feels relatively successful. To work on Jane's schema about herself and others, try focusing first on Jane's professional relationships or on her relationships with her girlfriends. These are arenas in which she is relatively successful, has a more balanced view, and will have a relatively easier time obtaining items to put on the Positive Data Log.

(c) *What types of evidence from the work arena would be appropriate entries on Jane's log of "I'm likable"?* Good items for the Positive

Data Log include lunch invitations from colleagues, acceptance by colleagues of lunch invitations Jane issues, enthusiastic greetings from colleagues who seem happy to see her, colleagues' initiating or responding to personal chitchat at business meetings, solicitous inquiries from colleagues when Jane has a cold or has been absent from work, expressions of interest from colleagues when Jane volunteers a bit of personal information, or positive reactions from staff people when Jane makes assertive requests of them (see Exhibit 6.6).

(d) *On the basis of Jane's schema of "I'm not likable," what types of automatic thoughts might get in the way of adding entries to her Positive Data Log?* Jane's therapist asks her to add items from her professional life to a Positive Data Log to support a view of herself as likable. In this type of intervention, patients often invalidate information about one arena because it is drawn from another. That is, Jane may tend to invalidate evidence from a professional arena about her personal qualities. She might discount a business invitation from a colleague by saying, "He asked me to lunch for business reasons, not because he likes to be with me." Other disqualifying automatic thoughts might include "Colleagues have to be pleasant whether they like me or not" and "Subordinates have to be nice because I have power over them." The therapist can use cognitive restructuring, including reviewing the list of cognitive distortions (see Exhibit 5.3) and the "ask for the evidence" intervention (see chap. 5), to point out and help Jane counter her tendency to disqualify positive evidence.

GUS

(a) *What alternative or balancing schema could the therapist work on with Gus?* "I have something to offer." "Others are interested in me." "I am as good as other people."

(b) *With which balancing schema might the therapist begin?* Collaboration is an important consideration; therefore, if the patient has a clear idea of where to start, that is probably a good place to begin. The patient is likely to be more motivated to work on a balancing schema that he or she has identified. Another strategy is to work with the patient to determine which balancing schema appears to be the most relevant to his or her presenting problems and start there. When doing Thought Records together, the patient and therapist may notice that a particular maladaptive schema comes up often. If the maladaptive schema is being activated often, it is probably creating many problems

EXHIBIT 6.6

Jane's Positive Data Log

Instructions: Describe your maladaptive schema and alternative schema in the space provided. Then, write down each piece of evidence in support of your alternative schema and the date and time when you observed the evidence. Be as specific as you can. For example, rather than writing "Someone said something nice to me" write "Tom said he liked the shoes I was wearing." Remember, you are to write down all evidence in support of the alternative schema, regardless of how small or insignificant you might think it is.

Maladaptive schema: "I'm unlovable, unlikable."

Alternative schema: "I'm likable."

Date and time	Evidence in support of alternative schema
1/14, 11:45 a.m.	"I asked Jean, my office mate, to lunch and she accepted."
1/15, 11:50 a.m.	"I went early to a big staff meeting and chatted with Peter and Sam who seemed to enjoy talking to me."
1/16, 3:30 p.m.	"I asked Dolores, a top woman in the company, to meet with me and offer some career advice; she got back to me right away and said *yes*."
1/19, 8:10 a.m.	"I called Esther to welcome her back to work after her new baby, and she really seemed to appreciate it."

© 2000 San Francisco Bay Area Center for Cognitive Therapy.

for the patient. Work on the balancing schema for that maladaptive schema.

At times, the therapist may be aware of an area of the patient's life in which he or she has fewer problems. Evidence in support of the balancing schema is usually easier to detect in an area of the patient's life that seems to be going okay. Start there and later move to more problematic areas of the patient's life. For example, the therapist might want to focus on Gus's successes in managing his investment portfolio rather than on his relationship with his girlfriend.

Ultimately, the answer to this question is an empirical one. Begin a Positive Data Log focused on one schema and monitor the outcome. Shift to another schema if the intervention is not having any effect on an index of change (i.e., the patient rates his or her mood on a 10-point scale).

(c) *Suppose Gus comes to his therapy session reporting that he did not put anything on his Positive Data Log. When asked about this by the therapist, Gus states that nothing happened during the week that would prove he has something to offer. What might the therapist do?* Several strategies are useful. The therapist can assume that something did happen during the week that supported Gus's balancing schema, but Gus did not see it because of his information-processing bias. The therapist might say, "I'm guessing some things did happen, but because of your self-prejudice, you didn't see them." Then the therapist could ask Gus to walk through his day or week to see if together they could discover something that is suitable for an entry on his Positive Data Log.

The therapist can also ask direct questions about areas of Gus's life in which the therapist knows Gus has had some success. The therapist might note that whereas Gus's work history is erratic, he always seems to be able to find work when he needs to. The therapist can then ask Gus specific questions about how he does this. Does he have specific skills (i.e., Does he network easily? Do people like him and remember him? Do people like his work and always want to send some his way?). Or if Gus is completely unaware of his strengths, the therapist can use Socratic questions to help Gus see them.

The therapist can also use the third person perspective to discover possible evidence for Gus's Positive Data Log: "Is there someone in your life who acts like you have something to offer, such as clients, family members, friends, and employers?" Or through Socratic questioning and the use of a Thought Record (see chap. 5), the therapist could ask Gus a series of questions (e.g., about a recent successful interaction with a client) to teach

Gus that because others value his input, this is evidence that he has something to offer.

SUSAN

(a) *Suppose that Susan came to her therapy session with nothing on her Positive Data Log and that the therapist learned that one reason for this was that Susan did not do any writing during the week. How might the therapist handle this?* Behavioral activity scheduling (see chap. 4) can be used to schedule writing in the future. The therapist can work with Susan to schedule times during the week she could allocate for writing and to plan what she will work on during those times. The activity scheduling intervention is most likely to be successful if Susan schedules one or two brief writing periods during the week at times she is most likely to be successful at completing the task (often this is first thing in the morning). If Susan's problem is that she sits down to write and then feels unable to do so, she might benefit from using a Thought Record to elicit and respond to the thoughts that block her writing.

(b) *Suppose that when the therapist questioned her about the fact that she had not entered anything on her Positive Data Log, Susan minimized the positive feedback that several members of the congregation gave her about a letter she wrote. What strategies can the therapist use to address Susan's tendency to discount evidence that she is a good writer?* Here are several ideas: Use Socratic questioning to point out to Susan that schema-driven thinking may be causing her to disqualify this and other pieces of positive data. As an antidote to "buying in" to schema-driven thinking, suggest to Susan that whenever she wishes to disqualify a piece of data she instead should enter it on her log followed by a question mark and review it in her next therapy session.

Propose a behavioral experiment to test the hypothesis that Susan's view of the quality of her letter is distorted. Encourage Susan to ask someone whose judgment she trusts to provide a blind review of her letter. Suggest that she ask that other person to give a grade (*A, B, C, D,* or *F*) to her letter. Use Socratic questioning to explore with Susan, such as the following: "If another person who was worried about her writing skills got the positive feedback she received, should that person disqualify this feedback?" The therapist could ask Susan to agree that if another person should accept this piece of positive feedback, Susan should too.

(c) *Suppose Susan came to her therapy session saying that "I think we*

EXHIBIT 6.7

Susan's Positive Data Log

Instructions: Describe your maladaptive schema and alternative schema in the space provided. Then, write down each piece of evidence in support of your alternative schema and the date and time when you observed the evidence. Be as specific as you can. For example, rather than writing "Someone said something nice to me" write "Tom said he liked the shoes I was wearing." Remember, you are to write down all evidence in support of the alternative schema, regardless of how small or insignificant you might think it is.

Maladaptive schema: "I'm incompetent (as a writer)."

Alternative schema: "I'm a good writer."

Date and time	Evidence in support of alternative schema
11/2/99, 9:00 a.m.	"The chair of the PTA called to say how much she liked the brochure I wrote."
11/2/99, 11:30 a.m.	"My editor commented that it was a pleasure to work with me because my writing is solid."
11/2/99, 6:30 p.m.	"My cousin called me to tell me to do another Christmas newsletter this year because she enjoys what I write."

should talk about my Positive Data Log next week. Nothing came up this week that I could put on the log, but I'll keep working on it." How might the therapist handle this? Do not be put off by Susan's reluctance to review her Positive Data Log. It is important to review her log every session (see Exhibit 6.7). Not reviewing her log sends a message to Susan that this intervention is not important and neither is homework. Even more important, it sends the message that her negative schema that she is not a good writer is true (after all, no data contradict it).

To address this issue, the therapist can begin by asking Susan's permission to discuss her Positive Data Log, even though Susan does not see this as worth doing. The therapist can use Socratic questioning to show Susan that putting her Positive Data Log aside is not a neutral behavior; it actually strengthens her belief that she is not a good writer (after all, no data were added to the log this week). If Susan is agreeable, the therapist could then spend time working to generate an item or two that might be added to her log and then ask Susan to try again next week.

Further Readings and Videotapes

Beck, A. T., Rush, J., Shaw, B., & Emery, G. (1979). *Cognitive therapy of depression*. New York: Guilford Press. Chap. 8, Cognitive techniques.

Beck, A. T., Freeman, A., Pretzer, J., Davis, D. D., Fleming, B., Ottaviani, R., Beck, J., Simon, K. M., Padesky, C., Meyer, J., & Trexler, L. (1990). *Cognitive therapy of personality disorders*. New York: Guilford Press.

Beck, J. S. (1995). *Cognitive therapy: Basics and beyond*. New York: Guilford Press. Chap. 11, Core beliefs.

Freeman, A. (1987). Understanding personal, cultural and religious schema in psychotherapy. In A. Freeman, N. Epstein, & K. Simon (Eds.), *Depression in the family*. New York: Haworth Press.

Ingram, R. E., & Hollon, S. D. (1986). Cognitive therapy for depression from an information processing perspective. In R. E. Ingram (Ed.), *Information processing approaches to clinical psychology* (pp. 259–281). New York: Academic Press.

Landau, R. J., & Goldfried, M. R. (1981). The assessment of schemata: A unifying framework for cognitive, behavioral and traditional assessment. In P. C. Kendall & S. D. Hollon (Eds.), *Assessment strategies for cognitive–behavioral interventions* (pp. 363–399). New York: Academic Press.

Padesky, C. (1994). Schema change processes in cognitive therapy. *Clinical Psychology and Psychotherapy, 1,* 267–278.

Tompkins, M. A., Persons, J. B., & Davidson, J. (2000). *Cognitive–behavior therapy for depression: Schema change methods* [Videotape]. Washington, DC: American Psychological Association.

Young, J. E. (1999). *Cognitive therapy for personality disorders: A schema-focused approach.* Sarasota, FL: Professional Resource Exchange.

APPENDIX 6A: POSITIVE DATA LOG

Instructions: Describe your maladaptive schema and alternative schema in the space provided. Then, write down each piece of evidence in support of your alternative schema and the date and time when you observed the evidence. Be as specific as you can. For example, rather than writing "Someone said something nice to me" write "Tom said he liked the shoes I was wearing." Remember, you are to write down all evidence in support of the alternative schema, regardless of how small or insignificant you might think it is.

Maladaptive schema: _____

Alternative schema: _____

Date and time	Evidence in support of alternative schema					

A Case Example: Nancy

7

The art of living is more like wrestling than dancing. (Marcus Aurelius)

n this chapter, we present a complete therapy from beginning to end. The primary goal of this case presentation is to illustrate the assessment, conceptualization, and intervention methods presented in the earlier chapters; therefore, the presentation emphasizes those aspects of the treatment. We particularly emphasize several ways the therapist uses the individualized case formulation to guide his or her thinking and decision making and to tailor interventions to the needs of the patient.

The Initial Contact

Mr. A. telephoned to discuss the possibility that I (J. B. P.) might treat his daughter, Nancy.[1] I spent about 20 minutes on the telephone with Mr. A.; he told me how bright and talented his daughter was and described his concern about the difficulties she was having that were impeding her ability to excel at her new job at a prestigious publishing house. He quizzed me to verify that I was competent to treat her, and he indicated that he would pay for the treatment if I would send the bills to him. I took note of the fact that Mr. A. took the trouble to call to check me out and generously offered to pay for his daughter's treatment. However, he seemed to be particularly intent on informing me

---

[1]Mr. A. and Nancy are pseudonyms. Names and details have been modified to protect the identity of the patient and her family.

that his daughter had beat out many competitors to get her job at the prestigious publisher. He repeatedly described her as especially talented and unusually bright but did not say anything about any distress or unhappiness she might be experiencing. These observations helped me to establish some initial schema hypotheses about Nancy. I speculated that she might believe that she must be especially accomplished to be acceptable to others and that her feelings and distress were unimportant and did not deserve attention.

The Initial Session

A couple of weeks later, Nancy called and we agreed to meet for a consultation session. Nancy arrived on time and brought with her the measures I had mailed her and asked her to complete before the session: the Symptom Checklist 90 Revised (SCL-90-R; Derogatis, Lipman, & Covi, 1973), the Beck Depression Inventory (BDI; Beck, Ward, Mendelsohn, Mock, & Erbaugh, 1961), the Burns Anxiety Inventory (BAI; Burns, 1998), a brief measure of substance use (a modification of the CAGE Questionnaire; Mayfield, McLeod, & Hall, 1974), and a demographics questionnaire (see chap. 2, Individualized Case Formulation and Treatment Planning).

My major goals in this interview were to begin to collect a problem list, obtain information needed for diagnostic purposes, develop more formulation hypotheses and test the ones I had already developed, establish rapport with Nancy, offer some initial treatment recommendations if possible, and—if I recommended cognitive–behavior therapy (CBT)—give her some information about it. In addition, if we agreed to move forward with treatment, I wanted to give her a homework assignment before she left the office. These were ambitious goals, so I was aware I that might not accomplish them all.

Nancy was a 25-year-old, single White woman who had recently begun working as an editorial assistant to a well-known publisher after graduating near the top of her class from a top undergraduate school. She was an attractive young woman with curly dark brown hair and a perky, engaging, almost childlike quality. She related in a frank, open, pleasant way, and she had excellent social skills except at times she seemed overly compliant and timid. Although Nancy presented herself as generally cheerful, her mood shifted at several points during the interview. When she was talking about upsetting topics, particularly her relationship difficulties, she looked distressed and was close to tears.

When I reviewed her scores on the various measures, I found that Nancy had endorsed many of the items on the BDI. She reported that she felt sad all the time, felt discouraged about the future, felt guilty all the time, was self-critical, cried often, had difficulty making decisions, had difficulty getting anything done, and had early morning awakenings. Her total BDI score was 21, indicating a moderate level of depressive symptoms.

On her BAI, Nancy had endorsed feelings of anxiety and tension, difficulty concentrating, and fear of criticism or disapproval. She reported several somatic symptoms, including palpitations, restlessness, tight muscles, rubbery feelings in her legs, dizziness, headaches, and fatigue. She had a total score on the BAI of 25, indicating moderate anxiety symptoms.

On the SCL-90, Nancy endorsed symptoms similar to those described on the other inventories. On the CAGE questionnaire, Nancy denied any concerns or problems involving alcohol use. She reported that she drank half a glass of wine a week on average and did not use illicit drugs.

When I asked Nancy to tell me in her own words what had brought her in to see me, she replied "I feel trapped by my relationships." Nancy reported that she was particularly troubled by her relationships with her ex-boyfriend and her roommate. The onset of her most significant distress was tied to her breakup, about 2 months ago with Morrison, a young man she had dated for about 6 months. The relationship with Morrison had been uncomfortable for her because he had obviously been more enamoured of her than she was of him. After considerable agonizing, Nancy had finally summoned the courage to break up with him, but she was having difficulty making the break final. Morrison kept calling, wanting to talk about their relationship, wanting to spend time with her, and wanting her to be his confidante. Nancy found herself feeling torn and trapped by this situation; she feared that Morrison would be devastated if she refused to be his friend, but she realized that maintaining such a close connection with Morrison was not fair to Pete, her new boyfriend.

Nancy was also struggling with her new relationship with Pete. She had repeatedly told him she "didn't want to get serious," but she admitted that she was fooling herself when she insisted she was not seriously involved with him. She said that she held the relationship at an arm's length because she feared that "If I get involved and then I decide he's not the right one, I'll want to break it off and he'll get hurt."

Nancy's relationship with her roommate Connie was also a source of tension. Nancy described Connie as someone she liked well enough, but Connie wanted to spend much more time with Nancy than Nancy did with her. When Nancy had recently said *no* to an invitation, Connie was visibly hurt and told her bitterly "now that you have a boyfriend, you don't want to spend time with me anymore."

Nancy said she felt she was "messing up" in all these relationships and felt trapped in them. In fact, she considered ending them all, saying "If I can't be a perfect friend/girlfriend/roommate, I'd rather just live alone."

At work, Nancy reported that she had a heavy workload and always felt behind and fearful of not meeting her boss's expectations, which were very high. Nancy had a major project looming, a presentation she would make to her boss and other high-level editors presenting the results of her reviews of several important manuscripts; she was extremely nervous about this presentation. Nancy had performed poorly when she had made a similar presentation a few months ago; a factor contributing to her poor performance on that occasion was that she had been in the middle of a major relationship crisis when she was trying to prepare the presentation. Aside from these difficulties, Nancy reported that she was doing well at her job and was well regarded by her colleagues and superiors, several of whom had recently consulted with her about possible collaborative projects.

At this point in the interview, I had the beginnings of a problem list: Nancy had symptoms of depression, she had relationship difficulties, and she had difficulties at work. Diagnostically, I had not yet completed a full assessment. However, Nancy appeared to meet the criteria for major depressive disorder, as described in the *Diagnostic and Statistical Manual of Mental Disorders* (4th ed. [*DSM-IV*]; American Psychiatric Association, 1994). She was also anxious, although it was not clear yet whether she met the criteria for an anxiety disorder (generalized anxiety disorder and social phobia seemed the main possibilities).

I reviewed with Nancy the results of my assessment so far, including my diagnostic hypotheses, indicating that I was basing my recommendations on the information I had and that things might change when I got more information. On the basis of my view of her as having major depression with some anxiety symptoms or an anxiety disorder, I offered Nancy information about her treatment options and suggested that CBT might be helpful to her (for more information about the issue of informed consent for treatment, see Pope & Vasquez, 1998).

I suggested to Nancy that I spend a few minutes in the session giving her a first notion about how CBT would address her difficulties to help her decide whether she wanted to pursue it; she agreed to this. To teach the cognitive model (see the chap. 5 section entitled "Teach the Cognitive Model"), I mapped onto a Thought Record the situation Nancy had described to me earlier when her roommate Connie looked hurt when Nancy turned down Connie's invitation to go out to dinner (see Exhibit 7.1). I asked Nancy a short series of Socratic questions to show her how these thoughts made her feel guilty, inadequate, and trapped and how they could lead to behaviors of agreeing to do things with

EXHIBIT 7.1

Teaching Nancy the Cognitive Model

Date	Situation (event, memory, attempt to do something, etc.)	Behaviors	Emotions	Thoughts	Responses
	I turned down Connie's invitation; she looked hurt and said "now that you have a boyfriend, you don't want to spend time with me anymore."	*Urge to break off the relationship*	*Guilty, inadequate, trapped*	*I'm messing up (again).* *If I were a good friend, I would go out with her.* *If I can't be a perfect friend and roommate, I'd rather just live alone.*	

Connie that she did not want to do as well as to urges to break off the relationship. I let her know that in therapy we would work together to develop cognitive and behavioral coping responses that would help her feel less guilty and inadequate in this type of situation and to handle it better. I recommended that we meet weekly, and I pointed out that homework between sessions would be a key component of her treatment.

Nancy indicated she wanted to try CBT, so we agreed to move forward with treatment. She indicated that she had tried Prozac in the past and found it increased her anxiety, so she did not want to take medication at this point. I told her that I was willing to try CBT alone as a treatment plan, but if we did not make good progress, I would want to revisit the pharmacotherapy option; she agreed to that.

As the session came to a close, I proposed an initial homework assignment: I asked Nancy to read the first 3 chapters of David Burns's (1999) book *Feeling Good* and to let me know her reactions to it when we met the next time. I also asked her to think about what she would like to accomplish in her therapy and to draft a list of treatment goals and bring it the next time. As a first step on the basis of her scores on the BDI (21) and BAI (25), I suggested that we include on her list the goal of reducing her symptoms of anxiety and depression. To track our progress, I asked her to complete the BDI and BAI scales for me weekly before the session. I asked her to come 5 minutes early for her session and to fill out the measures, kept on clipboards in the waiting room, and give them to me at the beginning of each session, starting with her next session.

As her first session came to a close, I asked Nancy for feedback about how the session had gone. She said that she liked the idea of a treatment approach that would teach her skills for managing her mood and solving her relationship problems. I felt we were off to a good start.

Summary of the Initial Session

I accomplished the goals I had set for the initial session. In particular, I collected some important information for the initial case formulation: I collected the beginnings of a problem list: Nancy had symptoms of anxiety and depression, she was distressed about relationship problems, and she was having some difficulties at work. I obtained a few details about some of the cognitive, mood, and behavioral components of Nancy's relationship problems and a bit of information about her work problems.

Some information I obtained in the session led to a revision of the schema hypotheses I had developed after the telephone conversation with Nancy's father. My initial hypothesis had been that Nancy believed she must achieve at a high level to be accepted by others. However, Nancy's distress when Connie was angry at her, her difficulty breaking off with Morrison for fear of upsetting him, and her reluctance to attach herself to Pete for fear of disappointing him later suggested that Nancy believed that "I must meet others' needs to be acceptable to them" and that "if another person is unhappy, this means I did something wrong." These beliefs are similar to the "self-sacrificing" schema vulnerability described by Young (1999).

I noted that although Nancy was clinically depressed, she had a bouncy, perky mode of interacting. I hypothesized that this perkiness was a compensatory strategy that she had developed to protect others' feelings and to hide her distress from them. Similarly, I hypothesized that Nancy's compliance, which made her pleasant to work with, was also part of her mode of accommodating to others. I noted as a potential obstacle to treatment that Nancy might have difficulty asserting herself if she disagreed with me about something.

Early Sessions: Beginning to Intervene and Continuing to Assess

Assessment, formulation, and treatment occur in tandem throughout treatment, as the therapist uses the hypothesis-testing mode of clinical work described in chapter 1. Of course, in the initial sessions, the proportion of time spent on assessment and formulation is higher than it is later. We attempt, in the first four sessions, to collect all the information needed for a complete psychiatric writeup, including a comprehensive problem list and a complete Cognitive–Behavioral Case Formulation and Treatment Plan (see chap. 2, Individualized Case Formulation and Treatment Planning). While collecting this information, the therapist also begins intervening both to get the treatment underway and to generate information based on the patient's response to the interventions, which feeds back to the formulation.

SESSION 2
BDI = 11

I went into the second session wanting to ask for Nancy's response to our initial meeting, follow up on her homework, continue to orient her

EXHIBIT 7.2

Progress Plot for Nancy

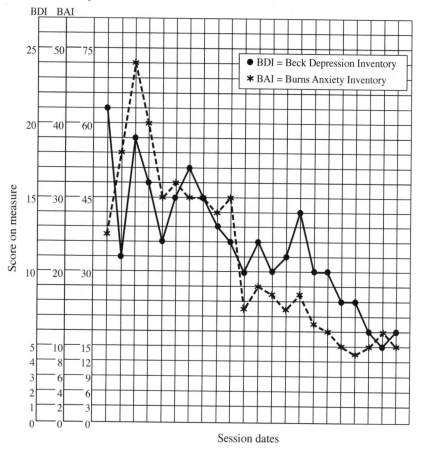

● BDI = Beck Depression Inventory

✳ BAI = Burns Anxiety Inventory

to the treatment, finish developing my problem list, begin to establish treatment goals and, if possible, begin intervening. I also wanted to make a new homework assignment.

Nancy came on time to the second session, and she brought a completed BDI but not a BAI. Her score on the BDI had dropped considerably (from 21 to 11). Such improvement often happens in the early sessions of CBT (see Ilardi & Craighead, 1994), for reasons that are not well understood, although the decrease in Nancy's BDI score was unusually large.[2] I entered this score on the Progress Plot I had set up after our first session (see Exhibit 7.2), and I showed her the plot and how

---

[2] I hypothesized that one factor contributing to this large improvement was Nancy's wish to meet my need to be a successful therapist.

we would use it to monitor her progress. I asked her to bring both a completed BDI and a completed BAI to her next session.

I began the session by orienting Nancy to the structure of the therapy session (see the chap. 3 section entitled Orient Patient to the Structure of the Session). I suggested that we begin with a check in because I would like to hear how things had gone during the week and any thoughts she might have about why her BDI score was so much lower. After the check in, I let her know that I would work with her to set an agenda for the session and, as part of that, I wanted to get her reactions to our last interview and to follow up on her homework.

During the check in, Nancy reported she was feeling considerably better because things were going more smoothly with her roommate. When she elaborated, I learned that things were going better because Nancy had found an apartment and planned to move out and she had been yielding to Connie's requests for time, so she felt less guilty. I was glad that Nancy felt better but was sorry to hear the reasons for her "improvement." My working formulation suggested that Nancy felt temporarily better because she had allowed her behavior to be driven by her maladaptive belief that she was inadequate unless she did what others wanted. The formulation also suggested that moving was (at least in part) maladaptive avoidance behavior, resulting from Nancy's discomfort in asserting herself with others and tolerating their negative feelings when they were unhappy with her. Because the decision to move appeared to be a "done deal" and Nancy and I were just getting our therapy underway and had not discussed my tentative formulation in any detail, I did not volunteer my speculations.

Next, I followed up on her homework. Nancy indicated that she had read and liked the first 3 chapters of *Feeling Good* and that she liked the approach Burns described. I asked her for her reaction to the previous week's interview; she indicated that she felt pleased at the way we had started and repeated that she liked the idea of a goal-oriented, structured therapy.

Another homework assignment had been to draft some treatment goals; Nancy had not done this, saying she had forgotten about this assignment. I was surprised at this because my formulation suggested that Nancy held a belief such as "I must meet others' needs"; this belief can contribute to excellent homework compliance. However, I realized that part of the noncompliance may have been due to my own failure to provide sufficient structure to the task. I also realized that another part of the formulation (Nancy's views of her own needs as unimportant) predicted that the task of asking herself what she wanted to accomplish in therapy might be particularly difficult for her. I suggested we spend some time in the session setting goals together; Nancy was agreeable to this.

I asked Nancy if she had any other topic she wanted to put on the agenda for the session today. (My working formulation predicted that this was a question that she might have difficulty answering.) Nancy indicated that she did not have any urgent business, so I proposed that I collect more information and we set treatment goals, to which she agreed.

To complete my problem list, I asked for more information about Nancy's work difficulties. Nancy indicated that she was well liked and well regarded at work; her problem was that she was chronically behind and anxious about being behind. In particular, she had trouble handling her quarterly report, a detailed summary of her assessments of all the manuscripts she had reviewed that quarter. Nancy always felt behind on this project and had to scramble at the last minute to put something together. Nancy reported that most editors at her (junior) level worked long hours, putting in lots of evenings and weekends and that she was having trouble doing this as much as she wanted to because she found herself agreeing to social dates with friends that she really did not want. This information supported my hypotheses that Nancy believed that she must meet others' needs to be acceptable to them and that her needs were unimportant. This information also helped me to understand how these two beliefs contributed not only to her relationship problems but also to her work problems (see the working hypothesis portion of Nancy's complete case formulation in Exhibit 7.5).

I also asked for more information about Nancy's relationship difficulties. Nancy indicated that her major interpersonal difficulties arose with Connie, Morrison, and Pete (she had described these in our initial session). Nancy also found her relationship with her father to be problematic at times. She described him as unpredictable: angry one moment, warm and supportive another. Nancy's job, although prestigious, was low paying, so she relied on her father, who was a highly successful businessman, to pay for extras such as therapy. Her mother had remarried and now lived on the East Coast, so Nancy had little contact with her.

Nancy stated that she suffered from migraine headaches about once a month but did not have any other significant medical problems. I collected some additional data and concluded that Nancy's anxiety symptoms, concern about her schoolwork, and difficulty in exam situations did not appear to meet the full *DSM-IV* criteria for generalized anxiety disorder or social phobia.

Nancy's psychiatric history showed that she had had several bouts of anxiety and depression and had received outpatient therapy on several occasions. She had received treatment for an episode of depression following the death of her maternal grandmother, to whom she was close. When her grandmother died, Nancy, who was 16 years old, was extremely upset and went into the bathroom; she poured out a bottle of aspirin, intending to take them, but did not. Nancy denied any subsequent suicidal behavior but said that at times when she was depressed, she did entertain thoughts of suicide. When she was not acutely depressed, Nancy frequently experienced a chronic low mood and energy state. Nancy had also been treated for panic attacks when she was 15 years old; she linked these attacks to feeling overwhelmed by pressures from both her parents to take sides in their contentious divorce.

Nancy and I used the last part of the session to set the following treatment goals:

1. Reduce symptoms of depression and anxiety (BDI, BAI).
2. Feel more comfortable and less pressured in relationships, less guilty; be less dependent in relationships; be more assertive and feel more comfortable being assertive, particularly when saying *no* to others.
3. Feel less anxious about work; work longer hours on a regular basis and be caught up at work; and finish the quarterly report more comfortably, without so much last-minute scrambling.

We agreed on a homework plan to continue reading *Feeling Good*. As we discussed *Feeling Good*, Nancy indicated that she liked the Thought Record concept and she seemed to grasp it; I had given her an initial orientation to it in the first session. So we agreed that she would fill out the first few columns of a Thought Record for any upsetting situation that might come up during the week, particularly one involving Connie, Morrison, or Pete. I recommended that she spend only 15 minutes on the Thought Record. I pointed out that because I had not spent much time orienting her to the details of the Thought Record, she might run into trouble but that if she did, she could bring whatever she could complete to the session and I would help her with it.

By working with Nancy on a Thought Record before teaching activity scheduling, I was modifying the standard Beck et al. (1979) protocol, which suggests that the cognitive therapist use activity scheduling interventions to help the patient make behavioral changes before using the Thought Record to promote cognitive restructuring. I began Nancy's therapy with cognitive interventions for several reasons. First, Nancy's level of day-to-day functioning was adequate; if she had been severely immobilized, spending a lot of time in bed, I would have begun with behavioral activity scheduling because individuals who are not functioning at all often cannot make good use of cognitive interventions. Second, she had asked to learn to use the Thought Record. Third, I had laid the groundwork for the use of the Thought Record when I used it in our first session to teach the cognitive model. Fourth, I believed she could benefit from it. Most decisions therapists make (e.g., whether to use activity scheduling or cognitive restructuring) cannot be made on an empirical basis. Therefore, the therapist makes decisions on the basis of a logical rationale, relying when possible on the case formulation for guidance, and monitors the outcome to assess whether the decision was a good one or not.

SESSION 3
BDI = 19, BAI = 48

I entered Nancy's scores on her Progress Plot (see Exhibit 7.2) when she gave me her measures at the beginning of the session. It was easy for both of us to see that her scores had gone up noticeably. When I asked her about this during the check in, Nancy told me that she had had a very stressful week due to lots of pressure at work; she had been behind in her work and had had to pull an all nighter to get everything done. I learned that this was a common problem, and we agreed to set a treatment goal of eliminating the need to stay up all night to meet a work deadline.

We set an agenda for the session: I recommended that we review her homework, I let Nancy know that at some point I wanted to collect additional background information, and then I asked Nancy what she wanted to put on the agenda. Nancy indicated that she had started a Thought Record on a situation with her roommate Connie that was upsetting her, and she wanted some help with it. We agreed to begin the session by working on the situation with Connie and to collect history if time permitted. I noted that Nancy had spoken up assertively with me to propose an agenda item, which suggested that Nancy might not need skills training to become more assertive; she might only need cognitive restructuring to overcome her obstacles and barriers to exercising those skills.

Nancy's Thought Record (see Exhibit 7.3) focused on a situation in which Connie had asked her to go out one evening when Nancy wanted to work. She yielded to Connie, went out, had a drink, did not get her work done, and had a headache and felt frustrated and upset with herself in the morning. This situation was an excellent one to work on for many reasons: It was an example of the interpersonal, work, and mood problems that appeared on Nancy's problem list and treatment goals, and it seemed likely to involve the schema in my working hypothesis that I had proposed were central to Nancy's difficulties (the need to please others, the tendency to ignore her own needs).

Nancy had written down the situation and a good set of automatic thoughts but no responses to the thoughts. As we looked at her Thought Record together, I used Socratic questions to show Nancy that her negative mood states and her behaviors stemmed from her thoughts, not

EXHIBIT 7.3

Nancy's First Thought Record

Date	Situation (event, memory, attempt to do something, etc.)	Behaviors	Emotions	Thoughts	Responses
	Connie asked me to go out, but I had work to do.	*I agreed to go.*	*Guilty, pressured*	*If I say no, it will hurt her feelings.*	Action plan: "NO THANKS. I'VE GOT A LOT OF WORK TO DO."
				If I say no, she will think I don't care about her.	I HAVE A DEADLINE COMING UP, AND I DON'T WANT A LAST-MINUTE SCRAMBLE.
				I said no last time she asked. I'm going to want to take a break anyway.	JUST BECAUSE I SAY NO DOESN'T MEAN I DON'T CARE ABOUT CONNIE'S FEELINGS. SO
				Maybe it will be fun.	I AM SAYING NO BECAUSE I HAVE A LOT OF WORK TO DO.
					IF A FRIEND TURNED ME DOWN BECAUSE SHE HAD LOTS OF WORK, I WOULDN'T SEE HER AS UNCARING.

Note. Italics indicate what Nancy wrote for her homework assignment, whereas all caps are what Nancy and her therapist wrote during the therapy session.

from the situation. This idea, simple though it is, is the heart of the cognitive model and a tremendously empowering notion (because Nancy's problem becomes her own thoughts, not something external). To convey this idea to Nancy, I asked her if another person in this situation could have felt differently and behaved differently in response to Connie's invitation to go out. Nancy agreed that another person could have refused Connie's invitation without feeling overwhelmingly guilty. I asked her if she would have liked to have been able to respond differently in this situation. She hesitated a bit before agreeing that she would have liked to have had the option to say *no* to Connie's invitation without feeling so guilty. I followed up this opening with more Socratic questions, and the following dialogue ensued.

Therapist: "Okay, let's see if we can work on that. I would say that what is needed is some responses to the automatic thoughts on this Thought Record. Let's see if I can help you find some. Does that sound useful?"

Nancy: [Nods] "Yes."

T: "Okay, good. Here's a question for you. Imagine another person who handles this situation differently, who responds behaviorally by saying 'I'd really love to go out, it would be really fun, but I've got a lot of work to do, and I really need to stay home and get it done.' How does that sound?"

N: "It sounds pretty good."

T: "Okay, let's put this down as a response—it's a behavioral response, so we'll call it an 'action plan' in the response column of the Thought Record, on the right. This is the new behavior you're shooting for. [The material Nancy brought to the session appears in italics on the Thought Record; material added during the session appears in all caps; Nancy writes 'NO THANKS, I'VE GOT TO WORK.'] Now here's the thing we have to figure out: 'What thoughts would that person need to have to drive or support that behavior?'"

N: "I don't know."

T: "Okay, right, that may be part of why you don't do that behavior! Let's try to figure it out. Think about it a moment. What might that person be thinking?"

N: "I guess that person would be thinking 'I really need to work. I've got a deadline coming up, and I don't want to have to scramble at the last minute to meet it.' That would be fine. But maybe that person would be thinking

'I have work to do, and I don't care if I hurt Connie's feelings.' That's where I run into trouble." [As I heard this concern, I speculated that Nancy's acute perception of how hurtful it can be when others act in an uncaring way stemmed from her own experience. I speculated that her parents expected Nancy to meet their needs (e.g., insisting that Nancy take sides in their divorce) and did not consider Nancy's needs or feelings. I made a note to test this hypothesis when I collected information about Nancy's family history.]

T: "Yes, I can see that would be hard. Let's look at your answer one piece at a time. Let's start with the first part: The person is holding onto the idea of how important it is to get the work done in an orderly manner, without a last-minute scramble. Would it be helpful to you to hold onto those ideas?"

N: "Yes."

T: "Okay, why don't you put that down in the thoughts column [Nancy wrote 'I HAVE A DEADLINE COMING UP, AND I DON'T WANT A LAST-MINUTE SCRAMBLE.'] Now you're worried that that person might not care about hurting Connie's feelings and you don't want to be like that, is that what you're saying?"

N: "Yes."

T: "Okay. Let me ask you this: 'Would it be possible to care about Connie's feelings and still say *no*'? Or if you care about her feelings, do you have to say *yes*."

N: [Hesitates] "Yes, I guess I could care and say *no*. Just because I say *no* doesn't mean I don't care."

T: "That sounds good to me. Do you believe that?"

N: "Yes, I do. [Hesitates] Some."

T: "Right. How much? Not 100%, I guess. What percent would you say?"

N: "Maybe 50%."

T: "Okay, fine, let's put it down [Nancy writes this on her Thought Record in the response column and writes 50% next to it.] Okay, now let's look at that. I hear you saying it's helpful, but we need something more here. Let me ask you this: '*Do* you care about Connie's feelings?'"

N: "Yes."

T: "Okay, let's put that down. [Nancy wrote 'I DO CARE' in her response column.] If you do care, why are you saying *no* to her?"

N: [Hesitates]

T: "Do you know the answer?"

N: [Silence.]

T: "Because you have work to do. Is that right?"

N: "Yes."

T: "Okay, should we put that down?"

N: "Okay." [With some help from her therapist to settle on the wording, Nancy wrote 'I AM SAYING NO BECAUSE I HAVE A LOT OF WORK TO DO.']

T: "So you are a person who does care about Connie's feelings, but you are saying *no* to her because you're putting your work at the highest priority on your list of things you plan to do on this particular evening."

N: "I guess so."

T: "This is hard for you, huh?"

N: "Yes."

T: "Think about this: If one of your friends said *no* to your invitation to go out for a drink because she puts meeting a work deadline higher in priority on her to-do list than spending some time with you that particular evening, would you conclude that your friend didn't care about your feelings?"

N: "No. It would be okay."

T: "So you wouldn't view it as a callous and uncaring way to treat a friend."

N: "No, it would make sense to me."

T: "Okay. So do you want to put that down in the response column? 'If a friend turned me down because she had a lot of work to do, I wouldn't feel she was uncaring.' [Nancy wrote this down.] Now let me check in with you and see how we're doing. Imagine that when Connie asked you out, you had these thoughts we just wrote down instead of the ones you did have. Would these thoughts help you to say *no*?"

N: "Yes, if I were having them, they would help me say *no*.

But they feel strange. I don't usually have thoughts like these!"

T: "Right! You don't usually have these thoughts, and you don't usually turn down this sort of invitation. The thoughts you usually have are the ones in the automatic thought column—the ones you started with. These words in your response column are foreign territory, so it's going to feel strange to imagine having them. Would you like to have thoughts like these more often? Would you want to be able to say *no* to invitations you don't want to accept?"

N: "Yes, I guess so."

T: "Okay, right, how can you do this?"

N: [Silence.]

T: "Well, I would suggest that one thing we can do is to use Thought Records to help you strengthen the line of thinking you need to support those behaviors. I'll give you a copy of this Thought Record to refer to [I made her a copy to take with her, and I kept one for my chart]. As we do more Thought Records, we'll develop more ideas to help you in this type of situation. How does that sound?"

N: [Nods and seems to like this idea.]

I suggested that Nancy set up a file folder for her therapy where she could keep the Thought Record from today's session and others we would develop later. We agreed that the issue of assertiveness, especially saying *no* to others, was an important one to keep working on. I suggested that she complete a Thought Record sometime during the week when she experienced an upsetting situation, especially when she felt pressured by a friend; she agreed to this assignment. We did not have time to take up the agenda item of information gathering, so we agreed to postpone it to her next session.

The intervention described here draws heavily on the strategies we described in chapter 5 (Using the Thought Record). I used the Thought Record both to teach the cognitive model and to promote change. I followed the guidelines for using a Thought Record described in that chapter: I focused on a concrete situation, and I relied heavily on Socratic questioning to help Nancy shift her thinking. I used the strategies of asking Nancy what thoughts would be helpful in this situation and what another person might do in this situation (see Exhibit 5.2, Questions That Promote Cognitive Restructuring).

This intervention is also similar to the "old view/new view" intervention (see Persons, 1989, p. 123). In this intervention, the therapist lays out three of four pieces of a puzzle: the old maladaptive behavior, the line of thinking that supports that behavior, and a proposed new behavior. The missing piece is a line of thinking that would support the new behavior. The therapist asks Socratic questions to help the patient obtain the missing fourth piece of the puzzle.

SESSION 4
BDI = 16, BAI = 40

The check in revealed that Nancy had moved and was pleased to be living alone. She had told her father how happy she was with me, and he asked to come to see me himself. He was upset when she told him that she did not think she would be comfortable with that. I thought it was terrific that she could assert herself with him about this, and I told her so. I reviewed her homework. Nancy told me that she had worked on a Thought Record focused on a situation in which a colleague had asked her for more help on his project than she had wanted to give. She reported that the Thought Record had helped her give him less help than she would have given in the past; she was pleased with this result. Unfortunately, she did not bring in the Thought Record so we could review it together; I asked her to bring it the next time so I could see how she was doing.

I wanted to finish collecting information for a complete family and social history, so I asked to put on the agenda some time for history taking. Nancy agreed to this and asked for time to discuss an upcoming trip to Puerto Vallarta that she was taking with her father, his new wife, and their two children. She feared that her father and his family would monopolize her time and that she would not be able to get any work done on the trip, which fell at a busy point in her work schedule. This was an excellent agenda item because it addressed Nancy's central interpersonal problem.

Nancy was anxious about the trip and in fact had not really wanted to go at all but had been unable to say *no* because her father had already bought the ticket (without consulting her), which was quite expensive. She feared that all her time would be spent babysitting her infant half sister, and she would not get her work done. To address her anxiety about getting work done during the trip, I asked Nancy if she thought it would be helpful to work out a concrete plan for combining work time and leisure time on the trip. She liked this idea, so I showed her how to use an Activity Schedule form to plan her time.

Nancy quickly decided that she wanted to allocate the morning of each weekday of the trip to work and spend the afternoon and evening with her family. She wrote out this plan on her Activity Schedule (see Exhibit 7.4). I suggested that it might be a good idea for Nancy to let her father know beforehand about her proposed schedule; Nancy agreed to tell him about this, as her homework assignment. Because we would have another session or two to prepare her for this trip and I wanted to spend some time on history taking, I did not initiate a discussion of the obstacles to success of her plan at that time, but I suggested that she think about any obstacles that might interfere with the schedule and we could address them at her next session.

We spent some time collecting her family history. Nancy had been born in a commune. Nancy's mother told her that she had used drugs when she was pregnant with Nancy; Nancy remembered her mother smoking marijuana in the car when she was picking Nancy up from school. When Nancy was 15 years old, her parents told her that they planned to divorce. "My mother was drunk when she told me. My father asked me if I could convince her to stay with him." Nancy reported that she felt good when her mother remarried when Nancy was in college "because I felt guilty leaving her to go to college." Nancy described her mother as often drunk when Nancy was a child, keeping her home from school "because she wanted me to do things with her." She described her father as "unpredictable; he could be really nice at times, and other times he yelled."

This disturbing information provided some support for my earlier hypothesis that Nancy's parents had placed their needs first and expected Nancy to accommodate to them. In fact, they had done this frequently, even when it caused Nancy emotional distress or threatened her physical safety. I placed some of this information in the origins section of Nancy's case formulation because it might explain how Nancy learned that her needs were unimportant and that she must meet others' needs. Nancy and I spent a short time discussing the link between her upbringing and her tendency to be overly accommodating to others' needs while undervaluing her own.

The Middle Phase of Treatment

By the end of the fourth session, I had completed all of my initial assessment tasks. At this point, I wrote up a complete formulation and treatment plan for my clinical record (see Exhibit 7.5). Nancy and I had settled down and established a good rhythm and way of working. We now embarked on a series of sessions in which I began working actively to help Nancy accomplish her treatment goals.

EXHIBIT 7.4

Nancy's Activity Schedule for Her Trip to Puerto Vallarta

	Monday Date:	Tuesday Date:	Wednesday Date:	Thursday Date:	Friday Date:	Saturday Date:	Sunday Date:
7–8 a.m.							
8–9 a.m.	Work	Work	Work	Work	Work	Free time	Free time
9–10 a.m.	→	→	→	→	→	→	→
10–11 a.m.	→	→	→	→	→	→	→
11 a.m.–12 noon	→	→	→	→	→	→	→
12 noon– evening	Lunch, free time for the rest of the day	Lunch, free time for the rest of the day	Lunch, free time for the rest of the day	Lunch, free time for the rest of the day	Lunch, free time for the rest of the day	→	→

Cognitive–Behavioral Case Formulation and Treatment Plan for Nancy

Name: Nancy
Identifying Information: 25 SWF editorial assistant living with a roommate. Referred by her father through another therapist.
Problem List:

1. Depressive symptoms. BDI = 21. Sad, discouraged about the future, guilty, self-critical, crying, difficulty making decisions, difficulty getting anything done, EMA. Suicidal thoughts. Typical automatic thoughts: "I'm a bad friend/girlfriend/ roommate if I don't meet others' needs." Typical problem behaviors: accepting social invitations pressed on her by others when she would rather work.
2. Anxiety symptoms. BAI = 25. Anxiety, tension, fears of criticism and disapproval, palpitations, restlessness, tight muscles, rubbery legs, dizziness, headaches, fatigue. Typical automatic thoughts: "I'm behind at work," "Connie will be angry with me if I don't spend time with her," "I'm not prepared for this presentation, and I'll mess it up." Typical problem behaviors: socializing with others when she would rather work, last-minute scramble to meet work deadlines.
3. Relationship difficulties. Felt trapped in her relationships and believed she handled them badly. Frequently felt guilty when others wanted to spend more time with her than she did with them, guilty about breaking up with boyfriend Morrison: "If I don't do what others want/need, they'll get hurt and it's my fault." Alternated between capitulating to others' wishes and avoiding contact with them. Good social skills, including assertive behaviors, but frequently avoids assertion for fear of hurting others.
4. Work difficulties. Was not working as many hours as she wanted/needed to do well at her job. Frequent (every 2 weeks) last-minute scrambles to meet deadlines. Unassertive (e.g., excessively deferential to others' opinions). Typical automatic thoughts: "I don't know what I'm doing," "If I don't do it his way, he'll be angry."
5. Financial stresses. Low-paying job left her dependent on her father for financial support for therapy and other extras.

Diagnosis:
Axis I: Major depressive disorder, recurrent
        Dysthymic disorder
Axis II: None.
Axis III: Migraine headaches.
Axis IV: Relationship difficulties, financial stresses.
Axis V: 60
Working Hypothesis:
Schema:
(self) "I am inadequate."
"I'm a selfish person."
"I must meet others' needs to be acceptable to them."
"My feelings/needs are unimportant."
"I am responsible for the happiness of those I'm close to."
(other) "Others' needs are more important than mine."
"Others are dependent on me for their happiness."
"Others expect perfection and are critical when I don't produce it."
(world) "The world is a burdensome place."
(future) "The future is unpromising."

(continued)

EXHIBIT 7.5 continued

Precipitants and Activating Situations:
Precipitants: breakup with boyfriend Morrison, demanding roommate.
Activating situations: pressure from others to meet their needs, for example, from friends/boyfriends/former boyfriends to be close, spend time together; deadlines at work, especially quarterly report deadline.

Origins: Nancy was reared by parents who expected her to meet their needs and disregard her own, (e.g., her mother drove her home from school after smoking marijuana and kept Nancy home from school when her mother wanted company; her father asked her to convince her mother not to divorce him).

Summary of the Working Hypothesis: Nancy's beliefs that paying attention to her needs and interests was a sign of selfishness and that others' needs were more deserving than hers, when activated by her interactions with her roommate, boyfriend, and others, caused her to feel guilty, inadequate, and trapped and to give in to their requests even when she did not want to. As a result, she felt trapped and pressured in relationships and at times coped by withdrawing (e.g., not returning phone calls). Her tendency to give in to others' requests for her time caused her to have difficulty getting her work done in a timely manner, which was anxiety provoking and sometimes meant she had to stay up all night to meet her deadlines. Financial problems were a result of her low-paying job coupled by her insistence on living alone (vs. with a roommate with whom she could share expenses). Living alone was in part Nancy's compensatory strategy for handling her difficulty being assertive.

Strengths and Assets: bright, attractive, personable, cooperative, collaborative, many good social skills

Treatment Plan
Goals (measures):
1. Reduce symptoms of depression and anxiety (BDI, BAI).
2. To feel more comfortable and less pressured in relationships, less guilty. To be less dependent in relationships. To be more assertive, and to feel more comfortable being assertive, particularly saying *no* to others.
3. To feel less anxious about work. To work longer hours on a regular basis, and to be caught up at work. To be better prepared (no last-minute scrambling), and to feel less anxious when making important presentations (e.g., on her quarterly report). No more "all nighters" to meet work deadlines (currently doing this twice a month). To be more assertive at work.

Modality: Individual cognitive–behavior therapy.   *Frequency:* Weekly.
Interventions:
1. Cognitive restructuring to address her views of self and others.
2. Activity scheduling to carve out time for work, to assist with saying *no* to others.
3. Role-plays to practice assertiveness.

Adjunct therapies: None at this time.
Obstacles:
1. Nancy's beliefs that her needs are unimportant and that she must defer to others' needs may cause her to be excessively compliant in therapy and then to feel resentful or trapped.
2. If Nancy's therapy results in increased assertiveness with her father, he may withdraw financial support for the therapy.

Note. SWF = single, White female; BDI = Beck Depression Inventory; EMA = early morning awakening; BAI = Burns Anxiety Inventory; score on Axis V = Global Assessment of Functioning Scale.

SESSION 5
BDI = 12, BAI = 30

Nancy reported that she had spoken to her father about her proposed schedule for the vacation, and she felt good that he had agreed to the plan. This, she felt, explained her lower BDI score. Nancy wanted to work on her guilt about her interactions with her ex-boyfriend Morrison. As we negotiated the agenda for the session, I suggested another possible agenda item: troubleshooting any obstacles that might arise during the Puerto Vallarta trip. Nancy agreed that this was a good idea but asked to do this in next week's session, pointing out that the issue with Morrison was very distressing and we had one more session before the trip. This plan made good sense (and I noted Nancy's good assertiveness skills in the negotiation process with me).

We began to work on the issue with Morrison. Nancy reported that she was feeling guilty for breaking up with him, hurting him, not wanting to get back together, not wanting to be his confidante, and getting involved with Pete after telling Morrison that she wanted to break off with him so she could be alone. As we discussed this situation, Nancy recalled that she had been repeatedly told by her parents that she was "selfish" and that her view of herself as a bad friend to Morrison was guided by the view that unless she put his needs first, she was selfish.

I suggested that we use a Thought Record to help her with this problem, and Nancy was agreeable to this. We developed a Thought Record focused on a recent situation in which she had spent a long time on the telephone talking with Morrison about his feelings for her, which caused her to feel guilty and upset in response to the automatic thought that she was being selfish if she did not meet his needs. After I asked her some Socratic questions, Nancy was able to write down the response "considering my own needs in this situation does not make me a selfish person."

However, as we focused on the topic of Nancy's needs, it became clear that part of Nancy's problem was that she spent so much time focused on *Morrison's* needs that she had not really thought about what *she* wanted. I suggested that we take up that issue. To help her focus her thinking, I asked her, "If you could set up this relationship the way you would want it, what would it look like?" After a brief discussion, Nancy was able to state that what she wanted was for Morrison to stop asking her to be his girlfriend. She wanted them to try being friends. This led to an action plan, which we wrote in the response column of her Thought Record. Nancy agreed to ask Morrison if he would agree to being friends and to stop asking her to be his girlfriend. I asked her to write down this action plan before she left my office because my formulation told me that it might be easy for her to lose track of what she wanted, especially if Morrison started pushing for his agenda again. Her homework assignment was to call Morrison and propose a friendship.

SESSION 6
BDI = 15, BAI = 32

Nancy arrived on time to the session, brought her measures, and reported that she had completed her homework assignment. This had worked out well, at least in part because Morrison had realized it was time to back off. The main agenda item for this session was the final planning for the upcoming Puerto Vallarta trip. We spent time thinking about any obstacles that would interfere with Nancy's proposed plan for managing her time on the trip. We practiced role-plays to help Nancy handle any pressure from her family to abandon her morning study plan or to stay up late playing cards and drinking.

SESSION 7
BDI = 17, BAI = 30

Nancy reported that she had followed through with her study plan on the trip to Mexico and was pleased at how well it had worked. She had experienced a bit of pressure early in the trip to give up her mornings, but after she held the line once or twice, she did not receive any more "arm twisting." She was anxious about her upcoming quarterly report and proposed this as our main agenda item for the session. It was due in 4 weeks, and she felt behind in her work and anxious about getting it done without major heroics at the end, as had happened last time.

I began by reviewing with Nancy how she had handled her previous quarterly report, so I could get more detailed information about what problems she encountered in that situation. I asked her for this information so I could develop a *miniformulation*—a hypothesis about the causes of a particular instance of a particular problem—in this case, the poor performance on the quarterly report (see chap. 2). A miniformulation describing the problems that arose with the previous quarterly report would be helpful in planning interventions to help with the upcoming report the next time around.

Nancy reported that a major reason she did not do well on the report (she had had to stay up all night the night before it was due and did not do as thorough a job as she had wanted to) was that she had been having a major relationship crisis (she was caught between two boyfriends) that had impeded her ability to focus on the project. Nancy agreed that she was in a better position in this regard now. But carving out time to get the report done remained a problem; she reported that she continued to "cave in" to requests from others, including colleagues at work, to socialize or help with their projects when she needed to carve out time to read manuscripts and complete her own report.

To address this problem, I suggested that Nancy make an Activity Schedule to block out her work on the report over the next week (see the graded task assignments intervention, as described in chap. 4). Nancy agreed that this strategy had helped her in Mexico and would be helpful again. I gave her an Activity Schedule form, and we spent the session blocking out times during her workday, evenings, and weekends over the next week to work only on her quarterly report, while still allowing some time for other projects and for socializing. Her homework plan for the week was to try to follow the schedule and to make notes of any problems that arose so we could discuss them the next week.

As I plotted Nancy's BDI score on the Progress Plot (see Exhibit 7.2) at the beginning of the session, I was reminded that at this point in the treatment Nancy's BDI and BAI scores had not improved much from her initial scores. I was a bit concerned about this and planned to continue to watch her scores carefully. However, I was not overly concerned for three reasons: (a) We were having productive sessions: Nancy was trying cognitive and behavioral interventions and finding them helpful; (b) we had a good, collaborative working relationship; and (c) the high scores might be a function of stress about her upcoming report, and I hoped the scores would drop after the report, especially if Nancy managed it successfully.

SESSION 8
BDI = 15, BAI = 30

During check in, Nancy reported that the Activity Schedule had been helpful in getting her quarterly report work done. Even though she had had to revise it as the week went on, the Activity Schedule had helped her stay focused on her work and gave her a bit of leverage to say *no* to activities that were not on the schedule. Because the Activity Schedule had been helpful that week, I suggested that she complete another one for the next week. She agreed to this readily and said that she could do this at home on her own, so we set it as a homework assignment.

We spent some time in the session working on her anxiety about the upcoming presentation of her report to the senior editors at the firm. Nancy reported that the last time she presented her report, her superiors had become, to her mind, overly focused on questioning her about certain minor issues, not allowing her to present the main ideas that she had about some of the manuscripts she had reviewed. She felt that she could have been more effective if she had been more assertive. Using a role-play practice, we developed some tactful ways that she might assert herself in this type of situation should it arise again; Nancy made notes about some of the strategies we developed so she could remind herself of them as she prepared for her presentation.

I also learned that Nancy had read the previous report verbatim rather than giving a talk based on the report. She did this in part because she did not have time to prepare a talk. She agreed to use the Activity Schedule form to carve out time to prepare and practice a talk based on her quarterly report. Nancy's homework assignment was to continue to use the Activity Scheduling form to work on her report and to prepare a talk based on the report.

SESSIONS 9–12

Sessions 9, 10, and 11 were spent helping Nancy with her report. Nancy used Activity Scheduling each week to schedule her work on the project, and we did role-plays to practice refusing unwanted invitations during this time. We also worked on her difficulty speaking up assertively to her landlord about a problem in her apartment. After we did a Thought Record and some role-plays, Nancy was able to handle the apartment problem successfully, which was satisfying for her.

In Session 11, Nancy announced that she had completed her report in good time and that the presentation had gone much more smoothly than last time. In response to this good news, Nancy's BDI and BAI scores showed a nice drop.

We began working on Nancy's telephone problem: She felt trapped by calls from Connie and others who wanted to spend 30 minutes or more talking on the phone. Nancy reported that she did not like talking on the phone to begin with and certainly did not want to spend 30 minutes or more of her evening talking on the phone; she preferred spending her evenings working or with her boyfriend. We worked on a Thought Record, tackling a situation in which she was on the phone with Connie and wanted to get off.

When I asked for feedback about the helpfulness of the Thought Record, Nancy admitted that the responses we developed, which focused on the logic that just because Nancy did not give Connie what she wanted did not mean that Nancy was a selfish person, were not very compelling. Nancy said that she believed this concept intellectually, but she had trouble really believing it at an emotional level and using it to guide her behavior when she was actually talking on the phone with Connie. In the actual situation, her maladaptive schema became activated and drove her mood and behavior.

We tackled the telephone problem again in Session 12, and we developed two responses to her negative automatic thoughts in this situation that Nancy found more compelling than the initial ones we had developed. Through a series of Socratic questions, Nancy saw that if she did not begin to set limits on the time she spent on the phone with Connie, she would be tempted to break off the relationship altogether (as she had done when pressured in other relationships) and that this was not what she wanted or what Connie wanted. Nancy found this response particularly compelling because it reminded her that it was in *Connie's* interest for Nancy to set limits that would allow her to be comfortable in the relationship. Nancy also saw that she was not being completely honest and in fact was leading people on if she spent more time with them than she wanted.

Nancy found these two concepts helpful, and we wrote them in the response column of a Thought Record that she took home with her (see Exhibit 7.6). A review of the formulation indicates why these notions were particularly helpful to her: They capitalized on Nancy's vulnerability (her concern for others' feelings and needs), while helping her be assertive and take care of her own needs.

Nancy's homework assignment was to log her calls so we could determine where her problems lay and track our progress at reducing her time on the telephone. The first time I suggested that Nancy keep a log of phone calls, she did not complete it. When I learned this, I suggested that we discuss it, saying,

> Therapist: "Nancy, I know you usually complete your homework and that this telephone problem is something you really want to solve. Let's think about what got in the way of your doing this assignment."
>
> Nancy: "I don't know."
>
> T: "I don't know either. But I think it would be good to find out. I suggest we put this on our agenda and spend a bit of time trying to figure it out. Would that be all right?"

When we discussed the assignment, I learned that part of the problem was therapist error; I had not followed one of the key guidelines for making a successful homework assignment (see chap. 3, Structure of the Therapy Session). I had not made the assignment sufficiently explicit, and Nancy was uncertain about what information to put on the telephone log.

However, therapist error was not the full explanation because Nancy could have made her own decision about how to structure the log or even called me to ask for guidance. I pointed this out; when I asked her to speculate about why she had not done either of these things, she responded with the following:

> N: "It would never have occurred to me to call you outside the session about a thing like this."

EXHIBIT 7.6

Thought Record on the Telephone Situation

Date	Situation (event, memory, attempt to do something, etc.)	Behaviors	Emotions	Thoughts	Responses
	On the phone with Connie, want to get off	Stay on the phone	Trapped	1. If I end the conversation now, Connie's feelings will be hurt. 2. I'm selfish not to want to spend time with her. 3. A few more minutes won't hurt.	1. I can't be sure how she'll feel; this is mind reading. 2. The fact that I don't give Connie what she wants doesn't make me selfish. 3. I need this time to work. *Also* If I don't set limits that are comfortable for me, I will want to break off the relationship, and this is not what Connie nor I want. If I just play along with Connie's agenda, I'm not being honest with her about my feelings. Action plan: I'll say, "Connie, I wish I had more time to talk, but I've got a lot of work to do tonight, so I'm going to have to get off the phone and go to work."

T: "Why not?"

N: "It's such a small thing! I'm sure you don't want to be bothered by little details like this!" [I speculated, on the basis of this evidence and what I knew about her upbringing, that Nancy believed, "others don't care about me and aren't willing to put out effort to meet my needs."]

T: "I don't? Are you sure?"

N: [Pause] "No, I guess I'm not sure."

T: "I will tell you that I would be happy to talk with you about this issue if you called me up. Remember, it's partly my fault that you don't have this information, so that makes it even more reasonable for you to call me about it."

N: "Okay" [but looking doubtful].

T: "Now let's think about another thing: Why didn't you just figure something out and set up a log on your own?"

N: "I don't know. I wasn't sure how you wanted it done."

T: "Okay, now this is an interesting statement. Do you see what's interesting about it?"

N: [Pause] "No."

T: "Because it's a log *you* are keeping to help *you* solve a problem. If you set up a log that is helpful to you, it doesn't really matter how I wanted it done, does it?"

N: "No, I guess not."

T: "Okay, now do you see why this piece is interesting?"

N: "No, not quite" [with a quizzical expression on her face].

T: "Well, you look like you have an idea, so take a stab at it."

N: "I'm focused again on other people's needs, not mine."

T: "Exactly!"

After this discussion, Nancy and I agreed on a format for the log that was clear, explicit, and helpful to her. She came to Session 13 with a completed log.

SESSION 13
BDI = 10, BAI = 17

During the check in, Nancy reported that she had begun to make some headway on the phone conversation problem. She reported that the log was helpful and that she kept it near the phone to remind her to complete it and of her goal to spend less time talking. The Thought Record we had completed a couple of sessions ago (see Exhibit 7.6) continued to be helpful. The fact that she had a lot of work to do also helped her get off the phone. She stated that she wanted to spend the therapy session on questions she was having about her career direction, and we agreed to start with that issue and take up the telephone problem again if we had time.

Before we began working on our agenda items, I proposed that in the next session, we review Nancy's treatment progress. I suggested that we both think about the therapy between now and next week and that in the next session, we review how we were doing in making progress toward her treatment goals. A systematic review of the patient's progress is of course central to the hypothesis-testing mode of treatment described here. Nancy and I had been monitoring her progress weekly by reviewing of the graph of her BDI and BAI scores, but these scores are not the whole story. It is also useful to schedule a formal time to review progress collaboratively with the patient. Nancy agreed to this.

When we discussed the career issue, I learned that Nancy was spending her time working on projects that she did not find particularly interesting, in part because she was unclear as to what areas interested her. As I collected information about the details of her problem, we learned that one reason Nancy had difficulty establishing her own interests was because several senior editors in various parts of the firm had asked her to work with them. The pressure from these editors made it hard for Nancy to ascertain what she found interesting. I proposed that we brainstorm to develop some ideas about things Nancy could do (e.g., individuals in her firm she could meet with) to clarify her interests and to learn more about what opportunities might be available at her firm.

In our brainstorming session, Nancy proposed several excellent ideas (e.g., attend a meeting focused on professional books, an area that she thought might interest her, and talk to a young colleague about what he was doing in the travel books department, another potentially interesting area). She agreed to a homework plan to follow up on one of those items during the coming week. I pointed out again, and Nancy could see, that her views of her own needs as unimportant or invalid and those of others as imperative and important were getting in her way. I suggested that we take up this issue directly a bit later in her therapy. We did not have time to take up the telephone conversation problem, but Nancy said she would continue to work on this problem by logging her phone calls.

Review of Treatment Progress

SESSION 14
BDI = 11, BAI = 15

The check-in portion of the session revealed that Nancy had gone to the professional books meeting, as she had agreed to do, and had kept her phone log. We agreed to begin the session with a review of her treatment progress, as planned, and then to work more on the phone call problem.

When we reviewed her treatment progress, Nancy and I agreed that overall she had made some good gains but had more work to do. The following is a list of her treatment goals and the progress she had made on each them.

1. Symptoms of depression and anxiety. These were improved, with Nancy's BDI score down from 21 to 11, and her BAI score down from 25 to 15.

2. Relationship difficulties: Nancy was pleased that she had been able to change her relationship with Morrison and with her assertiveness during her Puerto Vallarta trip, in talks with her landlord, and on the telephone. However, when I asked her for a rough figure, she reported only 60% progress on this problem. I was surprised that this number was so low, given the accomplishments we had listed. When I questioned her about this, Nancy reported that the evening telephone calls were still a major problem for her and that email was another problem area. These "sticky" spots caused her to continue to feel pressured and burdened by her relationships. I was glad to have this information because it gave me clear guidance about where we needed to work.

3. Work difficulties: Nancy reported that she was much more successful at handling her workload than before. She was pleased at how she had handled her recent quarterly report and felt more confident about handling these reports successfully in the future. She had not stayed up all night to complete a project since early in the therapy; this was a major accomplishment.

4. Financial difficulties: Unchanged.

I asked Nancy for feedback about what interventions had been helpful, and we made a list of them in the session. (I kept one for my own records and she kept one.) She reported that what had helped most was scheduling activities (e.g., work), clearly establishing why setting limits on relationships was good for the relationship, learning to use a Thought Record, and working on being more assertive with others.

In the remainder of the session, we returned to the telephone call problem. We reviewed her phone log and learned that although Nancy was doing a better job of getting off the phone more quickly, she frequently did this by promising to see the person for lunch the next day, for example; she wanted to stop doing this. To address this issue, we did some role-plays of getting off the phone without promising lunch or making any other commitment to see the person at a definite time. We practiced saying "I'll see you" instead of "let's have lunch tomorrow." Nancy agreed to try doing this as her homework assignment for the next week and to keep notes about any occasions on which she offered a lunch date or other meeting just to get off the phone.

Coming Down the Home Stretch

At this point in the treatment, Nancy had made some solid progress on her treatment goals. In the next several sessions, we continued working on the treatment goals, particularly the interpersonal issues, and began working on her underlying schema.

SESSIONS 15–17

We used Thought Records and role-plays to continue to work on Nancy's phone call problem and to address other problematic interpersonal situations. We worked on email communications, which absorbed more time than Nancy wanted. She felt compelled to write extensive email messages to everyone who sent email to her, including a young man she had known in high school who insisted on keeping in touch with her but whom she did not like.

It was striking how nearly all the situations Nancy needed help with were of the same type: She felt pressured into doing what others wanted her to do and guilty when she did not give in to this pressure. She was frequently unclear about what she herself wanted in the situation; when she was aware of her preferences, she often had difficulty asking assertively for them.

We continued to use many of the interventions that Nancy had found helpful in our previous work, introducing new ones as they were needed. In a situation in which Nancy needed to be assertive with a young man who was pursuing her for a lunch date, Nancy insisted that she needed to tell him in person that she had a boyfriend and did not want to date him; when I suggested that she tell him by email, she demurred because this method of communicating such information seemed rude to her. However, she found herself avoiding talking with him.

To handle this problem, I suggested that she do some contingency contracting (see Masters, Burish, Hollon, & Rimm, 1987) with herself: I suggested that she commit to tell him in person by Monday and that if she did not, she would tell him on the phone or with an email message on Tuesday before our session on Wednesday. Nancy liked this idea and agreed to it (she told him in person). To solve her email problem, Nancy used activity scheduling; she made a plan to limit her email communication to 30 minutes a day after dinner; she reported that this strategy worked well.

Although Nancy had not reported her relationship with her father as particularly problematic, it was not surprising that problems in interactions with him might arise. We spent part of a session working on how upset she was about the fact that her father had agreed to help her pay for a laptop computer but was not keeping his promise. She was also upset about the fact that when she talked to him about how stressed she was about her work, he was unsupportive, saying "Aren't you in therapy?"

We did a Thought Record to help her with these situations. Her automatic thoughts included "He made a promise; he should keep it." "If he's not planning to follow through, he shouldn't make promises." "He should be more supportive when I'm upset." After we spent some time discussing Nancy's father and I asked her a number of Socratic questions to open up her perceptions of him, we developed responses to her automatic thoughts and wrote them on a Thought Record. These responses included "He is unreliable; that's a fact, and it probably doesn't have much to do with me." "He has a history of making promises to others that he doesn't keep." "He is not good at providing emotional support when others are upset; he's more supportive when things are going well." "This is a drag, but if I can accept it, we can have a better relationship." As part of her work on this issue, Nancy read chapter 6 of *Feeling Good*, which offers an astute account of the cognitive underpinnings of anger and some excellent strategies to help alleviate it.

SESSION 18
BDI = 8, BAI = 10

Overall, Nancy was doing well. Her relationship with her boyfriend Pete had smoothed out, and work was going well too; in fact, she had already begun to work on her next quarterly report and felt confident about it.

Nancy reported that her 30-minute email schedule was working well, and she was pleased to see that even when she carried out a behavioral experiment (see chap. 4) of sending very brief emails, her friends did not seem offended. She had been able to ignore or delay responding to people she did not want to communicate with; this was a big step forward for her.

I suggested that at this point in the therapy, we begin working directly on the schema that seemed to underpin Nancy's difficulties, particularly the interpersonal problems. We had already identified that Nancy viewed herself as selfish, and we noted that the automatic thought "I'm selfish" had appeared repeatedly in her Thought Records. I suggested that we spend some time working to develop and strengthen an alternative, a less distorted view of herself, and she agreed.

I introduced the Positive Data Log, and Nancy agreed to try it. I took some time to introduce the log carefully, using some of the strategies illustrated in the *Schema Change Methods* video (Tompkins, Persons, & Davidson, 2000), including using the "prejudice" example borrowed from C. Padesky (1993a) and illustrated in the video. Nancy and I chose an alternative to "I'm selfish," which was "I set limits/take care of my needs in a way that is respectful of myself and others." We spent some time fleshing out the term *respectful of others*; Nancy decided that by this she meant not leading others on, being honest about what she could offer others in a relationship, and not being maliciously hurtful or carelessly inconsiderate. We began the Positive Data Log with the following item: Refused an invitation from Susan to go biking on Saturday (I had already promised Pete I would go with him).

SESSIONS 19–21

Nancy's BDI and BAI scores continued to be low, namely, in the 5–10 range on the BDI and occasionally as high as 12 on the BAI. Our focus in this phase of her treatment consisted of working on additional (mostly minor) difficulties that arose and reviewing the Positive Data Log weekly. Nancy at first struggled to find items to put on her Positive Data Log, but after I spent time with her in Sessions 19 and 20 helping her add items to the log and overcome obstacles (e.g., "That's too small an event to enter—it doesn't count") to adding items to the log, she found it easier to do this herself. Over time, she created the Positive Data Log seen in Exhibit 7.7.

We also spent some time working on Nancy's increasing feelings of boredom at work. We followed up on some of the things she had done to learn more about her career interests. She decided that she wanted to ask for a change in assignments, but she had difficulty deciding which department to ask for. To help her with this, I used a decision-making

EXHIBIT 7.7

Positive Data Log

Instructions: Describe your maladaptive schema and alternative schema in the space provided. Then, write down each piece of evidence in support of your alternative schema and the date and time when you observed the evidence. Be as specific as you can. For example, rather than writing "Someone said something nice to me" write "Tom said he liked the shoes I was wearing." Remember, you are to write down all evidence in support of the alternative schema, regardless of how small or insignificant you might think it is.

Maladaptive schema: "I'm selfish."

Alternative schema: "I set limits/take care of my needs in a way that is respectful of myself and others.

Date and time	Evidence in support of alternative schema
4/3	Refused invite from Susan to go biking on Saturday (I had already promised Pete)
4/4	Booked conference room at the time best for my client but inconvenient for my colleague
4/6	Stayed home from work yesterday when sick, although it was hard on my boss not to have me at a big meeting
4/8	Asked dry cleaner to redo a blouse that had a stain they had failed to remove
4/13	Told Pete I could have dinner with him on Thursday, not Wednesday

strategy described by David Burns (2000), in which she listed advantages and disadvantages of two options and then used them to make her decision. Nancy decided that she wanted to ask for a transfer to the travel section of the firm. Making this request required some assertiveness and required fighting against her fear of selfishness because she knew that the head of her current department would be unhappy about losing her. We did a Thought Record and a role-play to help Nancy with this situation, which she handled successfully.

As we discussed her professional interests and career direction, we learned that Nancy had difficulty pursuing her own interests in part because she was encountering a certain sexism in her company. The senior male editors, she reported, pushed her toward areas of the field that were not interesting to her but that they believed were more suitable for women editors; it was draining to "swim upstream" continuously against them and to experience their subtle lack of support for her interests. A Thought Record on this topic led to a new intervention, one that involved changing the Situation column, as it were. I suggested that to feel more supported at work, Nancy might benefit from cultivating collegial relationships with her female colleagues, particularly senior editors who could serve as mentors and role models.

This intervention is an interesting one. Although it emerged from the use of a Thought Record, it is not described in chapter 5 and is not a routine Thought Record intervention. However, the intervention flows firmly out of the cognitive–behavioral model (which states that external events activate schema to produce problems) and Nancy's individualized case formulation (which states that she has difficulty in situations in which she experiences pressure from others to meet their needs). Although most of the therapy's interventions focused on changing the automatic thoughts, behaviors, and schema components of Nancy's problems, interventions intended to change the external environment itself were clearly consistent with cognitive theory.

A general point is that the cognitive–behavior therapist is free to develop new interventions that are not described in any textbook. Novel interventions, particularly if they flow from and fit the nomothetic model and the individualized case formulation, are worth attempting. When using them, therapists can obtain feedback from the patient and monitor the outcome to evaluate their helpfulness.

Termination

At the end of Session 21, Nancy stated that she was doing well and felt ready to bring her therapy to a close. I agreed that this was appropriate but suggested that we schedule a final session to review her progress, summarize what she had accomplished and learned, and think ahead to prepare for any potential future difficulties. Nancy agreed to this.

SESSION 22
BDI = 6, BAI = 10

We began this session by reviewing Nancy's progress in general terms and as it applied to her treatment goals. Overall, Nancy was pleased with what she had accomplished in therapy.

1. Depressive and anxiety symptoms. Her BDI and BAI scores were significantly reduced and now in the normal range.
2. Relationship difficulties: Nancy reported she felt 85% improved, but she agreed that she needed to keep working on these issues. Her relationship with her boyfriend was more solid and comfortable, she had an easier time refusing invitations that she did not want to accept, she handled interactions with her father more successfully, she was more assertive and happier at work, and she had set good limits on her phone and email communications. Nancy felt confident that she could continue to make progress in this area on her own; she felt that the Positive Data Log was helping her here, and she planned to continue this intervention after her therapy ended.
3. Work difficulties: Nancy reported that she handled her workload much more effectively than before, and she no longer felt continually behind and anxious about it. She was meeting deadlines without panicky last-minute efforts.
4. Financial stresses: Nancy's increased assertiveness and productivity at work gave her some confidence, and she planned to ask for a raise sometime soon.

I suggested that we make a list of strategies Nancy had found helpful in her therapy that she could keep for later reference should she need them. The list read as follows:

1. About relationships,
   - Use Thought Records. In the response column, don't assume others are hurt or feeling rejected when I say *no*.
   - Remember that saying *yes* all the time will only lead to grief down the road if it is not honest and causes me to want to end the relationship.
   - I tend to see myself as selfish, but this view is not supported by the data I collected on the Positive Data Log.
   - Remember to ask myself what *I* want.

- Use the Activity Schedule to block out my time the way I want to spend it.
- When dealing with my father, remember he is more supportive when I let him know I am doing well and less supportive when I tell him that I am upset or unhappy.
- Be assertive and speak up for what I want.

2. At work,
   - When tackling big jobs, break them into parts (graded task assignments) and use the Activity Schedule to plan time to work on them.

3. When upset,
   - Do a Thought Record and look for distortions.

At the end of the session, I reminded Nancy that depression is a recurrent problem, and we reviewed how she would know if she needed to return to therapy. Nancy decided that if she felt her mood sliding, she would complete a BDI. If she scored 15 or over, she would begin to take action on her own to feel better (using the strategies she had learned in therapy). If she did not improve in 2 weeks, she would call for an appointment.

Nancy and I said goodbye. I had enjoyed working with her. It was a pleasure to see her do so well and finish up her therapy, but I would miss seeing her. I encouraged her to call me anytime that I could be of help in the future and to feel free to call me anytime, even if it was just to leave a message or send me a note to let me know how she was doing.

References

Agency for Health Care Policy and Research. (1993). *Depression in primary care: Vol. 2. Treatment of major depression* (Clinical Practice Guideline No. 5). Rockville, MD: Author.

American Psychiatric Association. (1993). Practice guideline for major depressive disorder in adults. *American Journal of Psychiatry, 150*(Suppl.), 1–26.

American Psychiatric Association. (1994). *Diagnostic and statistical manual of mental disorders* (4th ed.). Washington, DC: Author.

Antonuccio, D. O., Thomas, M., & Danton, W. G. (1997). A cost-effective analysis of cognitive behavior therapy and fluoxetine (Prozac) in the treatment of depression. *Behavior Therapy, 28,* 187–210.

Barlow, D. H., Craske, M. G., Cerny, J. A., & Klosko, J. S. (1989). Behavioral treatment of panic disorder. *Behavior Therapy, 20,* 261–282.

Barlow, D. H., Hayes, S. C., & Nelson, R. O. (1984). *The scientist–practitioner: Research and accountability in clinical and educational settings.* New York: Pergamon.

Basco, M. R., & Rush, A. J. (1996). *Cognitive–behavior therapy for bipolar disorder.* New York: Guilford Press.

Beck, A. T. (1976). *Cognitive therapy and the emotional disorders.* New York: International Universities Press.

Beck, A. T. (1983). Cognitive theory of depression: New perspectives. In P. J. Clayton & J. E. Barrett (Eds.), *Treatment of depression: Old controversies and new approaches* (pp. 265–288). New York: Raven Press.

Beck, A. T. (1999). *Prisoners of hate: The cognitive basis of anger, hostility, and violence.* New York: HarperCollins.

Beck, A. T., Emery, G., & Greenberg, R. (1985). *Anxiety disorders and phobias: A cognitive perspective.* New York: Basic Books.

Beck, A. T., Freeman, A., & Associates. (1990). *Cognitive therapy of personality disorders.* New York: Guilford Press.

Beck, A. T., Rush, A. J., Shaw, B. F., & Emery, G. (1979). *Cognitive therapy of depression.* New York: Guilford Press.

Beck, A. T., Ward, C. H., Mendelsohn, M., Mock, J., & Erbaugh, J. (1961). An inventory for measuring depression. *Archives of General Psychiatry, 4,* 561–571.

Beck, A. T., Wright, F. D., Newman, C. F., & Liese, B. S. (1993). *Cognitive therapy of substance abuse.* New York: Guilford Press.

Beck, J. S. (1995). *Cognitive therapy: Basics and beyond.* New York: Guilford Press.

Bellack, A. S., & Hersen, M. (1998). *Behavioral assessment: A practical handbook* (4th ed.). Boston: Allyn & Bacon.

Blackburn, I. M., Eunson, K. M., & Bishop, S. (1986). A two-year naturalistic follow-up of depressed patients treated with cognitive therapy, pharmacotherapy and a combination of both. *Journal of Affective Disorders, 10,* 67–75.

Blackburn, I. M., & Moore, R. G. (1997). Controlled acute and follow-up trial of cognitive therapy in out-patients with recurrent depression. *British Journal of Psychiatry, 171,* 328–334.

Blanchard, E. B., Schwarz, S. P., & Neff, D. F. (1988). Two-year follow-up of behavioral treatment of irritable bowel syndrome. *Behavior Therapy, 19,* 67–73.

Bloom, M., Fischer, J., & Orme, J. G. (1995). *Evaluating practice: Guidelines for the accountable professional.* Boston: Allyn & Bacon.

Bower, G. H. (1981). Mood and memory. *American Psychologist, 36,* 129–148.

Brown, G. P., Hammen, C. L., Craske, M. G., & Wickens, T. D. (1995). Dimensions of dysfunctional attitudes as vulnerabilities to depressive symptoms. *Journal of Abnormal Psychology, 3,* 431–435.

Brown, G. W., & Harris, T. O. (1989). Depression. In G. W. Brown & T. O. Harris (Eds.), *Life events and illness* (pp. 49–93). London: Guilford Press.

Burns, D. D. (1998). *Therapist toolkit.* Unpublished manuscript, Los Altos, CA.

Burns, D. D. (1999). *Feeling good: The new mood therapy.* New York: Morrow.

Burns, D. D. (2000, March). *And it's all your fault! How to overcome anger and interpersonal conflict.* Workshop presented by the Institute for the Advancement of Human Behavior, San Francisco, CA.

Burns, D. D., & Nolen-Hoeksema, S. (1991). Coping styles, homework compliance, and the effectiveness of cognitive–behavioral therapy. *Journal of Consulting and Clinical Psychology, 59,* 305–311.

Burns, D. D., & Nolen-Hoeksema, S. (1992). Therapeutic empathy and recovery from depression in cognitive–behavioral therapy: A structural equation model. *Journal of Consulting and Clinical Psychology, 60,* 441–449.

Burns, D. D., & Spangler, D. L. (2000). Does homework lead to changes in depression in cognitive–behavioral therapy? Or does improvement lead to homework compliance? *Journal of Consulting and Clinical Psychology, 68,* 46–56.

Chambless, D. L., & Hollon, S. D. (1998). Defining empirically supported therapies. *Journal of Consulting and Clinical Psychology, 66,* 7–18.

Craighead, W. E., Craighead, L. W., & Ilardi, S. S. (1998). Psychosocial treatments for major depressive disorder. In P. E. Nathan & J. M. Gorman (Eds.), *A guide to treatments that work* (pp. 226–239). New York: Oxford University Press.

D'Attilio, F. M., & Padesky, C. A. (1990). *Cognitive therapy with couples.* Sarasota, FL: Professional Resources Exchange.

Davidson, J., Persons, J. B., & Tompkins, M. A. (2000a). *Cognitive–behavior therapy for depression: Structure of the therapy session* [Videotape]. American Psychological Association.

Davidson, J., Persons, J. B., & Tompkins, M. A. (2000b). *Cognitive–behavior therapy for depression: Using the thought record* [Videotape]. American Psychological Association.

Derogatis, L. R., Lipman, R. S., & Covi, L. (1973). SCL-90: An outpatient psychiatric rating scale—Preliminary report. *Psychopharmacological Bulletin, 9,* 13–28.

DeRubeis, R. J., & Crits-Christoph, P. (1998). Empirically supported individual and group psychological treatments for adult mental disorders. *Journal of Consulting and Clinical Psychology, 66,* 37–52.

DeRubeis, R. J., & Feeley, M. (1990). Determinants of change in cognitive therapy for depression. *Cognitive Therapy and Research, 14,* 469–482.

DeRubeis, R. J., Gelfand, L. A., Tang, T. Z., & Simons, A. D. (1999). Medications versus cognitive behavior therapy for severely depressed outpatients: Mega-analysis of four randomized comparisons. *American Journal of Psychiatry, 156,* 1007–1013.

Detweiler, J. B., & Whisman, M. A. (1999). The role of homework assignments in cognitive therapy for depression: Potential methods for enhancing adherence. *Clinical Psychology Science Practice, 6,* 267–282.

Eells, T. D. (Ed.). (1997). *Handbook of psychotherapy case formulation.* New York: Guilford Press.

Eifert, G. H., Evans, I. M., & McKendrick, V. G. (1990). Matching treatments to client problems not diagnostic labels: A case for paradigmatic behavior therapy. *Journal of Behavior Therapy and Experimental Psychiatry, 21,* 163–172.

Elkin, I., Shea, M. T., Watkins, J. T., Imber, S. D., Sotsky, S. M., Collins, J. F., Glass, D. R., Pilkonis, P. A., Leber, W. R., Docherty, J. P., Fiester, S. J., & Parloff, M. B. (1989). NIMH Treatment of Depression Collaborative Research Program: General effectiveness of treatments. *Archives of General Psychiatry, 46,* 971–982.

Elstein, A. S., Shulman, L. S., & Sprafka, S. A. (1978). *Medical problem solving: An analysis of clinical reasoning.* Cambridge, MA: Harvard University Press.

Evans, M. D., Hollon, S. D., DeRubeis, R. J., Piasecki, J. M., Grove, W. M., Garvey, M. J., & Tuason, V. B. (1992). Differential relapse following cognitive therapy and pharmacotherapy for depression. *Archives of General Psychiatry, 49,* 802–808.

Fava, G. A., Rafanelli, C., Grandi, S., Conti, S., & Belluardo, P. (1998). Prevention of recurrent depression with cognitive behavioral therapy. *Archives of Genetic Psychiatry, 55,* 816–820.

Feeley, M., DeRubeis, R. J., & Gelfand, L. A. (1999). The temporal relation of adherence and alliance to symptom change in cognitive therapy for depression. *Journal of Consulting and Clinical Psychology, 67,* 578–582.

Fennell, M. J. V., & Teasdale, J. D. (1987). Cognitive therapy for depression: Individual differences and the process of change. *Cognitive Therapy and Research, 11,* 253–271.

Fischer, J., & Corcoran, K. (1994a). *Measures for clinical practice: A sourcebook. Vol. 1: Couples, families, and children.* New York: Free Press.

Fischer, J., & Corcoran, K. (1994b). *Measures for clinical practice: A sourcebook. Vol. 2: Adults.* New York: Free Press.

Fishman, D. B. (1999). *The case for pragmatic psychology.* New York: New York University Press.

Fleming, B. M., & Thornton, D. W. (1980). Coping skills training as a component in the short-term treatment of depression. *Journal of Consulting and Clinical Psychology, 48,* 652–654.

Foa, E. B., & Kozak, M. J. (1986). Emotional processing of fear: Exposure to corrective information. *Psychological Bulletin, 99,* 20–35.

Foster, S. L., Laverty-Finch, C., Gizzo, D. P., & Osantowski, J. (1999). Practical issues in self-observation. *Psychological Assessment, 11,* 426–438.

Frazier, H. S., & Mosteller, F. (Eds.). (1995). *Medicine worth paying for: Assessing medical innovations.* Cambridge, MA: Harvard University Press.

Goodman, W. K., Price, L. H., Rasmussen, S. A., Mazure, C., Fleischmann, R. L., Hill, C. L., Heninger, G. R., & Charney, D. S. (1989). The Yale–Brown Obsessive Compulsive Scale I: Development, use, and reliability. *Archives of General Psychiatry, 46,* 1006–1011.

Gotlib, I. H., & Krasnoperova, E. (1998). Biased information processing as a vulnerability factor for depression. *Behavior Therapy, 29,* 603–617.

Greenberger, D., & Padesky, C. A. (1995). *Mind over mood: A cognitive therapy treatment manual for clients.* New York: Guilford Press.

Haaga, D. A. F., DeRubeis, R. J., Stewart, B. L., & Beck, A. T. (1991). Relationship of intelligence with cognitive therapy outcome. *Behaviour Research and Therapy, 29,* 277–281.

Hammen, C., Ellicott, A., & Gitlin, M. (1989). Vulnerability to specific life events and prediction of course of disorder in unipolar depressed patients. *Canadian Journal of Behavioral Science, 21,* 377–388.

Hammen, C., Ellicott, A., Gitlin, M., & Jamison, K. R. (1989). Sociotropy/autonomy and vulnerability to specific life events in patients with unipolar depression and bipolar disorders. *Journal of Abnormal Psychology, 98,* 154–160.

Hammen, C., Marks, T., Mayol, A., & deMayo, R. (1985). Depressive self-schemas, life stress, and vulnerability to depression. *Journal of Abnormal Psychology, 94,* 308–319.

Harmon, T. M., Nelson, R. O., & Hayes, S. C. (1980). Self-monitoring of mood versus activity by depressed clients. *Journal of Consulting and Clinical Psychology, 48,* 30–38.

Hayes, S. C., Nelson, R. O., & Jarrett, R. B. (1987). The treatment utility of assessment: A functional approach to evaluating assessment quality. *American Psychologist, 42,* 963–974.

Haynes, S. N. (1992). *Models of causality in psychopathology: Toward dynamic, synthetic and nonlinear models of behavior disorders.* New York: Macmillan.

Haynes, S. N., Leisen, M. B., & Blaine, D. D. (1997). Design of individualized behavioral treatment programs using functional analytic clinical case models. *Psychological Assessment, 9,* 334–348.

Haynes, S. N., & O'Brien, W. H. (1990). Functional analysis in behavior therapy. *Clinical Psychology Review, 10*, 649–668.

Haynes, S. N., & O'Brien, W. H. (2000). *Principles and practice of behavioral assessment.* New York: Plenum Press.

Hedlund, S., & Rude, S. S. (1995). Evidence of latent depressive schemas in formerly depressed individuals. *Journal of Abnormal Psychology, 3*, 517–525.

Hewitt, P. L., Flett, G. L., & Ediger, E. (1996). Perfectionism and depression: Longitudinal assessment of a specific vulnerability hypothesis. *Journal of Abnormal Psychology, 105*, 276–280.

Hoberman, H. M., & Lewinsohn, P. M. (1985). The behavioral treatment of depression. In E. E. Beckham & W. R. Leber (Eds.), *Handbook of depression: Treatment, assessment, and research* (pp. 39–81). Homewood, IL: Dorsey Press.

Hollon, S. D. (1999, November). *Cognitive behavior therapy in the treatment and prevention of depression.* Presidential address at the annual convention of the Association for Advancement of Behavior Therapy, Toronto, Ontario, Canada.

Hollon, S. D., DeRubeis, R. J., & Evans, M. D. (1987). Causal mediation of change in treatment for depression: Discriminating between nonspecificity and noncausality. *Psychological Bulletin, 102*, 139–149.

Hollon, S. D., DeRubeis, R. J., Evans, M. D., Wiemer, J. J., Garvey, J. G., Grove, W. M., & Tuason, V. B. (1992). Cognitive therapy and pharmacotherapy for depression: Singly and in combination. *Archives of General Psychiatry, 49*, 774–781.

Howard, K. I., Moras, K., Brill, P. L., Martinovich, Z., & Lutz, W. (1996). Evaluation of psychotherapy: Efficacy, effectiveness, and patient progress. *American Psychologist, 51*, 1059–1064.

Ilardi, S. S., & Craighead, W. E. (1994). The role of nonspecific factors in cognitive–behavior therapy for depression. *Clinical Psychology: Science and Practice, 1*, 138–156.

Imber, S. D., Pilkonis, P. A., Sotsky, S. M., Elkin, I., Watkins, J. T., Collins, J. F., Shea, M. T., Leber, W. R., & Glass, D. R. (1990). Mode-specific effects among three treatments for depression. *Journal of Consulting and Clinical Psychology, 58*, 352–359.

Ingram, R. E., Miranda, J., & Segal, Z. V. (1998). *Cognitive vulnerability to depression.* New York: Guilford Press.

Jacobson, N. S., & Christensen, A. (1996). Studying the effectiveness of psychotherapy: How well can clinical trials do the job? *American Psychologist, 51*, 1031–1039.

Jacobson, N. S., Dobson, K. S., Truax, P. A., Addis, M. E., Koerner, K., Gollan, J. K., & Prince, S. E. (1996). A component analysis of cognitive–behavioral treatment for depression. *Journal of Consulting and Clinical Psychology, 64*, 295–304.

Jacobson, N. S., & Truax, P. (1991). Clinical significance: A statistical approach to defining meaningful change in psychotherapy research. *Journal of Consulting and Clinical Psychology, 59*, 12–19.

Jamison, C., & Scogin, F. (1995). The outcome of cognitive bibliotherapy with depressed adults. *Journal of Consulting and Clinical Psychology, 63*, 644–650.

Jarrett, R. B., Schaffer, M., McIntire, D., Witt-Browder, A., Kraft, D., & Risser, R. C. (1999). Treatment of atypical depression with cognitive therapy or phenelzine: A double-blind, placebo-controlled trial. *Archives of General Psychiatry, 56*(5), 531–537.

Kanner, A. D., Coyne, J. C., Schaefer, C., & Lazarus, R. S. (1981). Comparison of two modes of stress measurement: Daily hassles and uplifts versus major life events. *Journal of Behavioral Medicine, 4*, 1–39.

Kazdin, A. E. (1993). Evaluation in clinical practice: Clinically sensitive and systematic methods of treatment delivery. *Behavior Therapy, 24*, 11–45.

Kendall, P. C., Kipnis, D., & Otto-Salaj, L. (1992). When clients don't progress: Influences on and explanations for lack of therapeutic progress. *Cognitive Therapy and Research, 16*, 269–281.

Kingdon, D. G., & Turkington, D. (1994). *Cognitive–behavior therapy of schizophrenia.* New Guilford Press.

Klerman, G. L., Weissman, M. M., Rounsaville, B. J., & Chevron, E. S. (1984). *Interpersonal psychotherapy for depression.* New York: Basic Books.

Lewinsohn, P. M., Hoberman, T., & Hautzinger, M. (1985). An integrative theory of depression. In S. Reiss & R. Bootzin (Eds.), *Theoretical issues in behavior therapy* (pp. 331–359). New York: Academic Press.

Linehan, M. M. (1993). *Cognitive–behavioral treatment of borderline personality disorder.* New York: Guilford Press.

Masters, J. C., Burish, T. G., Hollon, S. D., & Rimm, D. C. (1987). *Behavior therapy: Techniques and empirical findings* (3rd ed.). Fort Worth, TX: Harcourt Brace Jovanovich.

Mayfield, D., McLeod, G., & Hall, P. (1974). The CAGE questionnaire: Validation of a new alcoholism screening instrument. *American Journal of Psychiatry, 131,* 1121–1123.

McKnight, D. L., Nelson, R. O., Hayes, S. C., & Jarrett, R. B. (1984). Importance of treating individually assessed response classes in the amelioration of depression. *Behavior Therapy, 15,* 315–335.

Miranda, J., & Dwyer, E. V. (1994, September). *Treatment of depression in disadvantaged medical patients.* Paper presented at the 8th Annual NIMH Research Conference on Mental Health Problems in the General Health Care Sector, McLean, VA.

Monroe, S. M., & McQuaid, J. R. (1994). Measuring life stress and assessing its impact on mental health. In W. R. Avison & I. H. Gotlib (Eds.), *Stress and mental health: Contemporary issues and prospects for the future* (pp. 43–73). New York: Plenum Press.

Neimeyer, R. A., & Feixas, G. (1990). The role of homework and skill acquisition in the outcome of group cognitive therapy for depression. *Behavior Therapy, 21,* 281–292.

Nelson, R. O., & Hayes, S. C. (1986). The nature of behavioral assessment. In R. O. Nelson & S. C. Hayes (Eds.), *Conceptual foundations of behavioral assessment* (pp. 3–41). New York: Guilford Press.

Nemeroff, C. B., & Schatzberg, A. F. (1998). Pharmacological treatment of unipolar depression. In P. E. Nathan & J. M. Gorman (Eds.), *A guide to treatments that work* (pp. 212–225). New York: Oxford University Press.

Nezu, A. M. (1986). Efficacy of a social problem-solving therapy approach for unipolar depression. *Journal of Consulting and Clinical Psychology, 54,* 196–202.

Nezu, A. M., & Nezu, C. M. (1993). Identifying and selecting target problems for clinical interventions: A problem-solving model. *Psychological Assessment, 5,* 254–263.

Ogles, B. M., Lambert, M. J., & Sawyer, J. D. (1995). Clinical significance of the National Institute of Mental Health Treatment of Depression Collaborative Research Program data. *Journal of Consulting and Clinical Psychology, 63,* 321–326.

Organista, K. C., Muñoz, R., & Gonzalez, G. (1994). Cognitive behavioral therapy for depression in low-income and minority medical outpatients: Description of a program and exploratory analyses. *Cognitive Therapy and Research, 18,* 241–259.

Padesky, C. A. (1993a). Schema as self-prejudice. *International Cognitive Therapy Newsletter, 5–6,* 16–17. (Available from K. A. Mooney [Ed.], Center for Cognitive Therapy, 1101 Dove St., Suite 240, Newport Beach, CA 92660)

Padesky, C. A. (1993b, September 24). *Socratic questioning: Changing minds or guiding discovery?* Keynote address presented at the European Congress of Behavioural and Cognitive Therapies, London, UK.

Padesky, C. A. (1994). Schema change processes in cognitive therapy. *Clinical Psychology and Psychotherapy, 1,* 267–278.

Persons, J. B. (1989). *Cognitive therapy in practice: A case formulation approach.* New York: Norton.

Persons, J. B. (1991). Psychotherapy outcome studies do not accurately represent current models of psychotherapy: A proposed remedy. *American Psychologist, 46,* 99–106.

Persons, J. B. (1999, August). *The nuts and bolts of evidence-based practice.* Presidential address (Section 3, Division 12) presented at the 107th Annual Convention of the American Psychological Association, Boston, MA.

Persons, J. B., Bostrom, A., & Bertagnolli, A. (1999). Results of randomized controlled trials of cognitive therapy for depression generalize to private practice. *Cognitive Therapy and Research, 23,* 535–548.

Persons, J. B., Burns, D. D., & Perloff, J. M. (1988). Predictors of dropout and outcome in private practice patients treated with cognitive therapy for depression. *Cognitive Therapy and Research, 12,* 557–575.

Persons, J. B., Burns, D. D., Perloff, J. M., & Miranda, J. (1993). Relationships between symptoms of depression and anxiety and dysfunctional beliefs about achievement and attachment. *Journal of Abnormal Psychology, 102,* 518–524.

Persons, J. B., & Davidson, J. (2000). Cognitive–behavioral case formulation. In K. Dobson (Ed.), *Handbook of cognitive-behavioral therapies* (pp. 86–110). New York: Guilford Press.

Persons, J. B., Davidson, J., & Tompkins, M. A. (2000). *Cognitive–behavior therapy for depression: Activity scheduling* [Videotape]. Washington, DC: American Psychological Association.

Persons, J. B., & Miranda, J. (1992). Cognitive theories of vulnerability to depression: Reconciling negative evidence. *Cognitive Therapy and Research, 16,* 485–502.

Persons, J. B., Miranda, J., & Perloff, J. M. (1991). Relationships between depressive symptoms and cognitive vulnerabilities of achievement and dependency. *Cognitive Therapy and Research, 15,* 221–235.

Persons, J. B., & Silberschatz, G. (1998). Are results of randomized controlled trials useful to psychotherapists? *Journal of Consulting and Clinical Psychology, 66,* 126–135.

Persons, J. B., Thase, M. E., & Crits-Christoph, P. (1996). The role of psychotherapy in the treatment of depression: Review of two practice guidelines. *Archives of General Psychiatry, 53,* 283–290.

Persons, J. B., & Tompkins, M. A. (1997). Cognitive–behavioral case formulation. In T. D. Eells (Ed.), *Handbook of psychotherapy case formulation* (pp. 314–339). New York: Guilford Press.

Persons, J. B., Tompkins, M. A., & Davidson, J. (2000). *Cognitive–behavior therapy for depression: Individualized case formulation and treatment planning* [Videotape]. Washington, DC: American Psychological Association.

Pope, K., & Vasquez, M. (1998). *Ethics in psychotherapy and counseling: A practical guide* (2nd ed.). San Francisco, CA: Jossey-Bass.

Rehm, L. P. (1977). A self-control model of depression. *Behavior Therapy, 8,* 787–804.

Rehm, L. P., Kaslow, N. J., & Rabin, A. S. (1987). Cognitive and behavioral targets in a self-control therapy program for depression. *Journal of Consulting and Clinical Psychology, 55,* 60–67.

Robins, C. J., Block, P., & Peselow, E. D. (1989). Relations of sociotropic and autonomous personality characteristics to specific symptoms in depressed patients. *Journal of Abnormal Psychology, 98,* 86–88.

Robinson, L. A., Berman, J. S., & Neimeyer, R. A. (1990). Psychotherapy for the treatment of depression: A comprehensive review of controlled outcome research. *Psychological Bulletin, 108,* 30–49.

Rossello, J., & Bernal, G. (1999). The efficacy of cognitive–behavioral and interpersonal treatments for depression in Puerto Rican adolescents. *Journal of Consulting and Clinical Psychology, 67,* 734–745.

Sackett, D. L., Richardson, W. S., Rosenberg, W., & Haynes, R. B. (1997). *Evidence-based medicine: How to practice and teach EBM.* New York: Churchill Livingstone.

Schulberg, H., Katon, W., Simon, G., & Rush, A. (1998). Treating major depression in primary care practice: An update of the Agency for Health Care Policy and Research guidelines. *Archives of General Psychiatry, 55,* 1121–1127.

Schwartz, J. M. (1996). *Brain lock: Free yourself from obsessive–compulsive behavior.* New York: ReganBooks.

Scogin, F., Hamblin, D., & Beutler, L. E. (1987). Bibliotherapy for depressed older adults: A self-help alternative. *Gerontologist, 27,* 383–387.

Scogin, F., Jamison, C., & Gochneaur, K. (1989). Comparative efficacy of cognitive and behavioral bibliotherapy for mildly and moderately depressed older adults. *Journal of Consulting and Clinical Psychology, 57,* 403–407.

Segal, Z. V. (1988). Appraisal of the self-schema construct in cognitive models of depression. *Psychological Bulletin, 103,* 147–162.

Segal, Z. V., Shaw, B. F., Vella, D. D., & Katz, R. (1992). Cognitive and life stress predictors of relapse in remitted unipolar depressed patients: Test of the congruency hypothesis. *Journal of Abnormal Psychology, 101,* 26–36.

Seligman, M. E. P. (1996). Science as an ally of practice. *American Psychologist, 51,* 1072–1079.

Seligman, M. E. P., & Johnston, J. C. (1973). A cognitive theory of avoidance learning. In F. O. McGuigan & D. V.

Lumsden (Eds.), *Contemporary approaches to conditioning and learning* (pp. 69–107). Washington, DC: Winston.

Shaw, B. F., Olmsted, M., Dobson, K. S., Sotsky, S. M., Elkin, I., Yamaguchi, J., Vallis, T. M., Lowery, A., Watkins, J. T., & Imber, S. D. (1999). Therapist competence ratings in relation to clinical outcome in cognitive therapy of depression. *Journal of Consulting and Clinical Psychology, 67,* 837–846.

Simons, A. D., McGowan, C. R., Epstein, L. H., & Kupfer, D. J. (1985). Exercise as a treatment for depression: An update. *Clinical Psychology Review, 5,* 553–568.

Simons, A. D., Murphy, G. E., Levine, J. L., & Wetzel, R. D. (1986). Cognitive therapy and pharmacotherapy for depression: Sustained improvement over one year. *Archives of General Psychiatry, 43,* 43–48.

Speier, P. L., Sherak, D. L., Hirsch, S., & Cantwell, D. P. (1985). Depression in children and adolescents. In E. E. Beckham & W. L. Leber (Eds.), *Handbook of depression* (pp. 462–493). Homewood, IL: Dorsey Press.

Stark, K. D., Rouse, L. W., & Kurowski, C. (1994). Psychological treatment approaches for depression in children. In W. Reynolds & H. Johnston (Eds.), *Handbook of depression in children and adolescents* (pp. 275–308). New York: Plenum Press.

Startup, M., & Edmonds, J. (1994). Compliance with homework assignments in cognitive–behavioral psychotherapy for depression: Relation to outcome and methods of enhancement. *Cognitive Therapy and Research, 18,* 567–579.

Taylor, D. C. (1971). The components of sickness: Diseases, illnesses and predicaments. *Lancet, 2,* 1008.

Thase, M. E., Greenhouse, J. B., Frank, E., Reynolds, C. F., III, Pilkonis, P. A., Hurley, K., Grochocinski, V., & Kupfer, D. J. (1997). Treatment of major depression with psychotherapy or psychotherapy–pharmacotherapy combinations. *Archives of General Psychiatry, 54,* 1009–1015.

Tompkins, M. A. (1997). Case formulation in cognitive–behavioral therapy. In R. Leahy (Ed.), *Practicing cognitive therapy: A guide to interventions* (pp. 37–59). Northvale, NJ: Aronson.

Tompkins, M. A., Persons, J. B., & Davidson, J. (2000). *Cognitive–behavior therapy for depression: Schema change methods* [Videotape]. Washington, DC: American Psychological Association.

Turkat, I. D. (Ed.). (1985). *Behavioral case formulation.* New York: Plenum Press.

Turkat, I. D., & Brantley, P. J. (1981). On the therapeutic relationship in behavior therapy. *The Behavior Therapist, 4,* 16–17.

Turkat, I. D., & Maisto, S. A. (1985). Personality disorders: Application of the experimental method to the formulation and modification of personality disorders. In D. H. Barlow (Ed.), *Clinical handbook of psychological disorders: A step-by-step treatment manual* (pp. 502–570). New York: Guilford Press.

Whisman, M. A. (1999). The importance of the cognitive theory of change in cognitive therapy of depression. *Clinical Psychology: Science and Practice, 6,* 300–304.

Williams, J. M. G. (1992). Autobiographical memory and emotional disorders. In S. A. Christianson (Ed.), *The handbook of emotion and memory* (pp. 451–476). Hillsdale, NJ: Erlbaum.

Williams, J. M. G., Watts, F. N., MacLeod, C., & Mathews, A. (1988). *Cognitive psychology and emotional disorders.* New York: Wiley.

Wilson, G. T. (1996). Manual-based treatments: The clinical application of research findings. *Behaviour Research and Therapy, 34,* 195–314.

Young, J. E. (1999). *Cognitive therapy for personality disorders: A schema-focused approach.* Sarasota, FL: Professional Resource Exchange.

Young, J. E., & Beck, A. T. (1980). *Cognitive Therapy Scale and Cognitive Therapy Scale rating manual.* Unpublished manuscript, Beck Institute for Cognitive Therapy and Research, Bala Cynwyd, PA.

Zeiss, A. M., Lewinsohn, P. M., & Muñoz, R. F. (1979). Nonspecific improvement effects in depression using interpersonal skills training, pleasant activity schedules, or cognitive training. *Journal of Consulting and Clinical Psychology, 47,* 427–439.

Index

About the Authors

Jacqueline B. Persons, PhD, is the director of the San Francisco Bay Area Center for Cognitive Therapy and an associate clinical professor, Department of Psychiatry, University of California, San Francisco. Dr. Persons presented cognitive–behavior therapy in the Psychotherapy Videotape Series prepared by the American Psychological Association (APA) in 1995. Trained at the University of Pennsylvania, Dr. Persons has been a practicing cognitive–behavior therapist for more than 15 years and maintains an active clinical practice. She is an internationally known workshop presenter, author of the widely used basic teaching text *Cognitive Therapy in Practice: A Case Formulation Approach,* and author of numerous research and clinical articles on topics related to the outcome and process of cognitive–behavior therapy. Dr. Persons is the treasurer of the Academy of Cognitive Therapy. She has served as editor of *the Behavior Therapist* and associate editor of *Cognitive Therapy and Research.* She recently served as president of the Society for a Science of Clinical Psychology (Section 3, Division 12 of APA).

Joan Davidson, PhD, is the director of clinical services at the San Francisco Bay Area Center for Cognitive Therapy and an assistant clinical professor, Department of Psychology, University of California, Berkeley. She is a practicing cognitive–behavior therapist, specializing in the treatment of mood and anxiety disorders, and a clinical supervisor to graduate students learning to conduct cognitive–behavioral treatments. Dr. Davidson is a Founding Fellow of the Academy of Cognitive Therapy. She lectures, teaches, and consults on numerous topics about cognitive–behavioral treatment to both professional and lay audiences.

Michael A. Tompkins, PhD, is the director of professional training at the San Francisco Bay Area Center for Cognitive Therapy and an assistant clinical professor, Department of Psychology, University of California, Berkeley. He is a Founding Fellow of the Academy of Cognitive Therapy. Dr. Tompkins specializes in the treatment of anxiety and mood disorders in adults and children. He is the author or coauthor of numerous chapters and journal articles on cognitive–behavior therapy and has presented widely on the topic.